The Comedy of Philosophy

SUNY series, Insinuations: Philosophy, Psychoanalysis, Literature
Charles Shepherdson, editor

The Comedy of Philosophy

Sense and Nonsense in Early Cinematic Slapstick

Lisa Trahair

State University of New York Press

Published by
State University of New York Press, Albany

© 2007 State University of New York

All rights reserved

Printed in the United States of America

No part of this book may be used or reproduced in any manner whatsoever without written permission. No part of this book may be stored in a retrieval system or transmitted in any form or by any means including electronic, electrostatic, magnetic tape, mechanical, photocopying, recording, or otherwise without the prior permission in writing of the publisher.

For information, contact State University of New York Press, Albany, NY
www.sunypress.edu

Production by Marilyn P. Semerad
Marketing by Michael Campochiaro

Library of Congress Cataloging-in-Publication Data

Trahair, Lisa, 1962–
   The comedy of philosophy : sense and nonsense in early cinematic slapstick / Lisa Trahair.
      p. cm. — (SUNY series, insinuations—philosophy, psychoanalysis, literature)
   Includes bibliographical references and index.
   ISBN 978-0-7914-7247-7 (hardcover : alk. paper)
   ISBN 978-0-7914-7248-4 (pbk : alk. paper)
   1. Comedy films—History and criticism. I. Title.

PN1995.9.C55T68 2007
791.43'617—dc22

2006100229

10 9 8 7 6 5 4 3 2 1

Contents

	List of Illustrations	vii
	Acknowledgments	ix
	List of Abbreviations	xi
	Introduction	1
1.	The Philosophy of Laughter: Bataille, Hegel, and Derrida	15
2.	Restricted and General Economy: Narrative, Gag, and Slapstick in *One Week*	35
3.	The Machine of Comedy: Gunning, Deleuze, and Buster Keaton	59
4.	Fool's Gold: Metamorphoses in *Sherlock Jr.*	87
5.	Jokes and Their Relation to...	105
6.	The Comic: Degradation and Refinement in 1920's Cinematic Slapstick	125
7.	From Words to Images (Gagging)	147
8.	Figural Vision: Freud, Lyotard, and *City Lights*	169
9.	Preposterous Figurality: Comic Cinema and Bad Metaphor	191
	Notes	213
	Bibliography	241
	Index	251

Illustrations

Figure 1. *Go West* (1925) BFI Stills	14
Figure 2. *One Week* (1920) The Academy of Motion Picture Arts and Sciences	52
Figure 3. *One Week* (1920)	55
Figure 4. *The Paleface* (1921)	62
Figure 5. *Daydreams* (1922) BFI Stills	64
Figure 6. *Neighbors* (1920) The Academy of Motion Picture Arts and Sciences	65
Figure 7. *The Navigator* (1924) BFI Stills	68
Figure 8. *Steamboat Bill, Jr.* (1928) BFI Stills	78
Figure 9. *Steamboat Bill, Jr.* (1928) The Academy of Motion Picture Arts and Sciences	82
Figure 10. *The Playhouse* (1921)	90
Figure 11. *Sherlock Jr.* (1924) BFI Stills	97
Figure 12. *Sherlock Jr.* (1924) The Academy of Motion Picture Arts and Sciences	102
Figure 13. Photograph by Arthur Rice (1921) The Academy of Motion Picture Arts and Sciences	103
Figure 14. *Go West* (1925) The Academy of Motion Picture Arts and Sciences	142
Figure 15. *The Love Nest* (1923) The Academy of Motion Picture Arts and Sciences	142
Figure 16. "Buster de Milo" (1927) BFI Stills	157

Figure 17. *Sherlock Jr.* (1924) 166
Figure 18. *The Navigator* (1924) 193
Figure 19. *Sherlock Jr.* (1924) 208
Figure 20. *The Navigator* (1924) Photofest 209

Acknowledgments

This book has been written with financial assistance from the Faculty of Arts and Social Sciences at the University of New South Wales, The Power Institute at the University of Sydney and the Australian Research Council. Some chapters or parts thereof are revisions of previously published work. Chapter 1 appeared as "The Comedy of Philosophy: Bataille, Hegel and Derrida" in *Angelaki* 6.3 (2001); chapter 2 as "Short-Circuiting the Dialectic: Narrative and Slapstick in the Cinema of Buster Keaton" in *Narrative* 10.3 (2002); chapter 3 as "The Narrative-Machine: Buster Keaton's Cinematic Comedy, Deleuze's Recursion Function and the Operational Aesthetic" in *Senses of Cinema* 33 (2004); chapter 4 as "Fool's Gold: Metamorphosis in Buster Keaton's *Sherlock, Jr.*" in Lesley Stern and George Kouvaros, eds., *Falling for You: Essays on Cinema and Performance* (Sydney: Power Publications, 1999) and parts of chapters 6, 7 and 8 as "Figural Vision: Freud, Lyotard and Early Cinematic Comedy" in *Screen* 46.2 (2005). My thanks to The Academy of Motion Picture Arts and Sciences, BFI Stills and Photofest for images.

Of the many contributors to the realization of this project, Alan Cholodenko and Mick Carter, who supervised my doctoral work on Keaton, are undoubtedly the ones who put in the hard yards. Along with a handful of others at the University of Sydney, they created a vibrant and stimulating scholarly environment for both undergraduates and postgraduates, fostering an enthusiasm for thinking and writing about culture and philosophy that saw so many of us through to working in the academy, the kind of environment now sadly depleted by funding shortfalls and overbureaucratization. Laleen Jayamanne and David Wills provided generous and encouraging comments on the thesis and without them this book would not have evolved to the extent it has. I also benefited from teaching with Frank Krutnik at the University of Aberdeen in 1996. Others who directly helped in the preparation of the current work, either by reading chapters or providing comments on the project as a whole, are Sue Best, Toni Ross, Amir Ahmadi, Alison Ross, Andrew Murphie, Lone Bertelsen, Moira Gatens, Lisabeth During,

Richard Smith, Celine Surprenant, Richard Rushton, Lesley Stern, George Kouvaros, Jackie Stacey, and Paul Patton. I am immensely grateful to each of them. Simon Lumsden, Roger Dawkins, Rex Butler, Jim Davis, Gillian Fuller, John Golder, Dan Smith, Simon Critchley, Jenny Breukelaar, Sharon Mee, Adrian Hardingham, and Ros Diprose also provided invaluable assistance either by discussing aspects of the project, giving advice and encouragement, or otherwise contributing to my intellectual well-being. Lone Bertelsen and Effie Rassos devoted many hours to the preparation of the current manuscript, ostensibly checking references, copyediting and proofing, but in fact doing much more. Special thanks are due to Penelope Deutscher for sending my book proposal to Charles Shepherdson, to Charles for finding such helpful readers for me and including the work in his series, and to James Peltz and Marilyn Semerad at SUNY Press. Thanks also to freelance professional copyeditor Therese Myers.

Thanks, too, to my family, particularly Nick and Sally, for putting up with me and for reconciling themselves to the fact that it takes me almost twice as long as most people to do things. Others have contributed greatly to my understanding of comedy who cannot be named here. Mostly they are my students, especially those who have studied comedian comedy with me, generously offered their insights, and whose laughter I look forward to sharing in years to come. Finally, acknowledgment should be given to some very funny friends (particularly Annette Trevitt) who have compelled me to try to understand the power that has held me in thrall.

Abbreviations

C1	*Cinema 1: The Movement-Image*
"FRGE"	"From Restricted to General Economy: An Hegelianism without Reserve"
JTRU	*Jokes and Their Relation to the Unconscious*
L	*Laughter: An Essay on the Meaning of the Comic*
NFF	*Narration in the Fiction Film*
P	*Proximity: Levinas, Blanchot, Bataille and Communication*
"PAC"	"Pie and Chase: Gag, Spectacle and Narrative in Slapstick Comedy"
PFTC	*Popular Film and Television Comedy*
"TTM"	"The Third Meaning: Research Notes on Some Eisenstein Stills"
"WM"	"White Mythology: Metaphor in the Text of Philosophy"

Introduction

This book investigates some of the ways that the comic manifests itself in culture. Its main concern is with what the comic means, or, more precisely, what its relation to meaning is. Its broad area of substantive focus is the slapstick cinema of the 1920s (Charlie Chaplin, Harold Lloyd, and Buster Keaton), although it gives more attention to the films of Keaton than to those of his peers. It undertakes some analyses of Mack Sennett films and the Marx Brothers' comedy as well. With respect to both Keaton and his peers, this book concentrates on a group of films, which, although made eighty or so years ago and intended for an audience of their own historical circumstance, continue to be regarded as living evidence of the fact that having a sense of humor is a condition of being human. We get pleasure from laughing, and we thus regard comedy as an aesthetic form vital to our individual and social well-being. Indeed, the films of this period still exemplify today what the popular imagination deems to be comic.

What makes an investigation of these films perhaps even more timely now than when they were made is the recent dissemination of the theoretical approaches to the comic that were developed in the early twentieth century (in some instances almost coincidentally with the production of the films that interest us here, in others slightly earlier). These theoretical approaches have been developed in a variety of disciplinary areas (philosophy, psychoanalysis, anthropology, literary criticism, art history, and film theory), and most significantly in the discourses of poststructuralism and postmodernism.

Comedy, the comic, the ludic, the joke, play, and *laughter* are terms that have pervaded both poststructuralist and postmodernist discourse. The works of Jacques Derrida, Jean Baudrillard, and Jean-François Lyotard are only the better known examples of a more general contemporary phenomenon that incorporates the tenets of the comic into philosophical thinking. At worst, this trend merely "inserts" the comic into philosophy. At best, it attempts to theorize the specificity of the comic's formations. Yet, one could argue that lack of attention to the theoretical basis for understanding the comic has meant that the effects of its operations remain unacknowledged and unknown. This book therefore takes as one of its major projects the investigation of what has to date remained an insistent, yet in many respects, neglected figure in contemporary thought: the nature, terms, and logic of what I call "the operation of the comic."

The intellectual genealogy of poststructuralist and postmodernist preoccupations with themes associated with the comic are found in the work of Freud, Nietzsche, and Georges Bataille, and, to a lesser extent, Henri Bergson and Mikhail Bakhtin. The second major project of this book is to reexamine the work on the comic by two of these thinkers, Bataille and Freud. My intention here is to use their work to delineate two distinctive, yet not incompatible, ways of thinking about the importance of the comic. On the one hand, Bataille's insistence on a philosophy of laughter, his understanding of the comic as an operation of sovereignty, and his concepts of restricted and general economy, present compelling parameters for thinking about the relationship between the comic and meaning. His work raises the question of what implications comedy has for philosophy and also the converse, namely, the implications of philosophy for comedy. On the other hand, Freud's presentation of a theory of the joke as a distinctive manifestation of the comic constitutes a point of departure from classical conceptions of the comic. Indeed, it proffers two different and to some extent opposed strategies of the comic. One strategy emerges as a result of unconscious processes such as condensation and displacement and involves transformation. The other strategy takes place because of a preconscious ideational comparison between "the is" and "the ought" and a technique of degradation.

☙

Keaton began starring in films in 1917 when he left the vaudeville stage to join the studio of Roscoe "Fatty" Arbuckle. Working as a performer with Arbuckle, Keaton adapted his theatrical comedy for the cinematic medium. From the moment Keaton joined Arbuckle's studio, his fascination with the mechanics of cinematography and the technical possibilities of film was apparent. In 1920, Arbuckle's producer, Joe Schenck, bought Keaton his own studio. Between 1920 and 1923 Keaton made nineteen short films (two- and three-reelers), and between 1923 and 1929 he directed and starred in twelve feature-length (five- to eight-reeler) films. In 1929, Keaton's career as a performer-director effectively ended. The manifest reason for this was his descent into the depths of alcoholic stupefaction. He would spend almost the rest of his life clawing his way out of this. Yet other factors—such as marital difficulties, loss of control over the production of his films, and the industry's transition to sound—also contributed to his demise. Although Keaton continued to act in films after the 1920s, had many television gigs right up until his death in 1966, and worked as a gag writer for numerous film and television comedians, this book focuses exclusively on the films made at his own studio in the 1920s.

The Keaton of this period has been variously described as a comedian, dialectician, metaphysician, technologist, poet, and philosopher. This overdetermination of Keaton—the diverse characterizations that he embodies—makes him eminently suitable for an analysis of both the philosophy of comedy and the comedy of philosophy. Experts generally acknowledge that of all the film comedians, Keaton is the most cinematic. In this respect, an analysis of his comedy has implications for understanding cinematic comedy as such. Indeed, his unsurpassed predilection for exploring the inner working of things, whether a technological object, masculinity, the heterosexual couple, narrative form, or cinema itself, ensures that the field in which his vision of the comic operates is sufficiently broad for the analyses I conduct here. Keaton's significance for this book, therefore, lies in his exemplariness rather than his uniqueness. Much of my theorization here is relevant to performers such as Chaplin, Lloyd, and the Marx Brothers, and in some of the book's final chapters their contributions to the aesthetics of the comic are examined. On the other hand, although my primary concern is neither with Keaton's status as an auteur (an honor bestowed on him the day Andrew Sarris appropriated the concept from the French writers at *Cahiers du Cinéma*), nor especially with distinguishing his style of cinematic comedy from that of others, what I have to say inevitably indicates differences between his work and that of his contemporaries.[1]

The books that best describe the singularity of Keaton's aesthetic are Jean-Patrick Lebel's *Buster Keaton*[2] and Daniel Moews's *Keaton: The Silent Features Close Up*.[3] Both present, for the most part, correctly identified and always interesting ways of thinking about Keaton's comedy, which I address here. Lebel's monograph is to all appearances a very modest undertaking, but it offers an incisive description of Keaton's aesthetics, examining the dialectical structure of his gags, his transformation of objects and the significance of the graphic quality of his images, and proposes that these various aspects of Keaton's comedy are unified by his ethical approach to the comic. Perhaps the most important contribution that Lebel makes to our understanding of Keaton's work is his argument that Keaton's comedy departs from the classical definition of the comic as a form of degradation. Moews's book is less concerned with the physical qualities of the iconic Keaton (as the punning title of his monograph implies) than with the comedian's feature-length films. While claiming that Keaton more or less made the same film time and again, Moews nevertheless devotes a chapter to each of the features produced between 1923 and 1928. He characterizes Keaton's films as comedies of fine metaphysical wit and examines the construction of his gags, the significance of his choreography, the patterning of his narratives, the cinematic aspects of his comedy, and the centrality of metamorphosis as a theme, diegetic quality, and behavioral disposition of Keaton's characters. Whereas Lebel's and Moew's studies are entirely devoted to elucidating Keaton's aesthetic, my work situates that aesthetic in the broader context of the philosophy of the comic. This emphasis leads me to clarify some of their points, to disagree with others, but most of all to take their work a step further to deepen our knowledge of Keaton's contribution to what we understand by the comic in general.[4]

☙

When I began this project, the most substantial academic writings on cinematic comedy in general focused on the narrowly cinematic implications of the comic, whereas the constitution of the comedic or the comic was largely presupposed. They were, moreover, bound up with an unreflective evaluation of what constituted "good" and "bad" comedy, and the distinction between high and low comedy, somewhat modified for cinema, underpinned this evaluation. Thus, Walter Kerr[5] and to a lesser extent Gerald Mast[6] celebrated the slapstick of the 1920s, renowned for the virtuoso performances of Chaplin, Keaton, Lloyd, and Harry Langdon, while derogating the early Californian slapstick associated with the Sennett studios. Sennett's fascination with the grotesque and the bawdy, his delight in physical violence, especially as it was perpetrated on the bodies of the genre's comic performers, combined with what was perceived to be a lack of narrative structure and of characterization, meant it was deemed primitive and inferior to the tempered slapstick of Keaton. The feature length comedies of Keaton, Chaplin, Lloyd, and Langdon were deemed superior because they adopted the romance plot as the vehicle for moderate genteel comedy, developed more coherent narrative structures. and paid more attention to characterization. Writers such as Mast and Kerr, while generally dismissive of Sennett's aesthetic, could theorize the comedy of the 1920s performers because their terms of reference were derived more from classical Hollywood realism than from the aesthetics of the comic. But because the films they celebrated were separated from the lineage that generated them (that is, Sennett films), the analysis they undertook, although formally and cinematically astute, had no means to theorize the predominating comic aesthetic.

One of the most important contributions to the study of cinematic comedy written in the decade following the work of Kerr and Mast was Steve Seidman's identification and exposition of the genre, now commonly known as "comedian comedy." In this genre, the central comic protagonist is understood to transgress the conventions of classical Hollywood realism by adopting a performance strategy that derives from his or her simultaneous status as a character within the narrative and as an extradiegetic (extrafictional) persona.[7] As well as the comic performers of the 1920s already mentioned, the genre includes the films of people such as Mae West, Jerry Lewis, W. C. Fields, Lucille Ball, the Marx Brothers, Eddie Murphy, Steve Martin, Woody Allen, Rowan Atkinson, and Jim Carrey. In classifying such comedians and the tendencies that are conventional in their work, Seidman set the stage for a rigorous examination of the aesthetics of cinematic comedy and its departure from the norms of classical realism. In particular, Seidman's work made possible the investigation of the distinctiveness of performance in this genre and its difference from the realist acting of other Hollywood genres. It has been taken up and developed by subsequent theorists of cinematic comedy, most notably Frank Krutnik and Peter Kramer,[8] who have analyzed the interrelation between the central comic performer, his or her extradiegetic status, and the economy of narrative; and Dana Polan and Michael Selig, who have commented on the extent to which 1970s and 1980s film theorists studying Lewis's comedy confused the conventions of comedian comedy with modernist and postmodernist deconstructive strategies.[9] Although I agree with Polan and Selig, I suggest here that aspects of both postmodernism and poststructuralism have a largely unperceived debt to the tenets of the comic.

Another important factor contributing to the study of comedy is Tom Gunning's work on the cinema of attractions. In the 1980s, Gunning reworked Sergei Eisenstein's concept of attraction to account for the tendency of the earliest cinema to astonish its audience by envisaging and promoting film as a series of shocks. Gunning argues that early cinema was constituted by a completely different aesthetic imperative than classical Hollywood realism.[10] Although not directly concerned with comedian comedy, Gunning's revision of the history of early cinema has nevertheless had a significant impact on the understanding of the genre. It implicitly calls into question the dismissal of Sennett's comedies as merely primitive, and hence unworthy of scholarly attention, and demands that cinematic comedy in general be theorized by attending to both the continuities and discontinuities evident in its development. Furthermore, both Tom Gunning's and Miriam Hansen's historicization of the development of cinema in the late nineteenth and early twentieth centuries has meant that the perspective from which the emergent aesthetic can be viewed is no longer narrowly confined to what is specifically cinematic, but must take the wider cultural context into consideration.[11] The significance of their work is evident in the recent attention given to cinematic comedy's vaudevillian and music hall origins and can be found in Henry Jenkin's *What Made Pistachio Nuts? Early Sound Comedy and the Vaudeville Aesthetic*[12] and Robert Knopf's *The Theater and Cinema of Buster Keaton*.[13]

A second cluster of discourses on cinematic comedy are those that consider the nature of the comic aesthetic by elaborating on the philosophy of comedy and the comic. Jerry Palmer's *The Logic of the Absurd: On Film and*

Television Comedy[14] and Steve Neale and Frank Krutnik's excellent introduction to the mode, *Popular Film and Television Comedy*[15] followed a burst of interest in comedy in the late 1970s and early 1980s resulting from the journal *Screen*'s efforts to encourage discussion of the connections between film, politics, and critical theory in the wake of debates surrounding intersections between film and Marxism, feminism, psychoanalysis, and semiotics. These include the *BFI Dossier* on television comedy,[16] Neale's and Mick Eaton's *Screen* essays on comedy and psychoanalysis,[17] Claire Johnston's and Paul Willemen's work on Frank Tashlin[18] and Patricia Mellencamp's essay on the Marx Brothers.[19]

Much of this writing was devoted to questioning the ideological nature and transgressive potential of cinematic and television comedy, and included the appropriation of a Lacanian/Althusserian account of subjectivity to analyze the impact of these visual media on their audiences. This writing recognized that one of the crucial issues in the study of comedy was the operation of meaning in comic texts and theorists such as Eaton, Neale, and Mellencamp took up Samuel Weber's reading of Freud's *Jokes and Their Relation to the Unconscious* to theorize cinematic and televisual comedy. However, their use of Weber's work often ignored the specifically Freudian limits of his articulation, meaning that the complex implications of both Freud's writing and Weber's reading of it were subordinated to issues about the transgressive capacity of comedy. This transgressive capacity would be seen to be ultimately undermined by what had been established as the audience's interpellation by narrative structure, along with the audience's narcissistic relation to the cinema as a realm of imaginary plenitude. Moreover, this writing took up Weber's earliest essay, "The Divaricator" in *Glyph*, whereas his later essays on Freud's theory of the joke in *The Legend of Freud* and a special issue of *MLN: Modern Language Notes* were unfortunately published too late to be considered by this wave of film comedy theorists.[20] This is significant because Weber's thinking shifts from his early work on Freud, in which he characterizes the joke as the play with meaning by a triumphant narcissistic ego, to his subsequent theorization of the temporality of the joke process as something putting subjectivity itself into question. On the other hand, these writers' engagement with Freud's text meant the comic and the joke were identified as distinct formal processes. This led to Neale's attempt to account for the different kinds of subjectivity enunciated through film texts and Mellencamp's identification of the presence of the different aspects of the comic in various performance techniques (for her Groucho Marx is the exemplary exponent of the joke, Harpo of the comic). But this essentially closes the chapter on the impact of Freud's work on the study of cinematic comedy.

In taking up Freud's work on the joke again here to understand cinematic comedy better, I dispense with the Lacanian/Althusserian framework that dominated 1980s' film theory and situate Freud's study of the comic in the context of Bataille's philosophy of laughter. This allows me to address from the outset a residual anxiety that lingers in the work of many theorists of the comic regarding the seriousness of their object of study and particularly its relation to meaning. Despite the attempts to theorize cinematic comedy just noted, I maintain we still lack a convincing understanding of what constitutes comedy and the comic. This is why the main focus of this book is on what is at stake in comedic and comic processes and operations, along with their relation to meaning. True, the relationships between slapstick, gag, and narrative; the delineation of various kinds of gags; the distinction between anarchistic comedy and realist comedy; and the specificity of characterization in the genre are key issues that have emerged in the scholarship on film comedy. Yet, the imbrication of the comic and meaning, of sense and nonsense, has persistently demanded—but just as often eluded—the attention of writers seeking to define the parameters of the comic. My intention in this study is therefore to situate the issues and insights emerging from previous studies of cinematic comedy within a framework that takes the relationship between the comic and meaning as its central concern.

This book has been written with the aim of keeping a fundamental absurdity in view. This absurdity is that the anxiety over the meaning of the comic almost inevitably leads to a reduction of the comic object to its significance. What is intrinsically comic about the object is lost in the rational articulation of what the comic means. This condition unavoidably limits any intellectual investigation of the comic. Accepting that this absurdity is something in itself worthy of sustained scrutiny necessitates an examination of not just what the various instances of the comic mean, but what their relation to meaning is and what impact meaning has on them.

The first half of my analysis reflects on Bataille's notion of a philosophy of laughter, both because it delineates precise methods by which philosophy's capacity to reason and to articulate meaning are subject to comic degradation, and because it concerns itself with the entire problematic of the relationship between meaning and that which has claims to unlimit it. I use Bataille's work to address the manner in which the tension between the comic and meaning surfaces in specific contexts in the history and theory of film comedy, whether at the level of form, genre, or institution.

Chapter 1, "The Philosophy of Laughter: Bataille, Hegel, and Derrida," thus extracts from Bataille's philosophy of laughter a number of theoretical concepts for understanding the relationship between meaning and the comic. Meaning is taken to be that which is produced by the dialectical method in Hegel's *Phenomenology of Spirit*, and the comic comes to the fore through an analysis of the precise moments at which Bataille laughs at that method. By analyzing the effects of Bataille's laughter, particularly its capacity to turn sense into nonsense, in conjunction with Derrida's discussion of the conceptual coherence of this gambit, indeed, its complicity with Hegel's own method, I establish in turn the limits of the comic's capacity to intervene in the articulation of meaning.

In Bataille's writing the relationship between sense and nonsense comes to the fore in his laughter at the dialectic of the master and the slave and the risk of death that self-consciousness supposedly undertakes to enter into a meaningful relationship with the other. Bataille's laughter bursts out on the basis of this risk of death, thus inscribing it as a phony risk, a sham, or duplicity. If a real death were to result from the duel between two self-consciousnesses, there would be no meaning. Hegel himself is well aware of the sacrifice of meaning that the dialectical method entails and distinguishes between the two kinds of negativity that it generates. The first is sublative negation, the negation of the dialectic proper, that operates within the system and constitutes its method, producing meaning by interiorizing material existence and turning it into conceptual existence. The second is abstract negativity, death pure and simple, mute and nonproductive death, meaningless within the system and losing meaning in any effort to make it meaningful.

But whereas for Hegel the two kinds of negativity, sublative negation and abstract negativity, derive from one economy—that of the dialectic— and abstract negativity remains both powerless and ineffectual, Bataille brings the restricted economy of the dialectic into relation with general economy to show their mutual dependence and to define the effect that each has on the other. (In this way he gives what Hegel would call abstract negativity the capacity to impact on an economy of meaning.) But he does so by redefining it in relation to sovereignty. The operation of sovereignty is nothing other than the operation of the comic, and it derives from laughter. Bataille's laughter at the Hegelian dialectic produces an alterity within that dialectic; its effect is to ensure that the productive negation that interiorizes difference and allows transcendence nevertheless produces something it cannot contain. Sovereignty, thus understood, has little to do with its conventional usage. It does not, for example, convey an idea of self rule and is not used here to define the authority vested in an individual or legitimate body of governance. Most of all, sovereignty is not mastery. Sovereignty has no identity, is incapable of operating systematically, and erupts only at isolated moments in relation to the articulation of discursive meaning. Sovereignty is therefore the means of thinking about the relation between restricted and general economy.

Chapter 2, "Restricted and General Economy: Narrative, Gag and Slapstick in *One Week*," describes how the concepts of restricted and general economy are relevant to understanding cinematic comedy by analyzing the significance of narrative, articulated gags, and slapstick in Keaton's short film *One Week* (1920). It examines how the tension between narrative and the comic has been theoretically, historically, and cinematically articulated in accordance with the respective conditions of exchange in these economies. As such, this chapter argues that narrative in general functions in accordance with restricted economy, whereas the comic opens that economy to the destruction and waste associated with general economy. In advancing the argument for the operation of narrative and cinematic narrative in terms of restricted economy, I refer to the work of the Russian formalists, Roland Barthes and Hayden White, in addition to film theorists such as Raymond Bellour and David Bordwell. I also suggest that the tension between restricted and general economy, although never explicitly addressed in such terms, is the preeminent debate for theorists of cinematic comedy such as Bordwell, Neale, Krutnik, and Donald Crafton. These theorists focus their work on the question of the subordination of the comic to narrative and the attendant possibilities of the comic replacing conventional causal logic with surprise, fate, chance, luck, and so forth, as well as slapstick existing as a nonnarrative kind of cinematic attraction. The historical dimension of the relationship between restricted and general economy is evident in the transformation of the institutional and industrial base of cinema in the late 1910s and early 1920s and this transformation has been consistently cast in terms of narrative form taking precedence over the comic.

This reformulation of the tension between narrative and the comic as evidence of the relationship between restricted and general economy raises questions about the way producers of comedy themselves negotiated various historical contingencies, industrial pressures, and social imperatives in the course of their filmmaking. Chapter 3, "The Machine of Comedy: Gunning, Deleuze and Buster Keaton," retains the conception of narrative understood as restricted economy and considers how the need for a storyline, for narrative, forced Keaton, beyond seeking assistance from other directors, to relearn his comic repertoire between making short and feature-length films. In doing this, I reconsider Gunning's conception of the operational aesthetic in terms of Gilles Deleuze's discussion of the "recursion function." Gunning's thesis that the machine is not just one of the most prevalent objects of early cinematic comedy's mise-en-scène but also provides a structuring logic for rudimentary narrative form is consonant with the recursive logic underpinning Keaton's machine gags and trajectory gags. Keaton negotiates the problem of narrative by submitting it structurally to the operation of general economy. In other words, Keaton does not so much recast his gags within the dramatic form of narrative as mobilize them in such a way as to create a distinctive form of farce narrative.

As an operation of sovereignty, laughter has ramifications beyond the specific moments of the Hegelian dialectic at which it bursts out. By making laughter not an effect of the comic but its cause, Bataille also reverses the conventional articulation of causality envisaged in the production of the comic. The comic does not exist except through an affective outburst on the part of the subject, and the subject is dispersed in this outburst. Sovereignty in this sense has no claim to identity, and laughter is not an intentional or self-constituting act. Comic sovereignty consequently inflects our understanding of character and performer and subject-object relations within the genre of comedian comedy. Chapter 4 examines how film theorists seeking to account for the complexity of identity emanating from the tension between character and performer in the genre, and for the contradictions that emerge from the divergent capacities of these entities, have found interpreting the behavioral anomalies that result difficult. Lacking an adequate theory of the comic, film theorists fall back into realist, normative, subject-centered, thematically oriented interpretations of narrative to account for them. In "Fool's Gold: Metamorphoses in *Sherlock Jr.*," I supplement Bataille's conception of comic sovereignty with Baudrillard's discussion of the fatal strategies of the object to account for the nonidentity of the film's central protagonist and the special "privileges" that come with this nonidentity. These privileges include the capacity to short-circuit discursive meaning by replacing words with objects and the capacity to engage in metamorphoses.

The basis for the analysis of the comic in the second half of the book moves from philosophy to psychoanalysis, although my aim is to indicate a confluence between the two approaches. Where Bataille engages the operation of the comic as a means of rendering philosophical meaning indeterminate by producing something outside it that calls its structural coherence into question, Freudian psychoanalysis, particularly when read through a poststructuralist lens, provides a means of understanding the techniques of this operation in a more detailed way. The prime instigator of the comic in the second half of this study shifts from laughter to the unconscious. To the extent that psychoanalysis itself presumes a play of sense and nonsense, and indeed theorizes the imbrication of sense and nonsense in a variety of ways (whether in terms of the theory of cathexis, the irreducibility of the two topographies—the unconscious and preconscious-conscious systems on the one hand, and the id, ego, and superego on the other—the relation between the secondary and primary processes or the reality principle and the pleasure principle), Bataille's concepts of restricted and general economy are still significant.

Apart from the study of cinema, the significance of Freud's study of the joke's relation to the unconscious lies in its alteration of the conceptual basis of the comic Aristotle defined in terms of the degradation of the ideal or the real. For Freud, the joke uses the techniques of condensation and displacement to bring about the transformation of thought. Chapter 5, "Jokes and Their Relation to...," thus focuses on the way Freud distinguishes the joke from the comic in general and how the two categories of the comic emerge from distinctive psychical terrain supported by a richly articulated but nevertheless hypothetical system of processes. Moreover, the joke and the comic both inscribe different relations between sense and nonsense: the psychical operations of condensation and displacement in the joke in fact work to destroy sense in a more thoroughgoing manner than the mimetic degradation of "the ought" by "the is" in the comic. Freud's study of the comic and the joke is of interest to the study of cinematic comedy because the techniques involved in the comic and the joke appear to move in quite different directions. Chapter 6, "The Comic: Degradation and Refinement in 1920s' Cinematic Slapstick," and chapter 7, "From Words to Images (Gagging)," investigate the means by which the two techniques manifest themselves in film.

Chapter 6 considers the comic in terms of Freud's notion of degradation and Bergson's conception of as *la mécanisation de la vie* (which I argue is still implicitly a theory of degradation) to examine some of the historical contingencies that impacted the nature of slapstick in the 1920s. The valence of degradation is thus found in philosophical understandings of the comic; a range of comic techniques such as parody, travesty, mimicry, and caricature; and, significantly, in moral aspersions on the tastelessness of "primitive" slapstick. Whereas the notion of degradation has a conceptual breadth that allows it to comprehend diverse comic practices, the difference between the Sennett slapstick of the 1910s and that of Keaton and his peers represents a significant diminishment of comic degradation. The chapter considers Harold Lloyd's film *Safety Last!* as exemplary of the hybridization of cinematic slapstick and the more refined genre of genteel comedy. It also reflects on the convergence between what was happening in the genre and changes in the pictorial conventions of caricature in the late nineteenth and early twentieth centuries and how art historians have intrepreted such changes. The chapter finally argues that the refinement of comic degradation in the 1920s was not simply an attempt to accommodate the aesthetic sensibilities of contemporary audiences but was part of a movement toward visual abstraction and intelligibility that would prove to be crucial to the simultaneous development of the cinematic sight gag.

By contrast, chapter 7 investigates the pertinence of Freud's theory of the joke to understanding the operation of the cinematic gag and the sight gag in particular. While heeding that Freud's theorization of the joke focuses on the transformation of words and thoughts by the unconscious, and acknowledging that this emphasis on verbal material has been one of the primary reasons for the restricted application of Freud's work to the study of cinematic comedy, I argue that by situating the study of the joke in a broader psychoanalytic framework we get a sense of the unconscious's capacity to act on visual material as well. This chapter examines the significance of the visual in facilitating the operations of condensation and displacement and hence the generation of sense and nonsense. I propose that where Sennett-style slapstick produces the comic from the degradation of physical causality, and by negating the epistemological connection between vision and truth, the cinema of the sight gag takes a second step in the transgression of the cinematic articulation of the relationships between vision, knowledge, and truth. The latter produces laughter not simply through deceptive appearances but as deriving from the capacity of visual appearances to create multiple relationships between things and hence produce multiple meanings. The psychoanalytic regression from words to images is taken up with regard to cinematic comedy's predisposition to literalization gags and specifically the gags on framing and projection in Keaton's film *Sherlock Jr.* (1924).

Chapter 8, "Figural Vision: Freud, Lyotard and *City Lights*," further explores the significance of visuality in cinematic comedy by bringing Lyotard's commentary on the various imbrications of discourse and figure to bear on Freud's discussion of the primary and secondary processes, and of the reality principle and the pleasure principle. Lyotard's work gives Freud's hypothetical psychical processes an aesthetic reality so that the quasi-visual and quasi-physical processes of psychoanalysis become visual and physical operations that constitute the basis of cinematic comedy. Considered in tandem with the function of hallucination in the primary process, Lyotard's concept of figurality allows me to theorize the function of "figural vision" that makes 1920s' slapstick distinctive. This figural vision is contrasted with figurative vision through an analysis of Chaplin's film *City Lights* (1931).

In chapter 9, "Preposterous Figurality: Comic Cinema and Bad Metaphor," I continue to explore the significance of the comic displacement of the figurative by figurality. Yet in this chapter thought and meaning are taken as the primary point of focus rather than comic nonsense. I thus consider the contrasting articulations of metaphor proposed by structuralist (Roman Jakobson and Jacques Lacan) and poststructuralist (Lyotard, Barthes, Deleuze, and Derrida) thinkers. The Marx Brothers' gags here illustrate the way the operations of the primary process shift the register of cinematic enunciation from the demonstration of meaning to the exhibition of comic spectacle. 'The adventure of signification,' evident in these gags, is understood by Derrida to be what philosophy has traditionally decried as bad metaphor. Derrida's work allows me to theorize how cinema produces meaning in a distinctive kind of way and how the comic seizes on the visual medium of cinema to produce what has been called bad metaphor. An analysis of the operation of the maternal figure in Keaton's film *The Navigator* (1924) provides the means of demonstrating how cinema, in this instance at least, both deploys and hides comic figures.

❧

Readers will note some slippage throughout this book in the use of the terms *comedy* and *the comic*. In general, I consider *comedy* as a distinctive mode of drama and as a form of representation opposed to tragedy, and *the comic* as the broadest category of things that are laughable. For the most part it is the latter that concerns me, although I sometimes use the term *comedy*, as in the comedy of philosophy, when the comic is undoubtedly closer to my semantic intentions. Generally my justification for the slippage is that the comic of philosophy is not a particularly pleasant syntactical construction. In addition, in this case, I also wish to convey the sense of the drama that ensues when the comic comes into play in the field of philosophy. From chapter 5 on I note Freud's distinction between *the comic* as a form that is distinct from the joke and *the comic* as the broad category of humorous incidents.

Figure 1. *Go West* (1922). Courtesy of BFI Stills.

CHAPTER 1

The Philosophy of Laughter

Bataille, Hegel, and Derrida

Historically, philosophers, literary theorists, and ecclesiasts alike have as often as not greeted manifestations of the comic with condemnation. Comedy has been judged as a form of low art, as a genre inferior to tragedy, as appropriate only to the trials and tribulations of the lower classes, whereas the comic has likewise been condemned for expressing taste base enough to warrant the recommendation of abstinence. The admittedly infrequent counter to this broad characterization has championed the comic, arguing that it is indeed worthy of serious scholarly attention. This has usually meant either defining the specificity of the operation of the comic by delineating its techniques—whether irony, parody, satire, slapstick, degradation, jokes, or particular kinds of narrative structure—or focusing on the thematic content of individual works and uncovering the meaningful content buried beneath any number of comic façades.[1] Indeed, those advocates who aim to comprehend the comic in this manner relinquish addressing what is intrinsic to the comic as much as those who seek to dismiss it. To comprehend the comic, therefore, is to risk overlooking the structure of incomprehensibility that is crucial to its operation. Whether for or against it, the theoretical and critical reception of the comic has tended to subordinate it to the demands of meaning and reason. In this chapter, I consider the possibility of avoiding this subordination by pursuing the idea that the comic emerges from a relationship between reason and unreason.

BATAILLE'S PHILOSOPHY OF LAUGHTER

My starting point here is an examination and evaluation of the relevant insights of Bataille, most significantly his philosophy of laughter as a philosophy of *non-savoir*. One could argue that because Bataille starts with laughter, rather than the comic, he manages to retain the relation between knowing and unknowing crucial to the operation of the comic. Henri Bergson provides an interesting point of comparison in this regard. While Bergson's "Essay on the Meaning of the Comic" is entitled *Laughter*, he is never really able to reconcile fully his identification of the comic as *la mécanisation de la vie* with laughter itself, concluding that:

> From time to time, the receding wave leaves behind a remnant of foam on the sandy beach. The child, who plays hard by, picks up a handful, and, the next moment, is astonished to find that nothing remains in his grasp but a few drops of water, water that is far more brackish, far more bitter than that of the wave which brought it. Laughter comes into being in the self-same fashion. It indicates a slight revolt on the surface of social life. It instantly adopts the changing forms of the disturbance. It, also, is a froth with a saline base. Like froth, it sparkles. It is gaiety itself. But the philosopher who gathers a handful to taste may find that the substance is scanty, and the after-taste bitter.[2]

Bataille's contemplation of laughter is itself fragmented across the breadth of his work, being found in his anthropological and sociological essays: for instance, the collection of essays Denis Hollier edited, *The College of Sociology (1937–1939)*; his philosophical essays (those on *non-savoir* and Hegel); and in his works dealing with mystical experience (*Inner Experience* and *Guilty*).[3] Each of these treatments of laughter is specific to its context, although a consistency is found in the theorization of it across these works. Thus the sociological essays are concerned with laughter's relation to the sacred and the role it plays in the transformation of repulsive forces into attractive ones, the philosophical essays consider the intersection between laughter and epistemology, and the mystical works deal with laughter and sovereignty. This chapter concerns the comedy that emerges from Bataille's conception of laughter and the implications that such comedy has for philosophy. As the major arguments of the book develop, I also consider the implications of Bataille's work for the study of cinematic comedy.

Bataille, more than any other theorist of laughter, provides the possibility of displacing the lowly status of the comic. He does so not by elevating the comic to the level of art, but by bestowing on the operation of the comic nothing less than the status of sovereignty. For Bataille the 'beauty' of the poetic is still subordinate to the logic of reason and meaning, whereas he perceives laughter to exceed this logic to the extent that it occupies a position outside the system of philosophy, yet nevertheless produces effects within that system.[4] Bataille's laughter exposes the relationship between reason and unreason—the unknowing that constitutes the essence of the comic—by reversing the conventional method of inquiry into comedy. Rather than just attempt to philosophize comedy, Bataille treats philosophy as comedy.

As noted in the introduction, comedy and the variety of terms associated with the comic constitute a significant cluster of motifs for poststructuralist thought. This alone warrants and has to some degree effected an expansion of the interpretation of Bataille's oeuvre. Attention to his affinity with surrealism and celebration of cultural forms expressing the irrational, the unthinkable, and the impossible (such as death, ecstasy, ritual, sacrifice, the erotic, the comic, and the sacred) has been extended to theorizations that interrogate both the philosophical underpinning of his work and, indeed, its consequences for philosophical thinking.[5] I refer here to the work of Nick Land, Joseph Libertson, and Arkady Plotnitsky as well as Derrida. This relatively recent scholarship has deemed Bataille's laughter capable of resuscitating the Kantian noumenon, presenting a radical alterity to philosophy and reinscribing the Hegelian dialectic to the point where the quest for meaning is forsaken.

In his essay "From Restricted to General Economy: A Hegelianism without Reserve," Derrida questions the possibility of the comedy of philosophy that Bataille envisages. More specifically, he draws on the breadth of Bataille's writings to consider their relation to the Hegelian project. The impetus for Derrida's analysis of Bataille's laughter no doubt can be located in what Michel Foucault has called the "epoch" which "struggles to disengage itself from Hegel" or what Vincent Descombes has identified as a general preoccupation of post-68 French thinking with the problems arising from the specific nature of the dialectic in the Hegelian project—problems such as the reduction of the other to the same, the all-encompassing imperative of philosophical reason, and the end of philosophy.[6] Doubtless, Derrida also sees in Bataille's thought the possibility of undermining the concepts of presence and identity that dominate Western metaphysics and to which his work returns again and again. His essay is of interest to us here because of its theorization of Bataille's dispersed comments on comedy, laughter, and unknowing, but also because it evaluates the success and failure of Bataille's endeavor from a poststructuralist perspective. In this respect, Derrida's deconstruction of Bataille is relevant to understanding the operation of the comic in general.

Whether we call it Bataille's challenge to Hegel or, as Derrida prefers, the "constraint of Hegel" in Bataille's work, my interest in Bataille's writing is with the manner in which he envisages laughter undoing the tenets of metaphysical philosophy, relating concepts to their own baselessness, subjecting them to "inner ruination," and inscribing a nonteleological method of "backwardation" by referring the known to the unknown.[7] While the significance of laughter as an affective response to philosophical reason should not be underestimated, such laughter implies very specific operations of the comic, or as Bataille calls them, operations of sovereignty. An examination of the moments where Bataille invokes laughter reveals the comic operation that it engenders. After elaborating the significance of the comedy of philosophy, of Bataille's "philosophy of laughter," and his response to the Hegelian *Phenomenology*, I turn to Derrida's evaluation of Bataille's endeavor to consider the limits of its success.[8]

꩜

In his essay "Un-knowing: Laughter and Tears," Bataille audaciously declares that in as much as he is a philosopher, his is a philosophy of laughter.[9] To make laughter the very basis of philosophy might here be construed as an attempt to further perturb the happy marriage of philosophy and reason that was, until Nietzsche, still in its honeymoon period. In the place of reason, Bataille inserts its very antithesis, neither an enterprise, nor a disposition constitutive of a subject, only barely a mode of behavior. (In his essays on attraction and repulsion, for example, Bataille considers laughter under the rubric of the principle of contagion which constitutes human society around a sacred nucleus, a community whose fusion entails a loss of individual selfhood and thereby intentional agency.)[10] Bataille's self-characterization is further radicalized when one considers that he proposes that the cause of such laughter is both unknown and unknowable: "That which is laughable may simply be *the unknowable*."[11] And for Bataille this very unknowability is essential: "*the unknown makes us laugh.*"[12] In his efforts to produce a philosophy of laughter, a philosophy therefore of the unknowable, Bataille questions the conventional understanding of the philosopher as the lover or friend of wisdom, of knowledge, learning and erudition, and of soundness of judgment.

Bataille's philosophy of laughter, and the importance of his mobilization of the notion of *non-savoir*, has prompted commentators to relate his work not only to Hegel, but also to Kant. Bataille's laughter and the impact it has on philosophy has thus been described by Nick Land as a "fanged noumenon" and Libertson as an "altering incumbence of exteriority."[13] These characterizations allow us to grasp what is at stake in Bataille's reinvigoration of the Kantian noumenon—against Hegel's subsequent dismissal of it—and the performative nature of its operation.

Unknowing, such as Bataille invokes, has a philosophical precedent in the Kantian noumenon and, as we will see, a psychoanalytic one in the Freudian unconscious. In the Kantian distinction between phenomena and noumena, phenomena are appearances in the world of which we have knowledge through sensory experience. Noumena by contrast are things in themselves. They are unknowable because they are ungraspable by sensory experience. Diana Coole notes that Kant conceives noumena both positively and negatively, "In the negative sense, ... the noumenon is 'a thing so far as it is *not an object of our sensible intuition*,' whereas in its positive sense, it is 'an *object* of a non-sensible intuition.'"[14] For Kant the noumenon in this positive sense is the concept that makes sensible intuition possible, the concept of the object in general before its determination as either "something or nothing."[15] Hence it is an "empty concept without object" (*"ens rationis"*).[16] Land argues that Bataille's "fanged noumenon" is not the beginning of knowledge but its end; laughter, as the experience of *non-savoir*, has a *destructive* capacity not broached by Kant, constituting the "slide into oblivion," it is a "dissolvent immanence" that can be neither defined nor comprehended.[17]

Libertson has discussed unknowing similarly in terms of a philosophy of alterity. Libertson contextualizes Bataille's work at the point of the philosophical impasse where the inadequation between discursive representation and the alterity implicit in communication emerges. The very possibility of communication, Libertson argues, produces an opacity in its economy, which escapes comprehension and manifestation.[18] The spontaneity of consciousness that discourse engenders is limited by "the difference or discontinuity of the exterior thing, of the exterior subject or intersubjective other, and of the generality of existence in its excess over comprehension's closure" (P, 1). The attempt by discourse to register these limits (this alterity) both domesticates them and is necessarily eluded by them. The result, according to Libertson, is that inadequation becomes correlation, "the vicissitude of a larger adequation" (P, 1).

Importantly, however, this is not for Libertson the only experience of the relation of alterity to thought. The great anti-intellectualist thinkers (Nietzsche, Marcel Proust, and Freud, but also the subjects of his book—Maurice Blanchot, Bataille, and Emmanuel Levinas) attest not simply to an inability of formal discourse to represent alterity but also to alterity's "alteration of thought," which "weighs upon subjectivity in a communicational moment which is not yet or no longer comprehension" (P, 2). Libertson calls this experience an "altering incumbence of exteriority" which nevertheless remains subordinate in formal discourse. (P, 2) That is to say, this altering incumbence of exteriority alters the effect of formal discourse, but when represented by discourse is still subordinate to it. According to Libertson, the anti-intellectualists turn the formal (Kantian) and speculative (Hegelian) proposition of the noumenon or the thing-in-itself on its head. They regard alterity neither in terms of a power that nevertheless constitutes the basis of thinking phenomena (the Kantian noumenon), nor negation working toward the achievement of absolute spirit (the Hegelian in-itself). The anti-intellectualists refuse "to characterize alterity as a power or effectivity" and "thematize subjectivity itself as a radical passivity or heteronomy: not a dependence upon another power, but a pure passivity in a reality without power" (2). They heed "the approach of a powerless element over which consciousness nevertheless has no power—an element which changes and concerns thought on the basis of its very passivity and inactuality" (2).

The means of this "'altering incumbence of exteriority" will become clearer when consideration is given to the effects of Bataille's laughter as rupturing moments for Hegel's text. For Bataille's laughter is just such an "altering incumbence of exteriority." Laughter is that powerless element over which consciousness has no power, that element that changes thought on the basis of its very passivity and inactuality.

HEGEL AND BATAILLE: FROM DIALECTICAL DIFFERENCE TO COMIC COMPLICITY

For our purposes, Bataille's mobilization of laughter as unknowing finds its most profound relationship when compared with the apotheosis of metaphysical thinking—Hegel's *Phenomenology of Spirit*. That Bataille's understanding of Hegelian philosophy is derived from the lectures Alexandre Kojève gave in Paris in the 1930s and 1940s—and attended by so many of the French intellectuals who would subsequently take issue with the Hegelian dialectic—is nothing new.[19] I am not so much concerned with the correctness of Bataille's interpretation as with the relation to Hegel that he construes and the implications it has for understanding comedy.

Bataille's relation to Hegel is both concrete and elusive. To be sure, Bataille, at the outset, appears to make a significant break with Hegel—unknowing and knowing being the respective motifs that inaugurate for each thinker the beginning of philosophy. And many of Bataille's notions respond specifically to Hegelian concepts. Hegel's articulation of the relationship between philosophy and knowledge, as well as his concepts of experience or *Erfahrung* (as the movement that consciousness exercises on itself) and the dialectic (as the logical method of such conscious investigation) are the motifs that are transformed in Bataille's philosophy of unknowledge.

Set against the relationship between knowledge, truth, and consciousness in Hegel's work, Bataille's statements about his philosophy of unknowing could easily be misconstrued as glib or perfunctory. But to approach him superficially would be to fail to heed his stance on the anti-intellectualism against which he has been so outspoken.[20] Bataille's philosophy of unknowing is in no way a celebration of ignorance. It is rather a very precise interjection in response to Hegel's thought in, as Bataille professes, full knowledge of its consequences.[21]

Bataille's starting point is the unknowing manifest in the experience of laughter, the sacred, ecstasy, and so forth. What is significant here is that while laughter, like knowing, is subjectively experienced, it is experienced as *unknowing*. One can be conscious of one's experience of unknowing, but self-consciousness cannot supersede the experience of unknowing. (Hence, Libertson's characterization of the radical passivity of subjectivity.) Bataille's "philosophy" is concerned with "the effect of any proposition the penetration of whose content we find disturbing."[22]

The concept of experience provides a point of differentiation between the two philosophers. For Hegel, experience is related to the dialectical movement of self-revelation, the inner movement of the knowing process coincidental with the inner movement and transformation of the object known that constitutes the "becoming" of absolute Spirit. Unlike Hegel's dialectical experience, Bataille's is not developmental or progressive. In proposing that a philosophy of laughter should not confine itself to the object of laughter or its cause, but consider laughter in the context of other experiences of unknowing that form a continuum rather than a dialectic (such as tears, anguish, the feeling of the poetic, ecstasy, and so forth), Bataille writes, "I do believe in the possibility of beginning with the experience of laughter and not relinquishing it when one passes from this particular experience to its neighbor, the sacred or the poetic."[23] Hegel, on the other hand, sees experience as the movement toward the absolute, toward Science, and toward Spirit. While in the *Phenomenology* the trajectory of consciousness' knowledge is from the less well-known to the better known in that a presupposition is refined or shown to be known in some way, Bataille claims that his is a presuppositionless philosophy, that it begins with the suppression of knowledge, with nothing.[24] Bataille also at times considers this experience as a regression from the known to the unknown, a movement he calls *backwardation*.

Bataille's interest in Hegelian philosophy is also explicit to the extent that so many of his writings directly address issues that arise from the *Phenomenology*. Bataille engages with the work of the Hegelian dialectic and the logic of its economy and speculates about the implications of the project's success in giving an account of the attainment of absolute knowledge. In so doing he puts forward the unknown or unknowability as the inevitable blind spot of the completion of philosophy. On the one hand, he emphasizes the unknown that the *Phenomenology* must necessarily turn its back on, the poetry, ecstasy, and laughter that provide no satisfaction to self-consciousness, and on the other, he points to the fact that the condition of absolute knowledge, the very completion of the project, coincides with reaching a point where there is nothing else to know, reaching, that is, the unknowable![25]

Bataille thus identifies a conundrum in the work of Hegel. While the aim to think through the "totality of what is" and to account for "everything which appears before our eyes, to give an integrated account of the thought and language which express—and reveal—that appearance"[26] is without doubt the noble aim of philosophical thinking in general; for Bataille it is quite another thing to claim success, as Hegel does, to state that the project is complete, to turn in one's badge and close shop indefinitely because the end of philosophy necessarily entails the redundancy of the philosopher himself.

In "Hegel, Death and Sacrifice," Bataille argues for the general comicality of the task Hegel set himself. He sketches a double caricature, claiming that Hegel usurps the sovereignty of the divine and at the same time downgrades God to the status of regent. God as eternal and unchangeable becomes "merely a provisional end, which survives while awaiting something better."[27] It is the Sage, Hegel, who is rightly enthroned as sovereign because he is the one to whom "history revealed, then revealed in full, the development of being and the totality of its becoming."[28] Bataille, presuming to identify with Hegel, briefly imagines the despair he must have felt on realizing that the consequence of his insight was that there would be nothing else to know, but cannot help see the comic side of it: "In order to express appropriately the situation Hegel got himself into, no doubt involuntarily, one would need the tone, or at least, in a restrained form, the horror of tragedy. But things would quickly take on a comic appearance."[29]

Bataille claims the issue of death to be decisive for Hegel and he in turn subjects it to various comical interpretations. The fact that Bataille invokes laughter at the moment of death is consistent with his more general conception of the community being bound by the interattractive force of laughter that encloses the sacred nucleus of death.[30] Paul Hegarty notes that whereas Hegel and Heidegger argue that awareness of death is constitutive of humanity as such in that it "drives us to react against this initial negativity, by creating society as protection," Bataille on the other hand sees this "as a defense mechanism that allows itself to fail at certain points (in the festival, eroticism, laughter, drunkenness, sacrifice)."[31]

Bataille argues that the comic significance of death in the Hegelian system directly parodies the equally comic death of Christ. Death and eternal divinity, he points out, are irreconcilably contradictory: "to pass through death is so absent from the divine figure.... The death of Jesus partakes of comedy to the extent that one cannot unarbitrarily introduce the forgetting of his eternal divinity—which is his—into the consciousness of an omnipotent and infinite God."[32]

Bataille surmises that in Hegel's conceptualization of death, the attempt made by self-consciousness to achieve independence duplicates the implausibility of the merely rhetorical death of Christ. Death is dramatized by Hegel in consciousness' acquisition of a sense of self, a disposition only fully realized when consciousness obtains the recognition of the other. The demand for recognition of self-consciousness by another self-consciousness entails the infamous fight to the death, the duel that institutionalizes the relationship between self-consciousnesses as that between master and slave. In this duel, Hegel sidesteps the issue of mortality in exactly the same manner as the Christian myth of the death of Christ. That is to say, the outcome of the drama is predetermined: the stakes are bogus; in each case no possibility of death exists. The necessity of both risking death and staying alive are irreconcilable.

Derrida has argued that in laughing at this point of the Hegelian text Bataille focuses on the duplicity of Hegel's concept of death. In the dialectic of the master and slave, self-consciousness realizes that it cannot negate everything—that it is theoretically possible to be independent of everything but the life that is necessary in order to be.[33] Hegel writes "self-consciousness learns that *life* is as essential to it as pure self-consciousness."[34] The difference between real death and theoretical death is conceptually represented in the difference between abstract negativity and sublative negation. Hegel argues that the outcome of real death "is an abstract negation, not the negation coming from consciousness, which supersedes in such a way as to preserve and maintain what is superseded, and consequently survives its own supersession."[35] The risk of actual death would thus appear to be overcome, being superseded by the anticipation of the idea of death. At exactly this moment Hegel, Bataille implies, overextends himself. He fudges his logic by drawing a distinction between the abstract negativity that lies beyond consciousness and the negation that consciousness uses as a tool to further its quest for truth.

Just as the eternal divinity of God turns the sacrifice of Jesus into a sham, so too does self-consciousness' putting at stake of life rely a priori on the condition that it continues to live—hence, Bataille's analogy between the comedy of the death of Christ and the risk of death undertaken by self-consciousness. Although the dialectic of the master and slave would seem to dramatize a shift from materiality to conceptuality, Hegel purports to have no interest in pure materiality as the unknowable in-itself. The opening claim of the *Phenomenology* is that the truth of consciousness' knowledge of an object is not dependent on its relation to a world beyond cognition. How, then, within a single diegesis can Hegel make the distinction between real death and conceptual death, between abstract negativity and sublative negation? This is precisely what Bataille laughs at.

What does Bataille's scorn of one of the necessary stages of Hegelian self-consciousness' pursuit of the absolute tell us of laughter and its epistemological status as unknowing? Bataille's laughter is not based so much on a material figure exceeding a conceptual figure as on the simultaneous invocation and denial of the noumenon, the in-itself. If we follow Bataille's thought a bit further we find that his laughter at the master-slave dialectic is not simply a response to an isolated moment of the journey toward Spirit. He does not refuse to buy Hegel's argument at this particular point, laugh it off and move on. For Bataille, the master-slave dialectic is not merely one dialectic among others. He takes it to be *the* model for the dialectic in general. Whether rightly or wrongly, for him it defines the nature and role of negativity throughout the entirety of the *Phenomenology*. Hence the seriousness of his laughter; its object is both specific and fundamental. Beyond the relation between domination and servitude, it goes to the very heart of Hegelian negativity, undermining the success of the dialectical method and its ability to institute reason, truth and meaning.

Bataille's laughter at the master-slave dialectic focuses on the two kinds of negativity that operate in the Hegelian system. The first is the productive negation of sublation, the interiorization of material death into conceptual death and its transcendence. The second is abstract negativity, which Hegel, according to Derrida, freely admits is a "mute and non-productive death, this death pure and simple" ("FRGE," 255). In making this distinction between sublative negation and abstract negativity, Hegel attempts to remove abstract negativity from the endless interpretation of the system, even while including it as a concept ("FRGE," 257).[36]

RESTRICTED AND GENERAL ECONOMY

Derrida also shows us that the difference between these two forms of negativity structures Bataille's concepts of restricted and general economy. In restricted economy, to all appearances coincident with Hegel's economy in *The Phenomenology of Spirit*, the negative works toward the production of meaning. Restricted economy is geared toward production and expenditure for the return of profit. It is an economy of determinate meaning and established values where the dialectic, through sublative negation (the *Aufhebung*), provides its rule of exchange. General economy is not an economy of exchange but of waste, of expenditure without return, of sacrifice, of the destruction without reserve, of meaning. It bears witness to the mode of functioning of abstract negativity. Bataille's laughter therefore repudiates the economy of the *Phenomenology*—that is to say, the structure of evaluation and exchange that occurs in the dialectic, the expenditure of intellectual currency on defunct concepts provided the returns are worthwhile, on a real death, a mute and nonproductive death, for example, returned as a conceptual death. Just as self-consciousness needs the other and the recognition of the other, to end the cycle of the meaningless negation of nature, Hegel needs discourse to ensure the meaning of life. Bataille therefore contrasts between the restricted economy that characterizes the circulation of meaning in the *Phenomenology* and the general economy that envisages meaning exposed to its comic underside, wasted, destroyed without reserve.

Bataille treats the distinction between sublative negation and abstract negativity, and Hegel's use of the former to institute meaning and relegation of the latter to the beyond of reason and meaning as simultaneously comic and significant. In the first instance, one can draw from Bataille's laughter a technique well known in the world of comedy—the conceptual bifurcation between the two forms of negation has the structure of the pun or joke. In the second instance, abstract negativity, "death pure and simple," is not simply what Hegel discards, it is, Bataille's writing seems to suggest, the condition of the possibility of sublative negation.

SOVEREIGNTY AND THE OPERATION OF THE COMIC

In proposing the philosophy of laughter as a philosophy of *non-savoir*, Bataille links an affective response to an epistemological condition. Indeed, he situates laughter at the limit of epistemology. But Bataille's philosophy of unknowing is neither systematic nor systematizable. It is not found in a given book that can be picked up, read, and understood. It rather amounts to a process of backwardation; a writing of transgression; and a submission to the ecstasy, death, and sacrifice that can be glimpsed in the isolated moments of already received ideas. In this regard, Bataille's response to the *Phenomenology* exemplifies many of the broader concerns we find in his writing. Although Bataille chastises Hegel for failing to thematize the significance of laughter, for refusing laughter a place in his reputedly all-encompassing tome (laughter, he argues, should have been considered first), he also enjoys its exclusion.[37]

For all that Bataille's stance turns this traditional conception of philosophy on its head, importantly he does not presume a synonymy between the laughable and the comic. Although Bataille speculates that the laughable is the unknowable, he makes the qualification that we can nevertheless know the comic; "define the various themes of the laughable," subject it to both methodological and epistemological investigation, devise ways to provoke laughter and even make objects of laughter.[38] Indeed, between Bataille's laughter and the meaning of the *Phenomenology*, I have sought textual incidents that justify his amusement, incidents that are comic no less. We have witnessed Bataille's caricature of Hegel the philosopher, his attribution of a parodic dimension to the completion of the philosophical project and his attempt to turn the Hegelian dialectic into a joke. And whereas Bataille's emphasis is on laughter rather than comic technique and whereas comic technique is simply something that we have retrospectively inferred from his laughter, a more explicit interpretation of the comic can be gleaned from his linkage of the comic to sovereignty.

In his collection of Bataille's writings, Michael Richardson argues that sovereignty is an ongoing problem for Bataille in as much as he is concerned with how "human beings exist integrally for themselves while living in society with others upon whose existence their own depends."[39] Certainly Bataille's writings are replete with references to the "concept" of sovereignty. The caricature of sovereignty performed by rulers, the rebel's inevitable loss of sovereignty in the satisfaction of his aims, the near attainment of sovereignty by poetry and sovereignty's relation to beauty are all habitually revisited in Bataille's writings.

But for Bataille, the term *sovereignty* is much more complicated than is conveyed in its everyday usage. It is not just an issue of the individual's freedom and rights in society. Nor does it simply define the status of the monarch. What we see in Bataille's conceptualization of the confrontation between the two self-consciousnesses is an emptying out of sovereignty as it is exoterically conceived and the emergence (if only for an instant) of another notion of it.

In *Inner Experience*, Bataille writes "*sovereign operation* is the most loathsome of all the names: in a sense, *comic operation* would be less deceptive."[40] In his essay on Bataille, Derrida demonstrates how Bataille's conceptualization of sovereignty as the operation of the comic both relies on and undertakes the destruction of two of the central concepts of Western metaphysics—identity and presence. In other words, as the comic operation, sovereignty puts an end to determinate meaning. Bataille's laughter at self-consciousness' feigned risk of death is the condition that instantiates the emergence of sovereignty as a simulacral doubling of lordship. I would suggest that Bataille thus laughs at Hegel's concept of lordship in the name of an *other* to which it might be compared. In this instance, sovereignty is conceived by Bataille as a non-present other that provides the basis for comic comparison and justifies his laughter at the Hegelian dialectic.

More generally, Bataille's method of backwardation is significant because it means he reverses the relation between cause and effect. In this case, laughter does not emerge on the basis of comic sovereignty; the comic is rather constituted in the instant that laughter bursts out and in that instant alone. The comic here is not something that precedes laughter; it is rather an effect of it. Therefore, in spite of Bataille's claims that the techniques of the comic can be produced at will—much as we can define the conventions of comedy by considering its opposition to tragedy or account for the joke in terms of condensation and displacement—the temporal precedence that Bataille gives to laughter emphasizes the priority of the unknowable that conventional theories of the comic so often forget about but which Bataille argues is nevertheless the single cause of laughter.

That this laughter has no place in the Hegelian text is fundamental. Derrida explains:

> Laughter alone exceeds dialectics and the dialectician: it bursts out only on the basis of an absolute renunciation of meaning, an absolute

risking of death, what Hegel calls abstract negativity. A negativity that never takes place, that never presents itself, because in doing so it would start to work again. A laughter that literally never *appears*, because it exceeds phenomenality in general, the absolute possibility of meaning. ("FRGE," 256)

This laughter "that literally never *appears*" does so on the basis/baselessness of abstract negativity and in so doing gives rise to the doubling of the Hegelian text. Whereas laughter would be a moment that exists outside the Hegelian text, an alterity that has no place in dialectics, the manner in which it gives rise to sovereignty allows us to see precisely that "altering incumbence of exteriority" that Libertson describes. This is evident in Derrida's careful ascription of the burst of laughter to that which "makes the difference between lordship and sovereignty shine, without *showing* it however and, above all, without saying it" ("FRGE," 256).

If the laughter that gives rise to sovereignty and, indeed, if sovereignty itself is an "altering incumbence of exteriority," laughter and sovereignty would each constitute a "passivity" that nevertheless has "effects." With regard to laughter, this passivity is evident in the fact that it never takes place, that it is outside of dialectics, while its effects are evident in sovereignty and the inflection of comicality it imposes on reason. As a nonpresent simulacrum of mastery, sovereignty puts the concept of identity into question. Sovereignty does not itself have an identity but exists in the relation between laughter and death ("FRGE," 256). Derrida writes, for instance, "differing from Hegelian lordship, [sovereignty] does not even want to maintain itself, collect itself, or collect the profits from itself or from its own risk" ("FRGE," 264) and that "sovereignty has no identity, is not *self, for itself, toward itself, near itself*.... It must expend itself without reserve, lose itself, lose consciousness, lose all memory of itself and all the interiority of itself" ("FRGE," 265). Lordship and sovereignty are thus related to Bataille's concepts of restricted and general economy. In the restricted economy of the Hegelian dialectic, lordship has a meaning, lordship seeks meaning and makes meaning; whereas in the general economy sovereignty sacrifices meaning: "it governs neither others, nor things, nor discourses in order to produce meaning" ("FRGE," 264).

COMEDY AND THE TRANSGRESSION OF MEANING: THE EMPTY FORM OF THE *AUFHEBUNG*

In "From Restricted to General Economy," Derrida interrogates the possibility of getting beyond the powerful mechanism of the dialectic, not by directly deconstructing the logic of the Hegelian enterprise, but by examining the success of one of the most strategic and incisive treatments of it. Although Derrida begins and ends by demonstrating that Bataille does not so much oppose Hegel as manifest a complicity with him, and he argues that if Bataille's work is to some extent "free" of Hegelianism, it is also paradoxically constrained by it, in the course of his essay Derrida reinscribes their relationship within the thematic of Hegel's two self-consciousnesses. In fact, he sets the scene for the two philosophers to engage in a duel. Yet he envisages not so much a struggle to the death as a metamorphosis—of Bataille into Hegel and vice versa.

The turning point is Derrida's evaluation of the transgressive potential of Bataille's complicity with Hegel where he gestures toward the limits of Bataille's laughter:

> For at the far reaches of this night something was contrived, blindly, I mean in a discourse, by means of which philosophy, in completing itself, could both include within itself and anticipate all the figures of its beyond, all the forms and resources of its exterior; and could do so in order to keep these forms and resources close to itself by simply taking hold of their enunciation. *Except, perhaps, for a certain laughter. And yet.* ("FRGE," 252, my emphasis)

In focusing on the issue of transgression, Derrida's argument has relevance beyond evaluating Bataille's relation to Hegel because the transgressive capacity of the comic has precipitated its denunciation by moralists and its celebration by more anarchistically inclined critics. Derrida's critique of Bataille is instructive in this regard. Through Bataille's work he demonstrates quite precisely the limit condition of transgression; that is, the manner in which it becomes bound to what it negates.

Derrida brings the issue of transgression to the fore when he questions Bataille's claim that sovereign writing is able to neutralize the effects of discourse. Bataille, for instance, claims that such writing neutralizes meaning because it is neither this nor that, it destroys discourse, proceeds by means of backwardation, and so forth. Derrida says both yes and no. Yes, because sovereignty enunciates nothing ("FRGE," 274), but no because *discursive knowledge is neutral*. Discourse, for instance, neutralizes the real death that is put at risk in the dialectic. Language neutralizes the alterity of the other. Derrida argues that sovereignty's destruction of discourse is not an "erasing neutralization," but a multiplication of words, a process of "baseless substitution," a "potlatch of signs" ("FRGE," 274). Whereas the words and concepts subjected to the sovereign (comic) operation might well neutralize each other by canceling each other out, as is the case with lordship and sovereignty, they nevertheless, Derrida argues, affirm "the necessity of transgressing...discourse" ("FRGE," 274). Transgression consequently affirms a kind of negation.

This affirmation of negation leads Derrida to ponder Bataille's conclusion that transgression has the character of the *Aufhebung*, that it operates like the sublative negation found in the Hegelian dialectic. According to Bataille, the transgression of those laws of discourse that prohibit meaningless play and baseless substitution previously described "dispels the prohibition without suppressing it" ("FRGE," 275). A reader familiar with Derrida's moves might at this point expect him to perform his characteristic about-turn, that is, affirm Bataille's position, emphasize once again the immense enveloping capacity of metaphysics ("FRGE," 251) and lament Bataille's inability to elude it. But surprisingly Derrida does not make such a move. He heeds Bataille's acknowledgment that the operation of transgression here has the character of the *Aufhebung*, but rather than interpret this as more evidence of the complicity between Bataille and Hegel, Derrida argues the opposite—that "Bataille is even *less* Hegelian than he thinks" ("FRGE," 251, my emphasis). Certainly, the character of such transgression is sublative to the extent that it must affirm (that is, preserve and maintain) that which it negates. But Derrida indicates a fundamental difference between dialectical sublation and sovereign transgression:

> The Hegelian *Aufhebung* is produced entirely from within discourse, from within the system or the work of signification. A determination is negated and conserved in another determination which reveals the truth of the former. From infinite indetermination one passes to infinite determination, and this transition...continuously links meaning up to itself. The *Aufhebung* is included within the circle of absolute knowledge, never exceeds its closure, never suspends the totality of discourse, work, meaning, law, etc. ("FRGE," 251)

On the other hand, transgression does not maintain itself entirely within discourse and the circle of absolute knowledge, but in simulating the figure of the *Aufhebung*, "links the world of meaning to the world of nonmeaning." The distinction between real death and conceptual death only has meaning by recourse to a diegetic mise-en-abîme. Derrida writes:

> Bataille, thus, can only use the *empty* form of the *Aufhebung*, in an analogical fashion, in order to designate, *as was never done before*, the transgressive relationship which links the world of meaning to the world of nonmeaning. This displacement is paradigmatic: within the form of writing, an intraphilosophical concept, the speculative concept par excellence, is forced to designate a movement which properly constitutes the excess of every possible philosopheme. ("FRGE," 251)

Derrida suggests here that whereas dialectical sublation is composed of determinate meaning and continually links the world of meaning up with itself, sovereign transgression uses the "empty form" (the noumenal form) of the *Aufhebung* in an analogical fashion, thereby linking the world of meaning to the world of nonmeaning. Transgression (the nonpresent doubling of the sublative negation of the *Aufhebung* by laughter, for example) does not proceed from a determinate form to a more determinate form but produces an excess that cannot be incorporated into the restricted economy of determinate negation and that, moreover, renders the concepts of restricted economy indeterminate. This excess would be either the simulacrum or a "laughter, which constitutes sovereignty in its relation to death" ("FRGE," 256), both empty forms, empty concepts without objects. Their nondeterminateness, far from restricting the economy of meaning, opens it to its beyond. In other words, the empty form of the *Aufhebung* Bataille uses engenders comedy by transgressing meaning and engenders comedy to transgress meaning.

This difference between dialectical sublation and sovereign transgression is crucial to understanding the operation of the comic—not simply in Bataille's work, but in general. The operation of the comic simulates dialectical sublation and produces an excess that lies beyond classical logic. In general, this simulation, this unreason buried and exposed in the heart of reason and vice versa constitutes the comic, makes the text funny, and makes us laugh. The comic in sum opens restricted economy to the effects of general economy.

But lest one think that Derrida ultimately sides with Bataille, consider the closing remarks of his essay. Having established that Bataille is less Hegelian than he thinks, Derrida nevertheless ends by insisting that the *Phenomenology* is by no means left in tatters by Bataille's laughter. In the duel that Derrida stages for us, it becomes less and less clear who has the advantage. If the Bataille in Derrida's scenario seems livelier than Hegel to begin with, in Derrida's mind's eye his laughter reanimates the Hegelian text. The statue comes to life, not to fight with him directly, but rather to deny the stability of representation Bataille had supposed to be Hegelian. Derrida argues that given the form—the empty form—of the *Aufhebung* that operates in transgression "[i]t would be absurd for the transgression of the Book by writing to be legible only in a determined sense. It would be absurd...and too full of meaning" ("FRGE.," 276–7). Derrida thus draws a distinction between the book and writing as though the former were a determined form, the *énoncé*, governed by the conditions of restricted economy and the latter were something like the writing of *différance*, overdetermined, and operating under the conditions of general economy:

Thus, there is the *vulgar* tissue of absolute knowledge and the mortal opening of an *eye*. A text and a vision. The servility of meaning and the awakening to death. A minor writing and a major illumination.

From one to the other, totally other, a certain text. Which in silence traces the structure of the eye, sketches the opening, ventures to contrive "absolute rending," absolutely rends its own tissue once more become "solid" and servile in once more having been read. ("FRGE," 276–7)

Interestingly Derrida's reading of Bataille's relation to Hegel, particularly with regard to the emphasis placed on the master-slave dialectic, has come under fire by Joseph C. Flay and Judith Butler in an anthology edited by William Desmond, *Hegel and His Critics: Philosophy in the Aftermath of Hegel*.[41] Both authors criticize Derrida for limiting his focus to the master-slave dialectic, and mastery in particular. Flay argues that this is to the exclusion of other instances of the *Aufhebung* and on this basis rejects the claim that the master-slave dialectic is the model for the operation of the dialectic in general. Flay's argument assumes that Derrida's essay is a deconstruction of the Hegelian *Phenomenology*. Yet, Derrida's project in "From Restricted to General Economy" is arguably not so much a deconstruction of Hegel as a deconstruction of Bataille. The title of the paper uses concepts—"restricted and general economy"—first elaborated by Bataille rather than Hegel, and the subtitle—"a complicity without reserve"—far from suggests that Derrida is arguing that Bataille is simply opposed to Hegel. Moreover, we will come to see that "without reserve" suggests that the complicity between the two thinkers is in accordance with the operation of general economy.

As a means of clarifying the subtlety of Derrida's argument here we can examine the terms in which Flay and Butler also call Derrida to account for failing to see the comicality that operates in the *Phenomenology*. Flay isolates a couple of moments of comic irony, whereas Butler goes much further, claiming not only that the structure of the *Phenomenology* mimics the comic style of Miguel de Cervantes's *Don Quixote*, but also that interpreting the speculative concept of the *Aufhebung* as a comic device is possible. Butler's work is indebted to the Hegelian scholar Jacob Loewenberg who has argued that the successive conceptions of self that natural consciousness passes through in its journey toward spirit and the absolute are retrospectively revealed to be outrageous caricatures.[42] Flay criticizes Derrida for assuming that Hegel remains "with the seriousness of the negative, within the framework of a dialectic chained to the *Aufhebung*, rather than taking up the issue of sovereignty and its laughter with the rejected 'abstract negativity.'"[43] Yet, the very proposition that Derrida is suggesting that the Hegel of the

Phenomenology should have taken on abstract negativity, sovereignty, and laughter lacks feasibility because he goes to such pains to show that these "concepts" can be thematized only in relation to the death and mastery of the *Phenomenology*. Were they interiorized by the discourse of the *Phenomenology*, they would become indistinguishable from their counterparts in restricted economy.

Contrary to Flay's and Butler's accusation that Derrida maintains a narrow conception of the Hegelian *Aufhebung*, that he takes its operation in the master-slave dialectic to be paradigmatic and moreover paradigmatically appropriative and restricted in its economy, Derrida's comments here indicate that he is willing to admit different forms of the *Aufhebung*; in this instance, one that functions through determinate negation and the other through analogy. Furthermore, it cannot be emphasized enough that once Derrida has acknowledged the empty form of the *Aufhebung*, attributing to the *Phenomenology* a fully determined sense becomes nearly impossible. Plotnitsky furnishes us with some insight here by arguing that general economy is *in principle* one of unusable excesses: "*in principle*, rather than only in practice. Such losses in practice would be recognized within many classical or philosophical frameworks—*restricted economies*—specifically in Hegel and Marx, to which Bataille juxtaposes the *general economy*."[44] Following Plotnitsky, we might say that, practically speaking, the *Phenomenology* produces and indeed might rely on unusable excesses but that Bataille's laughter does so as a matter of principle. For Derrida, it is the necessary iterability of the Hegelian text that makes it powerless to prohibit Bataille's laughter and unable to resist the operation of the comic that wends its way through it, changing everything and nothing at the same time.

Derrida thus takes up one aspect of the thematization of death in Bataille's philosophy of laughter, marks the place where Bataille inscribes its relation to the Hegelian dialectic and the difference between sublative negation and abstract negativity, and shows how restricted economy is doubled by general economy. Derrida's formulation here, one could argue, suffices for the comic in general because it heeds the meaningless element that resides in comedy. Does Derrida here define the comic as just another formal mechanism? Yes and no. Yes, because he provides a rule for it; and no, because in indicating its meaninglessness he invokes the possibility of contagion that undoes formal constraint.

Bataille's laughter at the *Phenomenology* wreaks havoc with determinate discourse, letting loose in it a certain nonrelation to what is variously designated as the sovereign operation or the comic operation. By examining the points at which Bataille's laughter bursts out, we get a sense of the specificity of some of these operations and find that what constitutes the comic is the disruption of discourse, or, to put it another way, the subjection of meaning to a certain nonmeaning. In this sense the comic is essentially transgressive. The story, however, does not end here. Derrida's scrutiny of the sublative character of this transgression indicates that the transgression has a limit and that thinking such transgression either as a form of absolute negation or abstract negativity is not possible. In as much as transgression is affirmed, prohibition is sublated; the prohibition negated is also maintained in transgression. From a particular perspective, sovereignty likewise interiorizes mastery and the comic interiorizes meaning. Thus, the transgressive affirmation of the general economic operation of the comic needs a restricted economy of determinate meaning. The comic is not nonsense as such, but the relation of meaning to nonsense. Because of the inseparability of these two economies and the intimacy between sense and nonsense that defines the comic, the destruction of reason can itself be given a reason. That the comic is so easily reinscribed in the order of meaning explains why theorists of the comic so efficaciously illuminate its meaning for us. But that such theorists so often fail to reflect on the implications of their practice means that in the process of taking the comic seriously they demonstrate neither more nor less of an understanding of it than those who deem it to be a worthless or dangerous enterprise.

CHAPTER 2

Restricted and General Economy

Narrative, Gag, and Slapstick in *One Week*

If philosophy traditionally shows scant interest in producing the kinds of texts in which the restricted economy of meaning is subject to the effects of general economy, the case is somewhat different with regard to aesthetic and literary endeavors. The impact of Bataille's conception of laughter is evident, for example, in the manner in which cinematic comedy is constituted through the tension between restricted and general economy. In the following pages, this tension is considered in three spheres. The first is historical and can be illustrated immediately, although it will also be dealt with in the next chapter. It makes reference to the fact that by the time Keaton was directing cinematic slapstick, films had ceased being component parts of vaudeville and music hall entertainment programs and had become entities in their own right, and their patronage was changing from working-class to middle-class audiences. The industry's determination to advantage itself economically by dominating the market with lengthier products and selling viewing time to audiences with higher disposable incomes resulted in an increasingly critical opposition to slapstick in both the trade press and fan magazines. Significantly, this opposition was presented in ideological terms that celebrated narrative cinema as more edifying than slapstick.[1] Keaton's films were thus born of a period when the demand for narrative marked an end to the tradition of pure slapstick Sennett's Keystone comedies exemplify, and a forsaking of a cinema of pure energetics, of gags piled one atop the other, each upping the ante, exponentially increasing the pace, the violence, and the excess of what had come before.

The second sphere is theoretical and involves an overlap between narratological theory in general and as it pertains to film comedy. Although it has never been stated in such terms, the question of the relation between restricted economy and general economy haunts both narratological theory and film theorists' desire to understand the impact of the comic on narrative. The third sphere is aesthetic and concerns the actual relationship between the comic and narrative in one of Keaton's first filmmaking ventures. Although various examples would suffice for a demonstration of the generative tension between restricted and general economy in cinematic comedy, Keaton's film *One Week* was selected because it was made very early in his career. As a two-reeler that runs at approximately twenty minutes, this film affords an examination of his filmmaking at a time when slapstick still had the comparatively stronger hand, when his films, in other words, were not bound by the demand for narrative that imposed itself on his later features. The reorientation of cinematic slapstick toward storytelling is set out here in terms of a duel between slapstick and narrative, where the former is bent on exploring the multifarious possibilities of the anarchy of pure pleasure and the latter is determined to rein in that impulse, limiting it by subordinating it to the desire for meaning. Against this backdrop, I ask whether slapstick in Keaton's cinema is indeed subordinate to the mechanics of narrativity or whether it retains an element of autonomy. This chapter thus entertains the proposition that narrative can be understood as exemplifying the conditions of the restricted economy (even if this proposition has to be dismantled in subsequent chapters) and the comic those of general economy. In its course, we see the sovereign comic make light of meaning, and meaning, in the form of both narrative and theoretical discourse, definitively and determinately subordinate comic excess. It is not simply the case that each economy constitutes the limit of the other; each also bears the possibility of metamorphosing into the other.

THE RESTRICTED ECONOMY OF NARRATIVE

In his essay "Introduction to the Structural Analysis of Narratives," Barthes claims that narrative is the most universal of forms. Narrative "is simply there like life itself...international, transhistorical, transcultural."[2] At the most general and rudimentary level, narrative has been defined as a kind of knowledge, "a way of coming to grips with the meaning of events, of perceiving the transformative effects of an action, and grasping the role of time in human affairs."[3] Hayden White remarks that narrative is not just one code among others but *the* metacode.[4] Narrative, economically speaking, is a form of exchange that makes meaning possible. *Narremes* are the units of particular manifestations of narrative and can be linguistic, cinematic, musical, and so on. But what makes them function narratively is the support the concepts of space and time give them. In this sense the most minimal function of narrative is its representation of space and time but what derives secondarily from the orchestration of events in space and time is a causal structure. Narrative's own existence in space and time, its linear and continuous unfolding, endow its contents and events with meaning. Whether we call it a code or a form, narrative is a conceptualizing structure that sublates material conditions and through this process makes them meaningful. In this regard, it operates in accordance with the conditions of restricted economy. In Western storytelling, its restricted economic function is also bound up with the actions of protagonists, the integration and resolution of loose ends, and a drive toward closure.

The bulk of the work on cinematic narrative was undertaken in the 1970s under the influence of structuralist thinkers such as Barthes, Claude Levi-Strauss, and Algirdas Julien Greimas on the one hand, and Vladimir Propp and the Russian formalists on the other.[5] Theorists of cinema, including those undertaking structuralist and psychoanalytic approaches, whether concerned with classical Hollywood film or avant-garde film, have conceived the operation of cinematic narrative as an operation of restricted economy. As an example, Bellour's early work on classical Hollywood narrative conceptualizes it as a play of variation and repetition, a movement from heterogeneity to homogeneity, ultimately toward coherence and cohesion. Bellour developed the concept of alternation to account for the systematicity at the heart of narration in classical American cinema, the regulated play of sameness and difference throughout the entirety of the mise-en-scène and diegesis.[6] Furthermore, Bellour's concept of segmentation is obedient to the dialectical model of thesis, antithesis, synthesis in that it describes the logic of the narrative in terms of "a textual system in the sense of a dynamic, structuring logic according to which the narrative *extends, complicates, and resolves itself.*"[7] Similarly, the wave of psychoanalytic theories preoccupied with cinema's ideological effects that use either or both of Freud's expositions of the scenarios of the Oedipus complex and the fort-da game to interpret classical Hollywood narrative consider that narrative as an economy of repetition and variation, symmetry and asymmetry, installing a trajectory that moves from lack to mastery.

On the other hand, less than a handful of writers have attempted to theorize cinema in terms that would free cinema from the restriction this economy of narrative imposes. Although strictly speaking referring to movement rather than narrative, Lyotard, for example, contrasts the utilitarian movement of Hollywood cinema, "production in the widest sense," to the general economy of movement found in avant-garde and experimental cinema and emblematized by him in the figure of a child who perversely lights a match solely for the sake of watching it burn, for pure pleasure, jouissance.[8] Barthes also attempts to introduce some unrecoverable excess into the play of the cinematic text in his concept of the third meaning or *signifiance*.⁹ The third meaning, or the obtuse meaning as he also calls it, is more of a mystery than a meaning—"it compels an interrogative reading." ("TTM," 53) Barthes calls it *signifiance* because it is a signifier whose signified is neither located in the economy of narrative (whether the film's own or a broader historical or psychoanalytic narrative that the film participates in) nor attributable to the author's intentions ("TTM," 54):

> [T]he obtuse meaning appears to extend outside culture, knowledge, information; analytically, it has something derisory about it: opening out into the infinity of language, it can come through as limited in the eyes of analytic reason; it belongs to the family of pun, buffoonery, useless expenditure. ("TTM," 55)

The question that such work raises, however, which is pertinent to our inquiry here, concerns whether this excess operates simply as an abstract negativity, a limiting condition over which meaning is powerless to extend its dominion, or as a fanged noumenon, an "altering incumbence of exteriority" that disperses its effects within the text and subjects the order of signification to the possibility of its own destruction.

More recently it has been the "achievement" of Bordwell, and credit might be extended to the Russian Formalists Victor Shklovsky and Juri Tynianov, to tighten the restricted economic function of cinematic narrative by dividing the narrative into *fabula*, *syuzhet*, and *style*, thereby accounting at one and the same time for its universal and singular levels of articulation. Bordwell's work is of interest to us here for two reasons: first because its definition of style makes the conceptualization of slapstick possible, and second because this very conceptualization involves an interiorization of the comic that ultimately leads to its absorption by narrative function.

The fabula or story is inferred from the events presented, and more specifically from the inference of causal, spatial, and temporal links between events or situations and events. The syuzhet comprises the plot or the actual arrangement or presentation of the fabula in the text, "the patterning of the story as a blow-by-blow recounting of the film could render it."¹⁰ As inference, the fabula thus transcends the precise means of its delivery. Style refers to the specificity of the cinematic medium and the operation of particular aesthetic criteria in individual films. Style coexists and interacts with the syuzhet, customarily to support it but having the potential to disrupt it. (*NFF*, 52) This characterization of style as being usually subordinate to the blow-by-blow account of the story is limiting when it comes to considering the relationship between slapstick and narrative in cinematic comedy.

Bordwell also attempts to establish limits to the impact of film techniques on film meaning. Drawing on Noël Burch's concept of the parametric to account for the disruptive potential of style, Bordwell envisages parametric narration as a kind of narration where the "film's stylistic system creates patterns *distinct from the demands of the syuzhet system*" (*NFF*, 275). Parametric narration is "'style-centered,' or 'dialectical' or 'permutational,' or even 'poetic'" (*NFF*, 274). But in this kind of narration, "a film's stylistic patterning splits away from the syuzhet when *only* 'artistic' motivation can account for it" (*NFF*, 280). When such artistic motivation occurs the viewer can consider "style as present for its own sake, aiming to become palpable as such" (*NFF*, 280).

Significant for the study of cinematic comedy, Bordwell refuses to entertain the possibility that generic imperatives such as slapstick or comedy give rise to parametric narration. Narrative function derives from "'artistic' motivation" only when "the viewer cannot adequately justify the stylistic work as necessary for some conception of realism, for transtextual ends such as genre, or for compositional requirements" (*NFF*, 280). Whether slapstick, as a transtextual end of genre (as Bordwell sees it), has the potential to disrupt narrative, to exceed its logic, or to become palpable is thus unclear. What Bordwell seems to imply here is that, governed by generic convention, slapstick is neither part of the restricted economy of narrative, nor does it impact on it, much less does it have anything to do with general economy (*NFF*, 53). Bordwell actually uses the interplay between the syuzhet and style to excuse himself from having to pursue the possibility of excess of the kind he identifies in Barthes's *signifiance*. He notes, for example, Kristin Thompson's claim that film elements exist that fit neither into a film's narrative nor stylistic patterns and are thus unattributable to "aesthetic motivation," but says such excess, offering "little perceptual or cognitive payoff," is beyond his concern (*NFF*, 53).

One could easily conjecture that the waning interest of film theorists in the issue of narrative (excepting those theorizing comedy on the one hand, and David Bordwell and a few others inclined toward analytic philosophy on the other[11]), and the increasing attention currently paid to other less restricted rubrics (such as affect, attraction, spectacle, and audience) is bound up with narratology's all too-easy imposition of a restricted economy onto the cinematic text.

NARRATIVE IN CINEMATIC COMEDY

Bordwell's claims aside, the question remains of how we are to understand the impact of the comic on narrative function, and vice versa, if we suppose that narrative generally functions in accordance with the conditions of restricted economy and that Bataille is in some sense correct in pointing to the sovereignty of the operation of the comic. What case can be made for the specific modality of narrative comedy, for the insertion of gags into narrative structure, and for cinematic slapstick?

Certainly, narrative comedy itself does not necessarily elude the restricted economic conditions that define narrative in general. The form of narrative comedy, for example, receives implicit articulation as early as the fourth century by the grammarian Evanthius, who defines comedy's three significant moments in terms of *protasis* (exposition), *epitasis* (complication), and *catastrophe* (resolution). During the Renaissance, the theorist Scaliger added another moment, *catastasis*, following the *epitasis*, which is a new and further complication.[12] To the extent that narrative comedy is obedient to the thesis, antithesis, synthesis model, it seems at first sight to have a structure not dissimilar to the dialectic.

Northrop Frye's specification of the conventions of New Comedy is largely consistent with this model, whereby the premise of the genre is the affirmation of the unity of the sexes in marriage. Frye considers not just the convention of the happy ending but the plot structure in which the heterosexual couple is characteristically prevented from consummating their desire for each other by some kind of obstacle that must be removed or neutralized. The couple, however, is unified not so much through the goal-directed action of the hero (who is usually relatively neutral and uninteresting), but through a fortuitous turn in events.[13] Here the dialectic's conventional generation of meaning through the articulation of causality and a reliance on human agency to instigate history and destiny seems to be called into question by the chance nature of the resolution.

Neale and Krutnik have taken further steps toward problematizing a dialectical conception of narrative comedy. They criticize the overly schematic nature of Evanthius's model and indicate its applicability to genres other than comedy. They acknowledge that this general applicability is the result of the transgeneric Hollywood imperative of the happy ending, and note Bordwell's qualification that although Hollywood conventions demand that the happy ending be narratively motivated, in cinematic comedy "causal motivation can be abandoned for, or intermingled with, coincidence, Luck, Fortune, Fate or the intervention of the supernatural."[14] But they also take him to task for skimming over the methods by which comedy departs from Hollywood narrative conventions. What is lacking is an understanding of the dynamics of both comedic structures and narrative articulation within the genre itself, of the extent to which comedic forces are at odds with conventional narrative devices. Neale and Krutnik themselves state the case for comedy in much stronger terms, arguing, "it not only permits but encourages the abandonment of causal motivation and narrative integration for the sake of comic effect, providing a generically appropriate space for the exploration and use of *non-causal forms of motivation* and digressive narrative structures."[15] Thus coincidence, luck, fortune, and fate are motivational devices, supposedly noncausal ones, that come into play through the manipulation of audience expectations.

Neale and Krutnik also come up against the difficulty of locating the comic in a place completely beyond reason. This is apparent in their efforts to differentiate causal motivation from other kinds of motivation. Referring to Bordwell's work, they define the former in terms of narrative unity deriving from relations between cause and effect, and narrative closure as logically dependent on prior events. With regard to discussing the arbitrary or coincidental instigators of comedy such as fortune or fate, however, they refer to them not as causes but as motivators, indeed sometimes as nonmotivators. Yet in either case they have to acknowledge they are still "functional to the design of narrative" (PFTC, 33). By accounting for the comic disturbance of narrative terms such as coincidence, luck, fortune, and fate, Neale and Krutnik unwittingly extend the logic of restricted narrative over the very comedy they wished to see as undermining it. These motivational structures are not so much noncausal as they are indicative of different perspectives on causality. Coincidence, luck, fate, and so forth, are still causes to which narrative events can be attributed.

Regarding Bordwell's theorization of the relationship between comedy and narrative, we could say that it is the arrangement of syuzhet that brings to the fore the noncausal forms of motivation from which comedy emerges, whereas the fabula is governed by restricted economy to the extent that it is structured in accordance with the coherence of causal, spatial, and temporal links between events that are inferred. If the actual unfolding of the events of the syuzhet operates under the conditions of general economy, the rearticulation of such events in the fabula brings them back under the dominion of restricted economy. This is exactly what we see in Keaton's film *The Frozen North* (1922). A series of irrational plot events nevertheless cohere in the fabula. The film opens with Keaton emerging from a subway station plopped in the middle of a subarctic setting. The first narrative event has him holding up a saloon/casino by placing a life-size cardboard image of a gangster holding a gun at the window. A drunk patron soon discovers that Keaton's partner in crime is not all he is *cut out* to be (after trying unsuccessfully to swipe the gun from the gangster's hand he lifts him through the window and shows him to the other patrons). Keaton compliantly returns his bootie, tips his hat to bid them farewell, and is promptly ejected through the window. Next he wanders home, finds a man and woman amorously intertwined—a closeup shows him gesturing toward his broken heart in a display of emotion that is completely uncharacteristic of the man the French nicknamed "Firgo"—shoots them both in a fit of jealous rage, and then realizes he is in the wrong house. He finds the right house, acts contemptuously toward his wife, who screams in rage, then collapses to the floor when a jug falls and hits her on the head. When a passing cavalryman, who has heard her scream, comes by the house, Keaton starts the phonograph and lugs his unconscious wife around the room pretending to dance with her to convince him that nothing is amiss. Keaton leaves the house, spies another woman, puts on his suavest, most irresistible attire, and sets out to seduce her, picking, on his way, a beautiful rose stem from the snow. Despite his best efforts to woo the woman, she resists, and when her husband returns to the house to collect a forgotten item a fight between the two men ensues. When the husband leaves again he takes his wife with him. Keaton's sidekick, the Herculean Joe Roberts, appears on the scene from nowhere, and the two men follow husband and wife to the North Pole. From here several activities and gags follow that have neither narrative motivation nor consequence: Keaton's sled is pulled along by a scruffy set of mongrel mutts; he is booked for speeding by a policeman who drives a lightweight air-propelled sledlike contraption; he wears guitars on his feet in lieu of snow rackets, goes fishing, falls through the ice, catches another angler's catch, catches the angler, turns a snowball fight into a baseball match, and so on. Only when Joe starts sweeping the igloo is Keaton's memory of the woman he has chased to these extreme climes triggered (a cutaway shot shows that she herself is sweeping) and he determines to resume his former hunt, strengthening his resolve with a swig of soda. Keaton arrives at her house in no time and is about to have his way with her when her husband reappears and chases him out of the house. While Joe distracts the husband, Keaton gets back inside, metamorphosing momentarily into a distinguished officer and then back into himself before threatening the cowering woman. When he is interrupted a second time by the woman's husband, he dons a heavy beard in the hope of disguising himself and thus somehow deflecting the cuckold's wrath. Keaton's own wife suddenly appears from nowhere outside the window and shoots him.

This film progresses in a way uncharacteristic of Keaton's other films (shorts and features alike). Not only is Keaton's character both a tough guy and a regular Lothario (much more like the early Chaplin or Walrus characters in Sennett films), but both the mise-en-scène and the machines and contraptions (the North Pole, the single stemmed roses sprouting in a snow field, the hybrid sleds, the snowshoes) are more exorbitant than usual. These peculiarities are rationalized by the last shot of the film—a long shot establishing Keaton, alone and asleep in an empty cinema, pointing a program at the janitor as though it were a gun. An illogical syuzhet is thereby retrospectively reconfigured by the final event of the film as having the logic of a dream—a logic governed not by causality and spatiotemporal coherence but by the primary process and the operations of condensation and displacement (which we examine in the second half of this book). As the syuzhet jolts along, the film's spatial relations are similarly unsettling. Although point-of-view and shot/reverse-shot techniques are still used, mismatches of scale between such shots and the use of incongruous cutaways add to the film's surreality. Until the end, the syuzhet is more consistent with the conditions of general economy and the transgression of meaning, but the final plot element sublates lack of logical causality into the patterning associated with the dream. Palpable stylistic elements retrospectively become a function of syuzhet and fabula and general economy gives way to restricted economy.

In this film, and to a lesser extent in more conventional comedies, events might not be causally motivated, but they are still motivated, and are therefore still reducible to a linear structure, if not in the syuzhet then certainly in the fabula (in this case, the Keaton character falls asleep, imagines he can act in accordance with his unbridled desire, turns his life into a nightmare and awakens to find it was all a dream). In many of Keaton's other shorts, the entire narrative is generated by unlikely circumstance. In *Convict 13* (1920), the opening story of Keaton playing a round of golf is interrupted by a parallel story of a man breaking out of jail, then completely replaced when Keaton is knocked unconscious by his ricocheting golf ball, wakens to have had his identity stolen by the prison escapee, and ends up in jail. Such surprises or chance events might confound the logic of the syuzhet but they do not perturb the fabula in any way at all.

Film analysis itself contributes to the subordination of the comic to narrative because the attribution of comic surprises to any kind of motivating forces, even "noncausal" ones, rationalizes away the very force of the comic that had emerged from the fabula-syuzhet relationship. The process of exchange (of syuzhet for fabula or comedy for meaning) results in the subordination of general economy to restricted economy.

Nevertheless, although narrative comedy can be subordinated to the dialectic and seems to operate like it, the manner in which it simulates its organic structure and the contradictions that supposedly inhere in its components is important to note. In narrative comedy, obstacles emerge not because univocal or dialectical being confronts the fundamental truth of its own existence, not, in other words, through the movement of knowledge toward truth, but because events present themselves arbitrarily and in a limited way. Contradictions emerge not on the basis of real differences but because of spurious perceptions. The narrative that is consequently set in motion is based on misunderstanding (of the potential son-in-law by the father, for example, or of the man by the woman), however, this does not make the events that develop from it any less real. Hence, misunderstanding can give rise to tragedy as much as comedy. Frye and Neale and Krutnik all place more emphasis on spurious resolution as the marker of comedy, and that this spuriousness takes two forms or merges both forms together is worth noting—it is either not really a resolution at all (in *Sherlock Jr.* Buster Keaton gets the girl but the final shot of him jiggling two babies on his lap conveys a look of quiet dismay on his part over the turn of events) or it has been brought about independently of the agency of the character whose job we mistakenly thought it was to orchestrate it. Narrative comedy thus evacuates the significance of the identity of the protagonists and the determination of their existence as the embodiment of fundamental states of being. It reduces narrative to the barest components of time, space, event, and consequence so that coincidence and arbitrariness become the instigators of history and fate. If narrative exists to make our lives meaningful, narrative comedy (or perhaps more appropriately comic narrative) diminishes the agency of the individual to show that the world continues to work according to a logic that is unknowable and ungraspable.

THE GAG

A second means by which the restricted economy of narrative can be considered undermined by the comic is through the gag. Although never stated in such terms, the theorization of the relationship between narrative and gag that has preoccupied so many theorists of cinematic comedy can be understood as an attempt to articulate the relationship between restricted economy and general economy. However, because theories of cinematic comedy have been more concerned with ascertaining the extent to which one dominates the other, they have been less successful in understanding how the relationship between the two economies specifies the nature of meaning on the one hand and nonsense on the other.

The gag is one of those devices that every theorist likes to define according to his or her own criteria, stipulating whether it is improvisatory or planned, visual or performative, instantaneous or linear, distinguishable or not from other kinds of comic effects and so forth. In their conception of the gag, Neale and Krutnik include both sequences of events and one-off comic effects such as pratfalls and double-takes, both "improvised interpolation[s]" and "pre-prepared piece[s] of action," but all of their examples are strictly nonlinguistic pieces of funny business (*PFTC*, 51). As a result, their interpretation of the gag includes what is commonly known as slapstick.

Because the gag is not an essential component of narrativity, it is generally discussed as working toward different and often antithetical ends from those of the narrative. Neale and Krutnik, on the one hand, argue quite adamantly that the general tendency of gags is toward digressive and destructive ends rather than the resolution that gives narrative its distinctive form—

gags are "suited to constructing or marking a pause or digression in the ongoing flow of a story" (*PFTC*, 47-8)—yet, on the other, attend to the full gamut of narrative-gag relations. Gags not only interrupt the narrative, digress from it, and play a completely gratuitous role (*PFTC*, 52-3), but they are also able to "dispel digressive actions rather than build or prolong them" (*PFTC*, 54). As self-contained units, their own requisition of formal closure (akin to the punch line in jokes) makes them "structurally unsuited to narration" (*PFTC*, 47), yet we can find instances of running gags that are not restricted to a single narrative occasion but dispersed throughout the narrative (*PFTC*, 53). The gag can take a narrative precondition as its point of departure and can "switch back...in the direction of a plot" (*PFTC*, 54). Thus, despite claims for the digressive and destructive potential of gags (in accordance, that is, with the conditions of general economy), gags are by no means "restricted" to the function of opposing the narrative. As such, the problem of theorizing the gag's general tendency to disrupt the aims and operations of the narrative and the particular examples in which it does precisely the opposite remains. We are lead to the view that although the transgression of narrativity is certainly a common operation amongst gags, it is not an essential one.

The question that emerges in light of a consideration of laughter and transgression is whether the interest of comedy is simply elsewhere (in noncausal forms and digressive narrative structures) or in the active negation of narrative causality. Is the difference between narrative and comedy a mere divergence of interests—say closure in the case of the former and laughter in the latter—or is it rather a structured opposition? Although an analysis of comedy limited to examining the manner in which gags disrupt narrative causality rests on the assumption that the primary purpose of comedy is the transgression of narrative causality, Neale and Krutnik's delineation of the gag's relation to narrative suggests that the interest of the comic might possibly just be elsewhere.

SLAPSTICK FOR ITSELF

Donald Crafton presents a view of slapstick that contrasts rather dramatically with Neale and Krutnik's equivocality over the gag's relation to narrative. For Crafton, slapstick and narrative are diametrically opposed. As in the distinction between restricted and general economy, narrative evidences an economy of work, investment, and return, and slapstick one of excess, transgression, and absolute expenditure. Narrative comprises the horizontal domain of the story.[16] It is likened by him to the chase, the fuel of the film that propels it from beginning to end ("PAC," 111). Whereas narrative is centripetal, slapstick is centrifugal. Slapstick is violent, nonnarrative intrusion, an excess that cannot be subordinated to the narrative and that is incompatible with the logic that structures narrative ("PAC," 111) It comprises "the vertical domain," "the arena of spectacle" ("PAC," 107), which is full of "emphatic, violent and embarrassing gestures" ("PAC," 108) that are "overt, flagrant and flamboyant" ("PAC," 111).

The divergence that appears here between the claims Crafton and Neale and Krutnik make can to some extent be understood by recourse to each party's initial definition of what constitutes the form of the comic under examination. Neale and Krutnik include slapstick within their definition of the gag, envisaging the gag as a single rubric inclusive of all instances of nonverbal comic effects. Crafton distinguishes between slapstick proper, the kind that characterizes the films of the teens, and what Neale and Krutnik would call the articulated gag; between the kind of comedy that predominates in two-reelers and that found in feature-length films. Indeed, at one point in his essay, Crafton differentiates between slapstick, as "the generic term for...nonnarrative intrusions," and gags, as "specific forms of intrusions" which "may also contain its own microscopic narrative system that may be irrelevant to the larger narrative, may mirror it, or may even work against it as parody" ("PAC," 109).

Neale and Krutnik make a similar point in distinguishing between first and second wave comedian comedy. They identify the first wave as dominated by French performers such as André Deed and Max Linder, and the second as composed mainly of the progeny of Sennett's Keystone studios, exemplified not only in the films of those who actually learned their craft from him such as Chaplin, but also Lloyd and Keaton.[17] Although they are careful to point out that the historical shift does not result in a complete subordination of slapstick to narrative and note that in many respects, and even in spite of some of its practitioners rhetoric to the contrary,[18] slapstick continued to flourish in the 1920s, they argue at the same time for a weakening of its position to the point that it:

> no longer existed in anything like its original form or context by the mid-1920s (except in shorts and cartoons).... [T]he feature films made by Chaplin, Keaton, and Lloyd represent not so much the final flowering of an authentic slapstick tradition as the point at which it came to be either hybridized, combined with other components, or else industrially and institutionally marginalized. (PFTC, 131)

In this respect Neale and Krutnik's historical analysis reveals a point that they are unable to make quite so boldly in their conceptual reflection on comic entities; that is, their very general use of the term *gag* cannot accommodate nuances they deem to be significant in the history of cinematic comedy.

Even if the key to understanding the differences of opinion over the relationship between narrative and the comic in many respects relates to the way theorists have defined their terms of reference, apparently we have not yet adequately understood from these theorists what slapstick is. We are in no position, for example, to ascertain whether it is distinguishable from the articulated gag, where the force of its comicality lies, and so on. Too often, theorists of cinematic comedy seem content to categorize certain modes of comedy as slapstick, to acknowledge briefly that it relates to physical comedy and to end their inquiry there—as if the mode were so self-evident it required no further analysis or explanation. Even when they note a shift in the nature of slapstick or a diminution in its prevalence in the 1920s, they account for this change merely in terms of the imperative toward storytelling and an ever-increasing distaste for this particular kind of violent, bawdy, and base comedy, devoid of illuminating capacity. Closer attention therefore needs to be paid to slapstick and how it has developed in the cinema. This in turn should expand our understanding of its relation to general economy.

The term *slapstick* originally referred to a stage prop constructed of two wooden paddles, joined at one end, used by circus clowns to hit each other, thereby producing a slapping sound. Don B. Wilmeth notes "the literal slapstick was translated into a term to describe physical or broad comedy."[19] Larry Langman contends that a prompter used a slapstick device to cue the audience to laugh and argues that although slapstick is a kind of physical comedy, not all physical comedy is slapstick. Taking his cue from what he considers to be the original purpose of the object, he distinguishes slapstick by its requirement of expert timing. Slapstick, he also claims, "implies both the use of physical gags aimed against someone for laughs and a sense of unreality as a result of the broad gags and the improbability of the stunts."[20] Crafton concurs with this definition of the word and argues that "[t]he violent aural effect, 'the slap,' may be thought of as having the same kind of disruptive impact on the audience as its visual equivalent in the silent cinema, the pie in the face" (PAC, 108).

Neale and Krutnik define slapstick as a mode of comedy just like parody or satire. Slapstick, in other words, would be one mode of articulating comic narrative; parody and satire would be others. In this regard, whether slapstick provides the nuts and bolts of the mechanism of narrative, serves as a digression from narrative, or operates independently of it, matters little. Slapstick thus understood can, however, contribute to the acceptability of comic narrative. Slapstick makes comic narrative tolerable by establishing a tone of delivery that ensures we will not take it seriously. In *Jokes and Their Relation to the Unconscious*, Freud notes numerous conditions that must be satisfied for the comic to have its desired effect. He says that the comic will not bear being hypercathected and such preconditions as a cheerful temperament, a sense of humor (the ability to obtain pleasure from distressing circumstances[21]), and "an *expectation* of the comic, by being attuned to comic pleasure" (*JTRU*, 282), are necessary for the appreciation of the comic, whereas "any other pleasurable accompanying circumstances as though by some sort of contagious effect" (*JTRU*, 285) will facilitate it: "Anyone who starts out to read a comic book or goes to the theatre to see a farce owes to this intention his ability to laugh at things which would scarcely have provided him with a case of the comic in his ordinary life" (*JTRU*, 282–3). Understood as merely assisting the acceptability of the development of comic narrative, slapstick would therefore be regarded as a jesting mode, a playful treatment of the relations between cause and effect and so forth, possibly operating as a necessary diversion to the mechanistic, serendipitous, or fatalistic (nonorganic) structures of narrative that predominate in comedy.

With Sennett's Keystone films of the teens, the slapstick mode of comedy takes on a specifically cinematic dimension, and in descriptions of his work we find a fuller elaboration of the gamut of possible slapstick operations. Significantly, these descriptions present a continuum of action that spans from physical violence, to elemental decomposition, to mechanical repetition, to stylization. Although the last and in some respects the least of these operations—stylization—is something the critics themselves barely notice, stylization nevertheless appears to be inherent in all manifestations of slapstick.

Robinson proposes that Sennett's Keystone films produced a comedy that "is basic and universal," "uncompromisingly anarchic," "anti-authoritarian," relentlessly pursuing an "orgiastic destruction of goods and possessions."[22] His analysis of Sennett's slapstick focuses on elemental decomposition. He notes, for example, the way individual props became the means for physical abuse and comic improvisation: "a single prop (car, telephone, boat) or setting (grocery store, garage, kitchen or bedroom) was sufficient to set off seemingly endless enchaînments of comedy."[23]

Raymond Durgnat theorizes Sennett's slapstick in accordance with Bergson's conception of the comic as *la mécanisation de la vie*, arguing that Bergson's view accords with Sennett's slapstick to the extent that the laughable emerges from the point at which the body reminds us of a machine and comedy arises from *"the mechanical encrusted on the living"*[24] But in his description of poetic slapstick, stylization permits the physical universe rendered on film to take on a conceptual status. In the "delirium of physical and mechanical knockabout," Sennett's comedy is "gravitational, ballistical, geometrical. Trees, cars, people alike are analyzed down into objects whose fates become matters of weight, mass, trajectories, momentum, inertia, fulcrums and other impersonal qualities."[25]

Stylization is implicit in Doug Riblet's characterization of Sennett's slapstick. Although he calls it vulgar, sadistic, unsubtle physical comedy, and violent knockabout, involving performance styles featuring "exaggerated mugging and broad gesturing"[26] and "cruel assaults on the human body,"[27] he also acknowledges the way it relies on the construction of "the comedian's body as *stylized* and grotesque through the use of disheveled ill-fitting costumes and bizarre facial hair, often building on the comedian's extreme body type and/or distinctive facial features."[28] But this stylization of performance is not strictly limited to the physical body and its perpetration of violent deeds. The cinematic means by which the breathtaking delivery of slapstick's physical assaults are conveyed involve palpable formal interventions into profilmic reality through techniques such as undercranking the camera, "fast-paced editing," "quick cutting between adjacent spaces" and cross-cutting between different lines of action.[29]

Finally, consider, for example, James Agee's description of a simple pratfall:

> When a silent comedian got hit on the head...he gave us a figure of speech, or rather of vision for the loss of consciousness. In other words, he gave us a poem, a kind of poem, moreover, that everybody understands. The least he might do was to straighten up stiff as a plank and fall over backward with such skill that his whole length seemed to slap the floor at the same instant. Or he might make a cadenza of it—look vague, smile like an angel, roll up his eyes, lace his fingers, thrust his hands palm downwards as far as they would go, hunch his shoulders, rise on tiptoe, prance ecstatically in narrowing circles until, with tallow knees, he sank down the vortex of his dizziness to the floor, and there signified nirvana by kicking his heels twice, like a swimming frog.[30]

Slapstick, we might thus hypothesize here, always entails a comic stylization of performance.

ONE WEEK

Keaton's film *One Week* provides a means of considering further how narrative, gag, and slapstick are articulated in short films. As the second of the two-reelers that Keaton directed independently of Arbuckle, it was made at a time before the demand for narrative impacted strongly on Keaton's filmmaking. It has strong elements of slapstick at the same time that it clearly deploys articulated gags.

Considered as a story, Keaton's film *One Week* recounts the events of a couple's first week of marriage. The film, is segmented into seven parts according to the day on which the events occur. *At a stretch*, we might surmise that the film details the teething problems that a newlywed couple experiences in the first period of their life together and these constitute the kinds of obstacles that narratives in general attempt to overcome. These problems are primarily concerned with intimacy and exclusivity. From the first day it is apparent that the Keaton character's old rival for his wife's affection is the primary narrative obstacle that needs to be removed and issues about sharing surface in the manifest nesting instinct depicted in various domestic undertakings.

If we were to pursue the narrative line of the film we might well follow Bordwell's method and consider the relationship between syuzhet and fabula, and the interplay between syuzhet and style. The relationship between syuzhet and fabula is straightforward in the sense that the syuzhet presents events in chronological order, the cause-effect structure is uncomplicated and self-evident with no complication or blocking of the inferences the audience makes as the narrative progresses, and the space in which the story is articulated basically conforms with the laws of renaissance perspective. Even so, we find a sense in which the events of the syuzhet do not detail narrative progression as much as protraction. In other words, the relation of the syuzhet to the fabula is best understood as a kind of farce.

Although today the word farce refers to a dramatic work whose only object is to arouse laughter, "a proceeding that is ludicrously futile or insincere; a hollow pretence or mockery," as well as "to season or spice a composition or speech," it is worth recalling that the Old French substantive *farce* originally meant force-meat or stuffing, and as a verb had now obsolete meanings such as "to stuff with force-meat, herbs, etc.," "to stuff or force (something) into something else," "to paint the face" and "to cram the stomach with food and to fill out something lean or shrunken."[31] The lean narrative of the film might thus be considered to be filled out, indeed, to be crammed full, by the syuzhet.

The film begins with a denotative shot of a day marked on a calendar, which is followed by the intertitle, "The Wedding Bells have such a sweet sound but such a sour echo." This is in turn followed by another denotative shot of wedding bells and then by a long shot of a newlywed couple (Keaton and Sybil Seely) descending the stairs of a church lined with people who shower them first with rice but then, somewhat bizarrely, with shoes, one pair of which Keaton retains for himself. While easily read as an element of slapstick, Keaton's response builds his persona—he is not exactly indifferent to, but certainly less interested in, responding to causes and meanings than to what can be done with effects; he takes the world as a given, and this becomes his point of departure. The next shot introduces us to the closest thing the film has to a villain, Keaton's rival suitor, described by an intertitle as "Handy Hank: the fellow she turned down." The couple receive a telegram of congratulations from a relative with news of a wedding gift—their first house. Hank chauffeurs the newlyweds from the church to their new domicile, taking every opportunity to interrupt any intimate exchange between them. Keaton, fed up, initiates a shift to another car, which narratively speaking is not entirely successful, yet nevertheless results in the film's first articulated gag. The individual details of this gag certainly constitute elements of the syuzhet, but a digressive syuzhet that has little bearing on the fabula. In the end Keaton manages to get rid of Hank temporarily by engaging him in an altercation with a policeman. The first sequence ends with the couple arriving at their new address, the last box of their DIY (Do-It-Yourself) house dumped on the ground in front of them.

The second segment and the second day contain a crucial fabula/syuzhet element expressed by means of restricted narration. As Keaton goes about erecting his new house, Hank exacts his revenge by changing the numbers on the boxes that contain the pieces so that the audience anticipates that even Keaton's best efforts will be thwarted. The remainder of the events in this segment depicts Keaton building the house—the task of construction being in itself uninteresting for viewers, its syuzhet is peppered with slapstick.

The third segment, and the third day, begins with an iris opening of Keaton standing in front of his near-completed house. The audience's anticipation of some kind of debacle is exceeded by the surreal object that Keaton stands before. Classical proportion, ninety-degree angles, and scientific perspective have been driven away by rhomboids and trapeziums, diagonals, and obtuse and acute angles: a multiplicity of perspectives (aerial, oblique, and anamorphic) reminiscent of a cubist painting. Although Keaton's expression is characteristically nonplussed and unfazed, the house that looks back at him has the mocking countenance of a skewed face—the roof has become a thick shock of hair under which a window winks at us, while the half smile of the verandah and the bare teeth of the palings warn the audience of what is to follow. The rest of the day sees Keaton putting the finishing touches on his masterpiece, all articulated under the guise of slapstick and articulated gags.

The fourth day is much like the third. In terms of syuzhet and fabula, it is full of little events that are inconsequential in the scheme of things. More trials, more tribulations, more gags, and more slapstick.

The fifth day is Friday the thirteenth—time for Keaton to show off his house to his friends and time for the house, in cahoots with the forces of nature, to reveal its hidden logic and malicious intent. A subplot concerns Hank's inclusion on the guest list and Keaton's skillful deployment of the idiosyncrasies of the house to dispose of him. Rainy weather reveals several leaks in the roof and consequently interrupts the tour of the house. As the weather deteriorates, the house transforms itself from a place of hospitality and hearth to a Coney Island ride and then to a tornado that willfully expels all who have dared to enter. The segment ends with Keaton and his wife

Figure 2. *One Week* (1920). Courtesy of The Academy of Motion Picture Arts and Sciences.

taking the only refuge they can on the minimal prop of a wooden box, the house whirling round and round behind them.

The sixth day begins the next segment in the same diegetic space that ended the last one. Keaton and his wife awaken from their sleep on the box, the house behind them collapsed with exhaustion, crumpled and tattered. For the first time, Keaton and his wife are perturbed by its appearance, but are distracted by a man who enters the frame carrying a numbered sign indicating that they have confused Lot 66 with Lot 99 and that their correct address is elsewhere. With resignation, Keaton's wife retrieves the jack from the car, while Keaton starts to work on the house, dismantling this, modifying that, and ultimately mobilizing it by inserting barrels under its four corners.

Sunday the fifteenth is the last day of the week and the last segment of the story. Keaton tows the house out onto the street while his wife pushes it from behind. The towline breaks and the house stops short, digs in its heels, on the train tracks of all places, and refuses to budge, even in spite of

Keaton's efforts to nail the backseat of the car directly to its exterior wall and his wife's determination to keep pushing. These frustrated attempts to deal with immobility are dissected by a very mobile train that bears directly toward them. Audience expectations are surprised twice over when the trajectory of the train changes so that it sails by, leaving the house unscathed, and when another unforeseen locomotive careens right through it, leaving it as it was in the beginning (dust to dust, ashes to ashes), a pile of wood. Keaton places on the heap a For Sale sign along with the construction directions and, in a manner that Chaplin was to make his signature, leads his wife into the distance as an iris out closes the vignette.

My purpose in describing the film in this way has been to show that while clear syuzhet elements occur in the film, their relation to the fabula is relatively uncomplicated and uninteresting. I have intentionally avoided where possible going into any detail about the comic level of the narrative's articulation. Admittedly some of the gags do arise from fabula-syuzhet (story-plot) relationships—the final gag of the train demolishing the house is one such example—and usually can be accounted for in terms of audience anticipation and surprise. In this respect, some comedy is undeniably produced by the structure of narrative and can be accounted for by attending to narrative process. But we can also see that the narrative produced here is not so much one of meaning as almost entirely one of cause and effect. Even though the end responds to the beginning, in that the story has described the sour echo of the wedding bells, this has nothing to do with the pair's interactions with each other, is orchestrated by circumstances beyond their control, is expressed entirely through material gains and losses, and tells nothing of the psychological impact of the disaster on the characters. Indeed, Keaton and his wife are performers more than they are properly developed psychological entities. We have no sense whatever of the marriage having deteriorated or of events in any way being conclusive. If the couple's first home at the end is reduced to a pile of rubble, we are led to believe that this is merely the end of an episode in an ongoing series of events, and if Keaton's nemesis is momentarily out of the picture, we have no way of confirming that he is any further away than slightly offscreen.

Strictly speaking, Keaton's film *One Week* has what White has called the structure of a chronicle. It is more complex than the most rudimentary kind of reportage—the annals—that comprises a mere "list of events ordered in chronological sequence" because it has a central subject, but it is distinguished from narrative proper by its lack of closure.[32] It does not conclude, it simply ends.[33] Although the narrative is produced through the continuity of space, time, and cause-effect relationships, it is more of an excuse for the film's comic force. Without the comicality, the narrative in itself would have little impact on an audience, and no doubt such comicality accounts for the continued popularity of films such as this one with contemporary audiences.

It is at what Bordwell and others have called the level of style that the film's comicality comes to the fore. This style is evident in both the film's articulated gags and its slapstick. Consider the film's first articulated gag. When a passing car sidles up alongside Hank's as he ferries the newlyweds, Keaton seizes the opportunity to change their traveling arrangements and thereby avoid Hank's unwanted interference. The girl successfully switches cars, but as the distance between the two cars expands slightly Keaton is caught with a foot in each and is thus unable to make the move. A motorbike intersects the space between the two cars that Keaton straddles and carries him away with it. It progresses only a short distance before crashing, and driver and passenger fall onto the street. Hank in the meantime switches into the car with the girl. The scene cuts to a long shot of a streetscape where a policemen stands, arms expanded outward, directing traffic. Keaton, back on the motorbike, comes into the frame but leaps off while it is still moving, seizes the policeman's hat and baton, and gives him a swift, sideways, straight-legged kick from the hip so that he falls to the ground. Keaton assumes the policeman's identity and stands, arms expanded outward, directing traffic and, more particularly, the car with Hank and the girl, which has now come into frame. The car stops, and Hank alights. As the policeman on the ground starts to regain consciousness, Keaton bops him on the head with the baton and in a continuous action deposits the weapon in Hank's hand. The first car, previously abandoned by both passengers and driver, now rolls fortuitously into frame and Keaton and the girl hop back into it while Hank and the now recovered cop become embroiled in an altercation mischievously orchestrated by Keaton. The gag, as we noted, contributes to the mechanics of the narrative in that the problem Keaton's rival posed is disposed of, yet it is also obvious that Hank is constituted as an obstacle only to give provision for the gag.

Whereas this articulated gag is connected to the narrative in as much as Keaton conveys his wife from the church to what will be their first home, and in the process temporarily removes the obstacle Hank, other articulated gags are much more loosely connected to the narrative.

Halfway into the film, an extended gag develops as the Keaton character attempts to install the chimney on the roof while his wife takes a bath. The cross-cutting between two separate spaces establishes the components of the gag that will eventually intersect in the gag's penultimate moment. Numerous incidental and isolated gags occur while the extended gag is being articulated. Keaton cannot transport the chimney up the ladder to the roof except by wearing it on his head—he literally becomes a block head and somewhat phallic to boot—which causes him to lose his balance and fall.

Figure 3. *One Week* (1920).

Keaton's wife drops the soap on the floor and cannot retrieve it except by exposing herself to the camera. She motions to the camera, directing a hand to cover the lens until she is safely back in the bath. On the roof, Keaton now wears the chimney as a skirt (his sartorial extravaganzas contrast with his wife's nakedness) and slides down the eave, his legs catching the chimney hole and permitting him to appropriately insert the object. But carried by the momentum of action, Keaton slips through the chimney and lands in the bath in the room below. The coital image that seems to be propelling this gag is, however, ultimately unfulfilled. Keaton does not land atop his wife as we might expect because she has elusively taken refuge in the shower recess where she stands modestly clad in the curtain. As she scolds Keaton, he escapes through a doorway—unfortunately one that leads nowhere—and he ends up for the umpteenth time on the ground below, a puff of dust dramatizing his fall.

This extended gag contributes to the development of the film's narrative to the extent that Keaton has successfully completed the task of inserting the chimney in its appropriate place, but the sequence clearly has much more to it than this....

Whereas the first gag moves in the order of unity, separation and reunification, the chimney gag moves in the opposite direction—separation, unity, and reseparation. Both gags have a strong linear quality and in this way seem to imitate the mechanics of narrativity—that is, continuity of time and space, and a clear causal structure. But what really makes both gags funny is the slapstick that is deployed in various moments of their articulation. Bound up with this slapstick is a pictorial quality that relates more to the two-dimensionality of the cinematic image than the film's narrative significance. Importantly, too, both gags deliver a huge amount of action in a very small amount of time, the sense of which is difficult to convey in the narrative descriptions given here. The vehicular gag occurs in sixty-six seconds of screen time, the chimney gag in sixty-five seconds.

Considered as an example of stylized slapstick, the pictorial and graphic qualities of the image in the first gag come to the fore. These qualities emerge first from the symmetry of two bodies (two cars) moving in the middle of the frame, Keaton's body constituting a third or a bridge between the two, a body that is stretched and then conjoined with another intersecting body (the motorbike). As the initial pair of moving bodies (the cars) disappear from the bottom of the frame, the single body (Keaton), conjoined to the motor bike, moves toward the top. The slapstick is accentuated using a long shot and through the timing of the fortuitous joining and separation of these mobile entities. When the bike crashes, the bodies of Keaton and the rider splatter like mud on the ground, and when Keaton assumes the identity of the policeman, the gestures of his performance are large rather than diminished (as they will be when classical realism becomes the norm) and graphic rather than simply denotative. The slapstick thus seems to comprise not simply physical comedy, which it certainly is at its most general level, but the movement of matter—real objects in three-dimensional space inscribed on a two-dimensional screen—and the unstoppable momentum of that movement, its pace, tempo, and rhythm, and its role in subsequent displacements, conversions, and expulsions. Simply to describe articulated gags at the level of their narrative function therefore overlooks the significance of slapstick, which gives objects a graphic two-dimensional quality and events a momentum that does, indeed, in Lyotard's terms, seem to appeal to a jouissance of movement for itself. Furthermore, an analysis of the significance of style makes it apparent that narrative itself is as elemental as the bodies in space.

Slapstick, thus understood, is about much more than throwing custard pies or slipping on banana skins. It is not just that the early cinematic clowns are prone to falling over; slapstick is about the stylized physicality of the fall itself, the body's responsiveness to events in a manner approaching a kind of abstraction that necessarily exceeds the conventions of realism. This abstraction is sought through graphic qualities, choreography, editing, and rhythm. Keaton is a virtuoso physical performer who uses his body simultaneously to demonstrate the forces of the material universe, whether bounce, tension, liquidity, gravity, flight, and so forth, and, to a certain degree, to defy them.

Demonstration stylized in this way exceeds ever so slightly the basic functions of the material universe and starts to endow things with a life of their own.

If theorists of cinematic comedy have argued for the relationship between narrative and the operation of the comic as productive of the kind of tension that I have identified between restricted economy and general economy, where narrative starts out as restricted economy par excellence but is opened to the general economy of the comic and where the institution of meaning is transgressed by the intrusion of gags and slapstick, it is also the case that the operations of the comic and narrative do not always approach each other in such a combative way. Slapstick can in fact pursue its need for laughter quite independently of the narrative process. If the issue of cinematic comedy has been posed so often in terms of a duel between narrative and gag, and if the change in cinematic comedy between the 1910s and 1920s has also been cast in these terms, the duel is not essential to the comic and the narrative is not necessarily the target of the destructive propensity of the operation of the comic. Although many gags take narrative as the unit of meaning they transgress or destroy narrative in the process of making fun of something else, the comic targets meaning at other levels as well and may even rely on narrative to do so. When this happens—as in the case of articulated gags—whether the comic is subordinate to narrative, in which case the gag's purpose is to propel the narrative forward, or whether narrative form is being subtly deployed in the service of the comic, is unclear.

The next chapter examines this complicity between narrative and the gag. Whereas the tension between narrative and the comic has been addressed here as a source of intellectual curiosity for film theorists, it is for producers of comedy such as Keaton grounds for anxiety. His concern was not with the extent to which the meaning underwritten by the function of restricted economy could be unsettled by the comic, but precisely the opposite. The threat for him would not be that posed by the comic toward meaning, but rather that the demand for meaning would create conditions that made it difficult for the comic to flourish. In this sense, the challenge that Keaton experienced in shifting his production from two-reelers to feature-length films is one that involved a reconfiguration of the relation between restricted and general economy in a very distinctive way.

CHAPTER 3

The Machine of Comedy

Gunning, Deleuze, and Buster Keaton

Keaton's two-reeler *My Wife's Relations* (1922) is prefaced by an intertitle that reads, "In the foreign section of a big city—where so many different languages are spoken, the people misunderstand each other perfectly...." Following this, parallel editing connects two utterly disconnected situations. In the first situation, Keaton, playing a sculptor, vigorously absorbed by the demands of his work, accidentally collides with a postman. In the second situation, a couple "speaking" Polish call a celebrant on the telephone to ask if he is available to marry them forthwith. In the first situation, Keaton's collision with the postman has two outcomes, both of which drive the narrative on. Keaton is left with a letter whose addressee is encrypted in the smudged details on the envelope and the postman throws something at Keaton that, like the letter, misses its destination, and breaks the window of a neighboring building—the building, no less, where the celebrant of the second situation awaits his clients. Keaton's attempt to flee the scene of the crime is obstructed by a big, fat, burly, beast of a woman who has witnessed the flying projectile, assumed Keaton to have been responsible for it and marched him in to face the wrath of the owner of the property. And because the celebrant does not speak English, he in turn assumes they are the couple desperate to take their vows and marries them accordingly.

Keaton's new wife takes him home to her father and brothers, who all mistreat him terribly. His would be the lot of an overworked "Cinderfella" had the father not found the misappropriated letter, opened it, read of an inheritance, and assumed his son-in-law to be the beneficiary. Accordingly, the family reverses their attitude toward him and all together begin to live the life of Reilly. That is, until the family of the letter's real addressee determines to revenge itself.

In this film, the play of contingency and misinterpretation provides the means by which Keaton (the director) connects disconnected events. What he dubs the perfection of misunderstanding in his hands becomes both an admirable description of the film's comicality and the basis of narrative structure.

In *Cinema 1: The Movement-Image*, Deleuze describes this connective aspect of Keaton's aesthetic in terms of the recursion function.[1] The English edition of *Cinema 1* translates *fonctions récurrentes* and *series récurrentes*[2] as *recurrent function* and *recurrent series*,[3] respectively, but this leads to an unusual characterization of Keaton's gags and does not, in any case, fit with the analogy that Deleuze subsequently draws between Keaton's cinema and Rube Goldberg's cartoons. On the other hand, *series récurrentes* also corresponds to the mathematical term *recursion series*, and this term—*recursion*—is, in fact, more appropriate to Keaton's aesthetic and, indeed, Deleuze's explanation of it. The example of recursive language given by the *Oxford English Dictionary* is, "This is the house that Jack built. This is the mouse that lived in the house that Jack built. This is the cat that ate the mouse that lived in the house that Jack built" and so forth.[4] Deleuze says of the structure of Keaton's films, "[e]ach element of the series is such that it has no function, no relationship to the goal, but acquires one in relation to another element which itself has no function or relation" (*C1*, 177). The series, in other words, is not purposive but results from a pragmatic effort to link one moment to the next. Strictly speaking, the series can go on ad infinitum, but in Keaton's work the beginnings and endings of his films stand as two disconnected points, and within these broad points of disconnection one finds numerous other disconnected points. By way of explanation, Deleuze likens Keaton's comedy to Rube Goldberg's machine cartoons, the causalities of which "operate through a series of disconnections" (*C1*, 177). One such Goldberg cartoon, *Professor Butt's Automatic Dishwasher* (c. 1928), shows a contraption Professor Butt constructed for washing the dishes while at the movies. The cartoon depicts a proscenium view of a room housing a complicated arrangement of domestic appliances, connected by pulleys and levers and energized by the family pets. The caption reads:

> When spoiled cat (A) discovers he is alone, he lets out a yell which scares mouse (B) into jumping in the basket (C), causing lever end (D) to rise and pull string (E) which snaps automatic cigar lighter (F). Flame (G) starts fire sprinkler (H). Water runs on dishes (I) and drips into sink (J). Turtle (K), thinking he hears babbling brook babbling, and having no sense of direction, starts wrong way and pulls string (L), which turns on switch (M) that starts electric glow heater (N). Heat ray dries the dishes.

Another example of a recursion trajectory, perhaps the most elemental to be found in Keaton's films, occurs in another two-reeler, *The Paleface* (1921). The Keaton character's effort to flee the clutches of the American Indians is stymied when the chase maneuvers him toward the edge of a ravine. Its precipices are connected by a broken down bridge, consisting of two parallel ropes and a handful of planks, which provide a path for the distance of only one or two steps. Beyond this the ropes are bare and the bridge hollows out to the abyss below. Keaton has no means of escaping the American Indians except by this forsaken bridge, so he installs himself as a machine in it, removes a plank from behind him as he crosses it and replaces it in front of him, thereby continuing his trajectory in a repetitive and piecemeal fashion. The two sides of the ravine thus present the points of disconnection, and the planks of wood (his props), individually useless, are the elements of the series that provide Keaton's means of transportation.

While Deleuze is not explicit about the role of the comic or the comedic in his discussions of cinematic comedy in either *Cinema 1* or *Cinema 2: The Time-Image*,[5] this chapter explores the connection between the aesthetic that he identifies as specifically Keatonesque and the comic quality of Keaton's narratives. Keaton's unique formulation and deployment of the action-image is consistent with Deleuze's insistence that narrative is not something given in the cinema but "a consequence of the visible [*apparent*] images themselves and their direct combinations."[6] The recursion function manifests itself in Keaton's cinema as nondialectical and inorganic teleology. As such, recursion is therefore the comic means by which Keaton discloses the machine lying at the heart of narrative.

THE TWO-REELERS

By Keaton's own admission, his short films were often not much more than a compilation of improvised gags, sometimes with less than the barest bones of narrative structure. But such extemporizing, he observed, could not sustain a 100-minute film.[7] And although he shares the credits with other directors in his shorts as well as his features, Keaton himself has quite tellingly suggested that in his feature films other directors were largely brought in to assist with the development of a storyline.[8]

To show how Keaton's gags provide him with a structuring logic for his extended narratives, let me first very briefly provide details of the kinds of narrative that are found in his two-reelers. The preponderance of adventures and situations furnishes the "structure" of Keaton's short films with a more or less rudimentary narrative form. The films tend to chronicle the Keaton character's life rather than present fully formulated narratives. The narratives

Figure 4. A recursion trajectory in *The Paleface* (1921).

vary, however, in the degree to which they are linear and in the extent to which they are digressive or resolved, as well as in the way events are organized according to the rules of psychological and causal motivation. For the most part they are produced through building up humorous incidents or episodes; they are not properly structured interpretations of events, but formations that emerge as a result of nothing more than the continuity of time and space. Four kinds of narrative can be identified in the two-reelers, although they are not necessarily mutually exclusive. A consideration of the articulation of these narratives in turn will enable us to understand how, in addition to the external pressures associated with the demand for longer films that were brought to bear on his filmmaking, Keaton eventually arrived at a distinctive form of cinematic narrative.

The two-reelers of the first group are conventional in the sense that they are goal oriented, psychologically motivated, structured through the logic of causality, and resolved at the end. These quest narratives detail the Keaton character's attempt to achieve a goal, whether it is marriage (*Neighbors* [1920]; *Daydreams* [1922]; *Cops* [1922]) or the completion (successful or unsuccessful) of any kind of task (*One Week; The Electric House* [1922]). While these narratives are quite conventional, they are also farcical in as much as the narrative is rudimentary, and the plot is as voluminous as its events are inconsequential. Those of the second group are less structured by narrative flow than built around situations, much like the situation comedies we see on television. Keaton retains this kind of structure from the time he worked with Arbuckle. This is evident in films such as *Coney Island* (1917), *The Butcher Boy* (1917), and *The Garage* (1919), which were all made with Arbuckle, and continues to predominate in *The Playhouse* (1921), *The Blacksmith* (1922), *The Scarecrow* (1920), *The Haunted House* (1921), and *My Wife's Relations*. The third group— *The Boat* (1921), *The Balloonatic* (1923), *The High Sign* (1921), *Hard Luck* (1921), *The Goat* (1921), and *The Pale Face*—are adventure narratives with digressive trajectories brought about by comic processes. The Keaton character's narrative agency in these films is minimized—meaning that he does not so much set out on an adventure (in the way he does later in the feature film *Go West* [1925], for example), as he embodies the attributes of a nearly will-less man caught up in the flotsam and jetsam of the world at large, but doing his best to adapt to the ordeals that it presents to him. This characteristic gives provision for the digressive structure of such films and allows the comic free reign. The films of the fourth group, structured according to the "logic" of displacement, are without a rational basis for connecting events. In *The Frozen North, The Love Nest* (1923) and *Convict 13*, even the most tenuous narrative logic of coincidence and accident is abandoned and replaced by dream logic. Causality is more dramatically forsaken in *Convict 13* and *The Frozen North* than in *The Love Nest*.

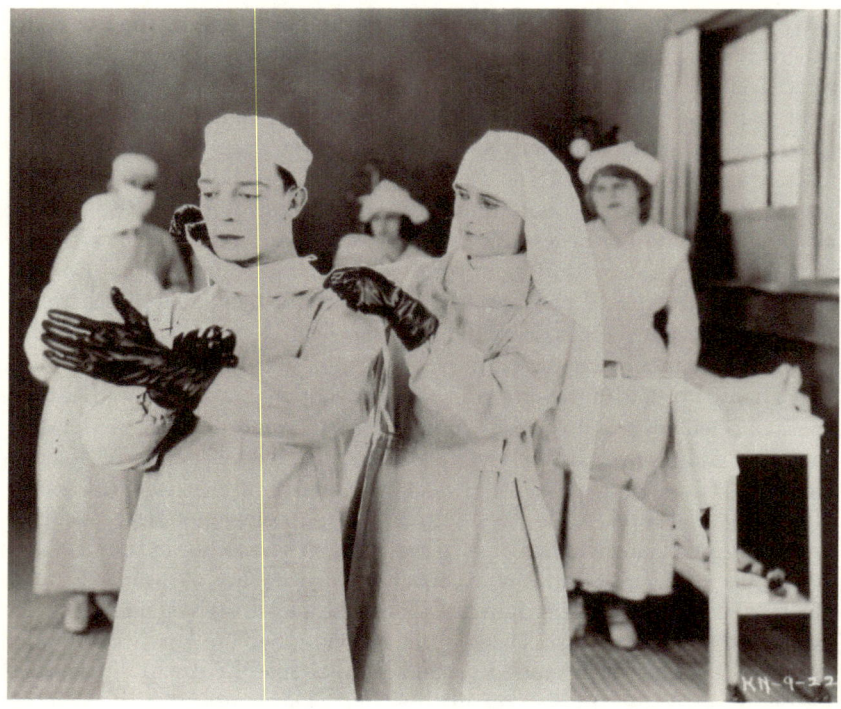

Figure 5. Evidence of dream logic in Keaton's quest films. *Daydreams* (1922). Courtesy of BFI Stills.

Keaton's two-reelers look back to Mack Sennett's aesthetics in their slapstick and chase sequences, in the creation of comedy from the interpenetration of situations which are parallel in space and time although wildly disparate in content, and in their experimentation with dream logic, particularly the imbrication of comic logic and dream logic. But the two-reelers also look forward to his features in their emphasis on props and in their construction of both stories and gags around the deployment of props. Indeed, the finest of the features are stories built around a single prop—the train in *The General* (1927), the ocean liner in *The Navigator* (1924), the steamboat in *Steamboat Bill, Jr.* (1928), the cinema in *Sherlock Jr.*, and the movie camera in *The Cameraman* (1928)—or a motif, which is in any case a concept that has a proplike status—athletics in *College* (1927) and marriage in *Seven Chances* (1925).

It is in the features that the problem of the tension between narrative and the comic presents itself most emphatically to Keaton. Evidence suggests that because the demand for a story was at odds with the methods he had previously developed for making audiences laugh, Keaton's shift to making

Figure 6. Keaton's quest to get the girl in *Neighbors* (1920). Courtesy of The Academy of Motion Picture Arts and Sciences.

feature-length comedies led him to reconsider the comic possibilities at his disposal. In his biography, he outlines how the need for a stronger storyline meant that between his two-reelers and features he had to relinquish implausible narrative structures and impossible gags. He had to curb his use of slapstick and work on developing believable characters. He also had to avoid gags that were discontinuous with the basic plot structure.[9]

Narrative linearity presented one of the biggest difficulties. Keaton learned through experience that in feature-length films audiences would not tolerate having their attention diverted from the hero's efforts to resolve the problems the narrative presented. To illustrate the point, he cites one of his favorite sight-gags, devised for *The Navigator*. It was to take place in the scene where Keaton, wearing a diving suit, plunges down to the bottom of the ocean to mend a leak in the ship on which he and the girl have been set adrift. At his disposal, he has numerous gags relating to the incongruity of situation and behavior (while underwater he puts up a barricade bearing the sign "Men at Work" and washes his hands in a bucket of water) as well as to the transformation of objects (he uses a lobster as a pair of pliers and a swordfish as a weapon to joust with another swordfish). The audience readily accepted all of these gags according to Keaton. The one they rejected, and which was cut from the film, involved the Keaton character playing a traffic cop. Pinning a starfish to his diver's suit, he held up his hand to halt a passing school of fish so that a big fish waiting patiently for clear passage could go on its way. When the gag was shown in the trailer, the audience's response was suitably mirthful, indicating that the gag itself was not lacking in comicality. But a subsequent test-screening of the whole film revealed that its placement in the narrative vitiated its comic potential. Keaton concluded that his "feature comedies would succeed best when the audience took the plot seriously enough to root for... [him] as ... [he] indomitably worked... [his] way out of mounting perils."[10] The challenge then was to devise a way of making gags while retaining a narrative structure that would guarantee the audience's attention.

While Keaton's feature films were more conventional in narrative structure than his two-reelers—not only more teleological but also more organized around the Keaton character as an agent of narrative development—an examination of his first forays into feature filmmaking indicates that it was not a straightforward transition. His first feature, *The Three Ages* (1923), a parody of D. W. Griffith's *Intolerance* (1916), is in fact three short films intercut with each other, each exploring the same theme but in different epochs—love in prehistoric, Roman, and modern times. The feature-length narrative of his next film, *Our Hospitality* (1923), was achieved largely by subordinating comedy to melodrama. The beginning of the film is firmly organized by the melodramatic mode; the narrative hinging on a feud between two families that provides the situation for a duel between the Keaton character and the brothers of his love interest. Comedy is injected into the duel structure; it breaks with conventional melodramatic realism, but its effects are comparatively insignificant in terms of narrative development, leading David Bordwell et al. to cite it for its exemplary narrative structure in spite of its genre.[11] The third feature, *Sherlock Jr.*, confirms that Keaton was, even at that stage, still uncomfortable with the feature-length narrative. This time he deals with the problem by inserting a dream within a film within the film, which allows him to retain the impossible gags and divergent logical structures of some of his earlier films. Only with his fourth feature, *The Navigator*, does Keaton makes the full transition to full feature-length comic narrative. Importantly, in this film he interweaves the narrative structure with a prop in a manner that he had not done so resolutely since *One Week*.

Both *The Navigator* and *The General* attest to a comparatively greater ease with narrative structure on Keaton's part and the story is implicated in nearly all of the incidents related. In *The Navigator*, Keaton plays a card-carrying member of the idle rich, Rollo Treadway. The plot of the film at its broadest level involves Rollo attempting to get the girl (Kathryn McGuire) he loves to marry him. While she initially rejects him, complication and coincidence sees them both set adrift on an ocean liner called *The Navigator*, thus conspiring to give them a second chance. Unnavigated, as it were, they are subjected to the will and whim of the elements. In the course of their adventure, Rollo and the girl must adapt to the scale of the ship, hazard fierce storms and vast seas, and fend off a tribe of hungry cannibals. A series of individual tests brings them closer until the final shot where their embrace affirms their love for each other.

Conventional narrative causality also appears to organize the unfolding of events in *The General*. The film presents the story of the heroic deeds of a Southern patriot in the American Civil War. Keaton plays an esteemed train engineer, Johnnie, who has but two loves: his engine, eponymously named *The General*, and a girl called Annabelle (Marion Mack). When Civil War engulfs the South, Annabelle's brother and father do the honorable thing and enlist. Annabelle expects Johnnie to do the same, but when he tries his application is refused because he is regarded as more valuable as a train engineer. Annabelle dismisses Johnnie's excuses and vows to have nothing to do with him until he is in uniform. From this point on, the narrative focuses on Johnnie's redemption.

Even though in both films all the events in some way pertain either to developing the character or to the films' narrative unfolding, nevertheless we sense that these feature-length narratives differ from their noncomedic counterparts. Chance, fate, luck, and coincidence are more significant factors in the orchestration of these films' narratives. For example, just when it becomes clear that the test of 'navigation' in *The Navigator* has overwhelmed the protagonists and death by drowning is inevitable, a submarine—the deus ex machina—comes to the rescue. And in *The General*, coincidence is the only reason that Annabelle journeys on Johnnie's train to visit her wounded father in a nearby town, and it is bad fortune that she remains on board when the Northerners steal it. When Johnnie makes it his mission to retrieve his beloved train, he does not know that Annabelle has been taken hostage and purely by luck is he privy to the Northerners' battle plans. Coincidence, not heroism, nor any self-transcending capability on Johnnie's part, enables him to rescue both Annabelle and his train as well as to warn the Confederates of the pending Yankee offensive. Coincidence and chance undermine the functions that causality and character agency have in narrative. In particular, such factors erase the way that conventional rational causality produces narrative meaning and, indeed, legitimates narrative's claim to meaning. However, this is not to suggest that coincidence and chance necessarily render the films nonnarrative or antinarrative.

Figure 7. *The Navigator* (1924). Courtesy of BFI Stills.

THE OPERATIONAL AESTHETIC

One of the most interesting arguments that can be brought to bear on the relationship between comedy and narrative structure in early cinema comes from Gunning's theorization of an operational aesthetic based on demonstrating the function of the machine. Whereas theorists such as Bordwell and Neale and Krutnik generally concur that in the relationship between narrative and the comic the abandonment of causal motivation is more or less a generic convention,[12] Gunning, by contrast, actually makes mechanical causality the crux of the relationship between cinematic comedy and the operational aesthetic.[13]

The operational aesthetic extends Gunning's previous theorization of the cinema of attractions.[14] Gunning uses the latter concept to account for cinema's emergence from the specific cultural and technological conditions of the nineteenth century, noting in particular the vast array of optical toys and visual attractions that both culminated in the invention of cinema and established its audience as sophisticated urban pleasure seekers. The imperative of early cinema or the cinema of attractions was not, he argues, to tell stories as much as to arouse and to intensify the curiosity of its audience, to astonish and shock them.

The earliest evidence of the operational aesthetic is found in the audience's attraction to the cinematograph itself; Gunning deems the films the cinematograph screened to be "simply a demonstration of the machine's process and functioning."[15] This cinematographic machine similarly captured the process and functioning of other machines as we see in the Lumière brothers' 1896 *actualité*, *Arrivée d'un train en gare à La Coitat*. The fascination with the machine went hand in hand with cinema's illusory capacity. Gunning cites, for instance, early cinema's appropriation of the music hall's sausage machine routine where a pig is herded into one end of a box and comes out the other side as meat cuts and sausages.[16] The operational aesthetic also reveled in the reversibility of nature, as the brothers' film *Demolition d'un mur* (1896) illustrates, when a brick wall is erected and dismantled by manipulating the forward and reverse wind mechanism of the projector.

While many of the cinematic examples of the fascination with operationality have a comic element to them, it was in the plethora of mischief films produced between 1896 and 1905 that cinematic comedy really got under way. During this period narrative, gag, and mechanism became three means of ordering the temporal process in a way that was distinctively cinematic. Gunning identifies these three components of the operational aesthetic in his analysis of *L'Arroseur arrosé* (1895), a film often cited as the first piece of cinematic comedy. A basic narrative structure is formed through a single gag, while the gag itself is constructed on the basis of the deployment and redeployment of an apparatus. A man attempting to water his garden is prevented from doing so by a boy stepping on the hose. When the man examines the nozzle to see what the problem is, the boy steps off the hose so that water suddenly spurts in the man's face. The man reprimands the boy and finally chases him out of frame with the hose. The narrative emerges from the apparatus mediating between the two characters and inscribing action with temporal development in the operation of the device.[17] The gag, Gunning quite rightly suggests, emerges from the deployment of an apparatus that creates a detour of character action through an inanimate object, and of course from the man, initially oblivious to the boy's intervention, being caught unaware.

Gunning describes the antiproductivist ethos of mischief films such as this. Their primary aim was the derailment or interruption of intentional action. Indeed, this quality of interruption or derailment, and the fact that it was "structured around a quick payoff," constituted its gaglike structure and prevented the "flow...into a longer temporal progression."[18] As films increased in length, directors for a time strung pieces of mischief together in a kind of additive or parataxical structure, but ultimately this method proved unsustainable and the mischief film all but disappeared. Gunning argues, however, that the operational aesthetic continued to prevail into the 1920s in Chaplin's assembly lines and Keaton's locomotives: "[t]his fascination with the way things come together, visualizing cause and effect through the image of the machine, bridges the end of the nineteenth century and the beginning of the twentieth, shaping many aspects of popular culture."[19]

The Keaton films in which the operational aesthetic is most clearly foregrounded can be called *task films* (although all of Keaton's films have a task dimension).[20] The operational aesthetic is evident in most of the two-reelers. We see it in the articulated gags in *One Week* depicting the construction and transportation of the house; the gallows with the elasticized noose and the machine like performances of the rioting prisoners in *Convict 13*; the collapsible mast designed to allow the vessel to squeeze under the low bridges in *The Boat*; the trafficator made from a boxing glove and pantograph (extension scissors) in *Cops*; the constructive and destructive transformations of the house in *Electric House*; the demolition of the car and the invention of the sprung saddle in *The Blacksmith*; the hybrid balloon-boat in *The Balloonatic*; and finally Buster's lifeboat and his means of lowering it into the water in *The Love Nest*.

The most memorable exploration of the operational aesthetic occurs in Keaton's two-reeler *The Scarecrow*. The adaptation of objects and construction of apparatuses that shape so many of Keaton's ventures are here used to add a masculine touch to domesticity. The film opens with two men at home (Keaton and Joe Roberts), one with a toothache and the other with an idea of how to remove the offending tooth. After misconstructing an apparatus, but nevertheless succeeding in removing the tooth, the two men prepare for dinner. The house they share is completely, although somewhat unconventionally, mechanized. It is filled with transformable objects and apparatuses created to economize and masculinize domesticity. A phonograph is also a cooker, a table top doubles as a wall plaque, a sink converts into a lounge, a bed into a piano. Strings and pulleys connect the bottles of condiments set on the dinner table so that they can be efficiently exchanged and conveniently removed. While the plates are attached permanently to the table, the table itself is detachable so that food can be emptied from it and fed to the pets outside through a trap door before being hosed down.

Gunning's identification of an operational aesthetic in early cinematic comedy unquestionably provides a means of understanding the deployment of apparatuses in both Keaton's short and feature-length films. More importantly however, it can be used to explain how these apparatuses relate to Keaton's gags and narrative structures. For the operation of apparatuses often provides the substance of both the story and the comedy. Consider, for example, the two-reeler *The Electric House*. As a tale of retribution, narrative events are linked through misidentification and revenge. The Keaton character has just graduated as a doctor of botany but is mistaken for an electrical engineer and contracted to wire a house for electricity. The film is organized around the undertaking of a single task. Both the story and the film's comic dimension emerge from the demonstration of the uses of electricity. And both, literally and figuratively, are concerned with crossed wires. This film recalls the house of gadgets in *The Scarecrow*, and one can imagine that the diverse uses of electricity that the film explores would have dazzled contemporaneous audiences more than today's. (The poetic, often surreal, quality of images that emerge from this enterprise remains impressive.) Stairs become escalators; the bath travels to the bed to pick up its patron; dinner is distributed by train; the plates are cleaned in the dishwasher and returned to their cupboards by conveyor belt; the pool table is automated to set up the game; the library to distribute books; and outside the water level of the swimming pool can be altered by shifting a lever. The film's gags involve both the operationality and malfunctioning of these newly invented machines. As one would expect in a Keaton comedy, a few slapstick glitches temper the demonstration of such modern marvels. The real engineer gets his own back by unleashing the destructive underside of electricity. The circuit room is like a computer, which he reprograms to turn the house against its inhabitants. Keaton's attempt to carry his suitcase upstairs turns into a Sisyphean nightmare. With the trunk heavy on his back, he is unable to see that his interminable movement up the stairs is thwarted by their downward mechanization. And as the owner argues with one of his guests in the library, the automated book selector slaps the latter on the back with such perfect timing as to lead the man to believe his host is the perpetrator of the violent deed. Lights flash off and on of their own accord and the dining room furniture starts to pulsate. The rollaway bath seems to take offense at Keaton and the girl being alone together in the room and intervenes in the situation by sucking him in and ferrying him away while knocking her onto the bed, which in turn folds up and imprisons her in the wall cavity. The house that had been animated by electricity appears to those within it as suddenly animistic and, in this respect, it behaves in a manner not unlike the malevolent house in *One Week*.

Undoubtedly the contraptions and apparatuses in Keaton's films are the basis for his gags. Even if the operation of such machines does not always correspond with the Keaton character's intention (at times he unleashes an unstoppable destructive capacity), they are his primary means of adapting to the world in which he lives and they justify his continuing existence in the film. Related simply to tasks and the malfunctioning of apparatuses, the operational aesthetic appears to break out at isolated moments. The machines that Keaton constructs in his short films are mostly small gestures of intentionally directed behavior that accumulates to form the plot. Occasionally the aesthetic is pursued quite rigorously, such as in *One Week* or *The Boat*, but more often than not, its somewhat piecemeal form is closer to that of the turn of the century extended mischief films.

THE COMEDY OF THE DIALECTIC

In Keaton's early work, the operational aesthetic coincides with the films' status as farce comedies and its mode of functioning is no doubt a new means of accounting for the structure of farce. What is interesting is the way Keaton eventually manages to extend the form into some of his features as well. The operational aesthetic permitted Keaton to respond to the demand for longer films (and for greater adherence to the conventions of realism, characterization, and story) without abandoning what was essential to the comedy of his short films.

Gunning, for his part, hesitates over aligning this aesthetic with narrative structure. While arguing for the coincidence of comedy and a fascination with operationality, he nevertheless initially refuses to concede that the gag could be "an elementary building block of narrative."[21] Instead he holds on to the gag's predominantly disruptive role and antiproductivist basis—a role consonant with those gags just elaborated in *The Electric House*. But he nonetheless ends up considering the narrative component in such gags,[22] coming to the conclusion that "in their contact with narrative, gags do not simply lose their independence, but precisely subvert the narrative itself."[23] This is achieved "not through their nonnarrative excess, their detouring of narrative concerns into pure attraction [such as slapstick], but precisely through their integration with narrative, their adoption of narrative's form of logical anticipation, and then their subversion of it."[24]

While Gunning uses the concept of the operational aesthetic to demonstrate that causality and mechanism coincide in the gag, and that this ordering produces something like narrative, his emphasis is ultimately on crazy machines, absurdist mechanics and, hence, the gag's subversion of narrative's anticipatory logic. The gag, in other words, relies on a cause-effect structure but follows recognizable causes with unexpected effects. The gag's subversion of narrative remains part of an antiproductivist ethos. In addition, Gunning's interest lies not in the story or what the event means, but in how the operational aesthetic focuses on the functions and processes of the machine. Yet although he identifies the coincidence of causality, mechanism, and gag, he fails to reflect on their configuration in functional (as opposed to absurd antiproductive) causality—precisely the kind of coincidence that we saw at the beginning of this chapter in the series of gags that established the narrative of *My Wife's Relations*. Such coincidences produce a mechanistic kind of narrative in which meaning is indeed secondary to operationality.

One of Keaton's commentators, Lebel, goes a step further than Gunning. His observation that Keaton's gags often function as mechanisms for narrative resolution led him to label Keaton a dialectician. The gag registers a "'dialectical' form of adjustment on Keaton's part in the course of which the synthesis resolves the contradiction, through Keaton's masterful success.... The gag structure is not circular but dialectical."[25] Consider his account of a gag from *The General*:

> In pursuit of the Northerners, Keaton prepares to use against them the curious bombarder-mortar-cannon he has had the foresight to hitch on to the back of his train. He loads the weapon with elegant pinches of cannon powder (*first variation*: cannon charge assimilated into salt-cellar). Keaton lights the weapon's fuse. The cannon fodder pops out and, after describing a most graceful curve, drops a few feet away (*second variation*: simple turnabout, Keaton's fiasco. The cannon belches its projectile in a niggardly fashion).
>
> But Keaton isn't one to let himself be bested. This time he stuffs the cannon full to the brim. Now we'll see what we'll see. He lights the fuse and, while it burns, returns to his driver's seat.
>
> But on his way back to the tender he unfortunately uncouples the mortar truck, detaching it from the rest of the train. The liberated connecting hook drags along the track, jerking the weapon and causing the cannon to lower dangerously, until it's aiming directly at Keaton who tries to save himself. But in his panic he's ensnared his foot in the hook of the tender, and remains a captive directly in the cannon's line of fire. In a fit of panic he impotently throws a piece of wood at the cannon (a supreme detail this, adding to the gag's perfection). This solution proving ineffective, he faces the cannon, helpless.
>
> It is now that Keaton the director, compensating for his energy, makes the track curve. The positions are thus the following: Keaton's locomotive takes the curve and is no longer in the cannon's line of fire; the Northerners' locomotive, on the other end of the curve, is. And just before the cannon itself takes the curve, the shot goes off![26]

Lebel reduces this "double-trigger" gag to the three moments of the dialectic. The first stage comprises Keaton overloading the cannon; the second stage, or antithesis, occurs when the cannon turns on him; and the third stage, or synthesis, comes about because the cannon nevertheless hits its initial target.

Lebel thus delineates the gag in dialectical terms, identifying Keaton's behavior with dialectical sublation (the *Aufhebung*). The sublative process is exemplified in his statement that "[b]oth Keaton and the cannon surpass themselves, the former by his magnified action, the latter, its function enriched, by its added inventiveness and precision; Keaton makes the cannon do things it could never have done otherwise."[27]

Lebel's interpretation is salutary in so far as it demands further examination of the relation between the comic and the dialectic. Unlike many other theorists of cinematic comedy, Lebel argues (in this respect like Gunning) that the gag is not necessarily an interpolation—an autonomous insertion into the narrative—which bears no necessary relation to the narrative chain, but rather a necessary link in the narrative, a means of propelling the narrative forward. The frequency and the facility with which Keaton deploys this kind of comedy demands a consideration of the closeness of Keaton's comedy to the operation of the dialectic and more specifically, an examination of the means by which narrative is constructed in Keaton's comedy. At the very least it begs the question, what kind of synthesis is it that resolves the contradiction?

To account for the different positions of Lebel, who argues that Keaton is a dialectician, and Gunning, who implies that Keaton's aesthetic tends toward mechanism and mechanical causality, we need to examine the concept of the dialectic itself and the distinction Hegel makes between internal dialectic and sophistry.

For Hegel, an internal dialectic is the form of becoming of objective things and the "proper" form of becoming of concepts and categories. According to Hegel's commentator, Michael Inwood, the internal dialectic of objective things is internal to them in the sense that they "grow and perish" by virtue of their own contradictions. The internal dialectic of concepts is undertaken by the philosopher's radical development of flaws within them, thus making them pass over into other concepts.[28]

Inwood claims that by virtue of the dialectic's internal nature, the "dialectic is not a *method*, in the sense of a procedure that the thinker applies to his subject-matter, but the intrinsic structure and development of the subject-matter itself."[29] Dialectic purporting to be a method would be mere sophistry or an external application of the dialectic to concepts, "finding flaws in them that they do not really contain."[30] Comedies of misunderstanding, such as we see in Shakespeare, are doubtless sophistical in this sense.

In theorizing the relationship between the dialectic and comic narrative, the concept of teleology can be used to distinguish between the dialectical or organic form of dramatic narrative and the possibility of a nondialectical comic form. Teleology doubtless has a relation to the dialectic in so far as both are modes of becoming, but teleology is not necessarily concerned with the resolution of immanent contradictions nor with sublation as the preservation of that which is negated on a higher level. Teleology, for Hegel, pertains to mechanism and chemism[31] and in contradistinction to the dialectic can properly be either internal or external. Internal teleology is exemplified in living organisms and corresponds to the dialectic in so far as the realization of purpose is immanent to the object.[32] In external teleology, the purpose or goal is introduced from an outside agent rather than immanent. The agent consequently presupposes the object and intervenes in it by attending to the mechanical or chemical principles according to which it operates. The purpose that the object serves is not its own but that of the agent and often also that of another entity such as God.

Lebel's characterization of Keaton as a dialectian could therefore be challenged on the grounds he confuses the dialectic with teleology. Keaton's surpassing of himself, as Lebel puts it, is not, after all, the result of the development of internal contradictions but the outcome of nature conforming to narrative necessity through divine intervention (a curve in the track positions Keaton outside the cannon's line of fire), which in this instance means the intervention of Keaton the director, the metteur-en-scène who usurps the power of God. In Lebel's example of Keaton's "dialectical" gag structure, the character's action and its consequences would be more appropriately understood as the enactment of an external teleology rather than the operation of the dialectic. Although the gag has an undeniably teleological aspect, it is not strictly speaking internally dialectical.

To clarify further what is at stake in this mode of narrative that functions in accordance with the rules of external teleology, we can examine the ramifications of Deleuze's classification of Keaton's films in terms of the large form of the action-image—the form that he argues is properly an organic form in as much as it is self-generating and self-regulating. Deleuze's situation of Keaton's work in the context of the organic form of the action-image provides a pertinent backdrop for a consideration of comic narrative. Let us bear in mind, too, that dialectic, for Hegel at any rate, is necessarily organic and that the difference between internal dialectic and the external application of the dialectical method is ultimately a distinction between the organic and the inorganic.

The *action-image* is the phrase Deleuze uses for classical Hollywood narrative. His emphasis falls predominantly on the active, transformative structure of such films. Transformation occurs on the basis of two compositions of images of actions and images of situations that give rise to the large and the small forms. In the large form the relation between situations and actions has the formula SAS' (situation, action, new situation). The small form, by contrast, is expressed by the ASA' (action, situation, new action) structure. An action discloses a situation that demands a new action (*C1*,

144). As such, the large and small forms of the action-image articulate specific economies of narrative.

Deleuze in fact specifies five laws of the large form of the action-image, but does so quite separately from his discussion of Keaton. What is important to us here is the way Keaton's comedy both deploys and modifies them. This will be demonstrated by posing Deleuze's articulation of such laws against the narrative structure of Keaton's feature films. In this way, Deleuze's work can be extended to show that Keaton's comedy puts into question the organic quality of the large form.

In theorizing the large form of the action-image, Deleuze specifies the sign value of images of situations in terms of the Peircian concept of the *synsign*. The synsign or the encompasser, as Deleuze also calls it, signifies a real or determinate milieu, a place with actual qualities and powers that specify that subject's relation to the situation (*C1*, 141, 218). The qualities and powers of the milieu impinge on a character and make him or her respond to the situation to modify it. The fact that the situation impinges on the character in a particular way, and that the character is responsive, constitutes a second sign called the *binomial*. The binomial designates a duel comprising two individuated forces that intersect. One force comes from the synsign, which can manifest itself in an antagonist, the other in the protagonist (*C1*, 142).

To paraphrase Deleuze, the first law of the action-image pertains to the organic mode of the synsign, which forms a spiral of development and includes both spatial and temporal caesuras. This law of the organic structures the actualization of milieus at the level of situation, space, frame, and shot, and organizes the passage from the first situation to the subsequent one (S to S') (*C1*, 151). Not only is it self-generating and self-regulating, but the situation also issues forth challenges that will be responded to and that will cause it to change. The second law concerns the passage from situation to action. Here the synsign/encompasser contracts into a binomial or a duel by means of the convergence of parallel montage. Lines of action emanate from the encompasser and converge in the binomial to "make possible the ultimate individual confrontation, the modifying reaction" (*C1*, 152). The third law refers to the actual point of confrontation. At the climax, montage, even the shot/reverse-shot is forbidden. Rather, "two terms confront each other face to face and must be seized in an irreducible simultaneity" (*C1*, 153). The fourth law of the action-image is that the duel is neither single nor local; we find "a dovetailing of duels in each other. The binomial is polynomial" (*C1*, 153). The fifth and final law states that the breach between the encompasser—Deleuze also calls it the limit-image—and the hero is huge and "can only be bridged progressively" as the hero actualizes his potential powers (*C1*, 154). Implied in this progression is the development of the hero: "In general the hero must pass through moments of impotence, internal or external" (C1, 154). Insofar as the large form of the action-image is an organic form, it is synonymous with the Hegelian dialectic. It develops as a result of the emergence from the situation of internal, immanent contradictions, which are resolved in accordance with their own immanent qualities. That is to say, the resolution of contradictions is organic.

To see how these laws function in Keaton's cinema, consider the example of *Steamboat Bill, Jr.* The film's narrative is centered around Willie (Keaton), a college dandy, attired in Oxford baggies, bow tie, and beret, who visits the father he has not seen since early childhood. Steamboat Bill (Ernest Torrence), Willie's father, provides a parody of early- twentieth-century working-class masculinity. Big, beefy, and butch, he embodies the ideal that to be a man entails practical competence, and he is clearly repulsed by what he perceives as his son's effeminate qualities. The challenge presented to his son Willie (obviously so-named in accordance with his personal affectations) is to prove his worthiness to his father. This challenge is for the most part ignored by Willie, who is more interested in pursuing the affection of a girl (Marion Byron) he knows from college than in pleasing his father. The challenge is only responded to when the storm hits and engages him in a duel of hyperbolic proportion.[33]

In *Steamboat Bill, Jr.*, the synsign starts out as the idyllic quality of a town situated on the riverside of the Mississippi—which is immediately undermined by the place name "Muddy Waters." The pastoral idyll has been wrenched open by the progress of modernity, the old steamboat is obsolete in the face of its modernized counterpart, and the tradesman is superseded by the entrepreneur. The synsign thus contracts to form the two sides of the binomial: the redundant father, Bill, and the town's most prominent businessman, King (Tom McGuire), come head to head on several occasions. What is distinctive in Keaton's oeuvre, and this no doubt prevents his comedy degenerating into pure parody, is that he never breaks the third law, the law forbidding montage. The confrontation with the cyclone, like the collapsing bridge in *The General* or the waterfall in *Our Hospitality*, is not conveyed through montage but is shot as continuous action. *Steamboat Bill, Jr.* in fact gives Keaton's most famous example of the confrontation and the risk of death it involves. The façade of a two-story building descends on Keaton in a single shot, the open upper window (the eye of the needle) becoming his escape hatch from a certain death. The fourth law is evident in the extension of the general antipathy between King and Bill to Bill and Willie, and to Willie and King (who also happens to be Willie's girlfriend's father). Minor duels escalate into slightly larger ones: Willie is forbidden to see his girlfriend; Bill gives Willie a return ticket to Boston and sends him on his way; a violent outburst between Bill and King sees the former incarcerated, and so forth. In *Steamboat Bill, Jr.*, the

Figure 8. Keaton smuggling getaway tools to his imprisoned father in *Steamboat Bill, Jr.* (1928). Courtesy of BFI Stills.

limit-image comes in the form of the cyclone. But while the Keaton character enters into a duel with the manifest dimensions of the cyclone and in so doing reinstalls harmonious relations, significantly, he does not convincingly meet this challenge through self-transcendence as the fifth law demands. Admittedly, in *Steamboat Bill, Jr.* (and *College*), Keaton accumulates greater competency than in his other features, but even though Willie rescues his father, and his girlfriend and her father, the director also reminds us that he still cannot tie a basic knot.

Consequently, Keaton's cinema is not properly obedient to one law of the large form of the action-image. In the Keaton character's bridging of the breach the synsign presents, he demonstrates little capacity for self-transcendence.[34] The issue of self-transcendence is a complicated one in the genre of comedian comedy because the narratives of such films are organized around the virtuoso performance abilities of already established live entertainment comedians, whether they be from vaudeville, the music hall, or the night club. The central performer has an existing extradiegetic persona that is grafted on to the identity of the character. Whether this persona is to be regarded as transcending the limitations of character identity is not altogether clear, but it is undoubtedly the case that the extradiegetic persona gives the character license to behave in a manner that is inconsistent with the conventions of fictional realism. Theorists such as Steve Seidman and Peter Kramer have argued that the narratives of comedian comedies develop in such a way as to create an opposition between the performative license of the comedian and the normative society of the diegesis.[35] More precisely, they suggest that the performative license is bound up with nonconformity, with aberrant and antisocial behavior and that the purpose of narrative development in these films is to ensure the subordination of such excess. The next chapter proposes that the tension between the extradiegetic persona and the diegetic character problematizes the notion of identity and the possibility of transcendence in a way that demonstrates not all of the narratives in comedian comedy function as Seidman and Kramer suggest. Here, though, the point I want to make concerns not so much the question of identity as the organization of the story. And in this regard, we could say that in Keaton's films the development of contradictions is organic, that both the constitution of the synsign and the development of the binomial are organic but their resolution is inorganic. In spite of Deleuze's claim that Keaton's comedy complies with the large form of the action-image, it by no means complies with all the laws of that form. And in breaking the fifth law, Keaton throws into question the organic quality of narrative that the form claims.

MINORATION AND RECURSION

How, without self-transcendence, does Keaton meet the challenge presented to him by the limit-image? Deleuze's emphasis on the machine and on the functions of recursion and minoration indicate the specificity of Keaton's response.

Minoration, or the conversion to the miniature, is the means by which Keaton diminishes the scale of his environment. To understand its implications fully we must first reflect further on the fourth of the five laws of the large form of the action-image because the dispersal of the binomial in the polynomial gives rise to numerous minor difficulties. In fact, we can see here that the *small form* of the action-image (the ASA') manifests itself in Keaton's feature-length films. That Deleuze's commentary on Keaton is not situated in the chapter on the large form of the action-image but in the one on the small form, suggests that one should be wary about polarizing the comedy of the small form and of the large form (polarizing, for instance, Chaplin and Keaton). Deleuze himself says in chapter 11, "Figures, or the transformation of forms," that whereas "[t]he distinction between the two forms of action is in itself clear and simple,... its applications are more complicated," and that although directors have a preference for one form or the other, they also at times use the form that is not their usual one (C1, 178). My argument is that even though Deleuze proposes that the distinctiveness of Keaton's comedy results from the audacity with which it tackles the large form, the small form is not only more prevalent in Keaton's shorts, but also is evident in the large form in what Deleuze calls *minoration*.

Let us turn for a moment then to the small form. Like the large form of the action-image, the small form is comprised of actions and situations, but in the latter variety the movement emanates from action to situation to new action. The small form, Deleuze writes, moves from "a mode of behavior, or a 'habitus,' to a partially disclosed situation.... A representation like this is no longer global but local.... It is no longer structural but constructed around events [*événementielle*]" (C1, 160). The ASA' form is comprised of a specific kind of sign, called the index, which provides the rationale for the images of actions and their disclosure of situations (C1, 160–3). The index itself is located in the action, whether it be a mode of behavior, a gesture, a habitus, or a fully articulated action. Two kinds of indexical actions exist: one refers us to something about the situation that is not present, to a lack or an absence of something; the other is equivocal or suggests two situations at the same time. In cinematic comedy the latter kind of index prevails. Deleuze illustrates the index of equivocity with a scene from a Chaplin film in which Charlie, seen from behind, appears to be sobbing convulsively until a subsequent shot discloses that he is shaking a cocktail. Certainly this is an apposite image of Chaplin's use of equivocity to produce pathos and comedy simultaneously. My argument is that Keaton's comedy also relies on the equivocity of the index.

The equivocity associated with the small form dominates most of Keaton's short films. For example, as the story of *The High Sign* develops, the Keaton character participates in two antithetical modes of employment, while it becomes apparent that the trajectory of the narrative necessitates the removal of this equivocity. In *One Week*, Lot 66 is confused with Lot 99, and the further perpetration of equivocal signification by Keaton's rival, Hank, changing the numbers on the house building kit, is the cause of the monstrous house and the debacle that results from its relocation. In many of Keaton's shorts, as well as in some of his features, the narratives are propelled by a misinterpretation of signs, misinterpretation made possible only because of equivocity. In *Convict 13* and *The Haunted House*, the confusion occurs at the level of costume; in *Cops*, at the level of the object (the bomb that Keaton apprehends as a cigarette lighter); and likewise in *The Balloonatic* (the hybrid balloon-boat) and *The Scarecrow* (the contraptions/objects). The

Playhouse is concerned with the equivocity of identity—Keaton not only plays the entire orchestra, but also his girlfriend is a twin. In *The Navigator*, Rollo ends up on the wrong ship because a sign has only been partially disclosed to him, and in *Battling Butler* (1926), the narrative is complicated by Keaton pretending to operate under the sign of someone he is not.

This overwhelming evidence of equivocity suggests that we should examine the specific relationship between the large and small forms more closely because by grasping the nature of the interaction between these forms, we can understand the distinctive relationship between narrative and gag in his films. Deleuze, in fact, accounts for the transposition of the small form into the large form in Keaton's cinema, proposing that Keaton's originality lies in the way he "filled the large form [of the action-image] with a burlesque content," indeed a content so at odds with the large form that Keaton's reconciliation of the two is as implausible as it is improbable.[36]

Although Deleuze himself does not say as much, the two forms intersect at the exact point that Deleuze attempts to theorize Keaton's comedy in terms of minoration. Even though Deleuze proposes that various instances of the synsign in Keaton's films are notable for their immensity and grandeur, he also argues that the hero of Keaton's films deals with this immensity, these limit-images, through a process of minoration. The gap between synsign and character is filled by minoring actions.

The notion of minoration is derived from the functioning of the machine. Deleuze writes of "Keaton's dream of taking the biggest machine in the world and making it work with the tiniest elements" (*C1*, 176), and says of *The Navigator*, "the machine is not merely the great liner by itself: it is the liner apprehended in a 'minoring' function, in which each of its elements, designed for hundreds of people, comes to be adapted to a single destitute couple" (*C1*, 176). Minoration results from the Keaton character's disavowal of what is essential to the constitution of the limit-image. Rather than the hero undergoing the self-transcendence necessary to rise up to meet the limit-image, he succeeds by diminishing its immensity. In diminishing it, he produces comedy.

Despite *Steamboat Bill, Jr.*'s indisputable presentation of the large form, discussing it without mentioning minoration is not possible. Not only is there the diminution evident in the names of the three male protagonists, King, Bill, and Willie, the dovetailing of duels that Deleuze discusses in regard to the fourth law must be understood in this film as the accumulation of minor duels. The passage from situation to action (the second law of the large form) similarly takes place through the accumulation of small details. In fact the antipathy between father and son is expressed in terms of costume and habitus (both of which are indicators of the small form). Keaton's father, disaffected with his son's appearance, takes steps to "redress" him. Willie's

Figure 9. Willie and Bill in *Steamboat Bill, Jr.* (1928). Courtesy of The Academy of Motion Picture Arts and Sciences.

whiskers are whisked away ("Take that barnacle off his lip," Bill Sr. instructs the barber), and new attire is sought for him. Bill Sr. attempts to alter the indices of his son's personality so that father and son might be more harmoniously connected. The small form is also the means by which Bill hopes to recognize Willie when he meets him at the train station. Willie writes his father that he will be wearing a white carnation, but because it is Mother's Day every man on the platform wears a white carnation. What should have been a sign of individuation becomes a sign of generality and sameness. When Willie and his father at last see eye to eye, Willie has, notably, given up his pansy outfits for the work gear his father wanted him to wear initially. And when King's ship sinks at the end of the film, the crown is the only part that remains above water, King clinging to it with all his might. These points confirm that the small form (the minor) is present in what Deleuze otherwise calls the large form of the action-image.

The concept of minoration can thus be interpreted as implying that Keaton inserts the small form into the large form, that he uses the small form as the means of apprehending the situation expressed by the limit-image of the large form. The operation of minoration can, in turn, be understood as Keaton's means of relating actions to situations—actions characterized by a refusal to acknowledge situations that border on sublimity, and, more important, actions that respond to situations *bit by bit* instead.

Keaton's most overt minoration of the large form is found in *The General*, which diminishes the epic through the combination of melodrama and slapstick. The narrative of the heroic deeds undertaken by a Southern patriot in the American Civil War combines with the story of the patriot's on-again, off-again romance with his sweetheart Annabelle so that monumental history is turned into the experience of a single couple.[37]

Two shots in the film illustrate this point. Johnnie has single-handedly taken on the group of thieves from the Northern army, chasing them by train. As his train advances north, a long shot captures him standing aloft the tender, facing the camera, chopping wood to fuel the boiler for his engine, while the whole Southern army and then the Northern army pass behind him. The shot is funny not simply because Johnnie has his back to the action, not just because he is oblivious to the *situation* and engaged in completing another *action*, fulfilling another function, but also because of the disproportion, the disparity between the two planes of the image, the epic grandeur of the armies in the background, and the banal and docile demeanor of Johnnie chopping wood in the foreground. Here the two forms, the large and the small, meet in the single frame. Interestingly, too, the scene has no dialectical point of confrontation; the two simply pass each other by.

The second image exemplifying minoration occurs when Johnnie, having rescued his train and girl, returns to Marietta to warn the Southern army of an impending incursion. As the Confederate general puts on his battle garb, Johnnie and Annabelle help him dress. Johnnie takes the general's hat and puts it on his head. He straps his sword to his waist while Annabelle buttons his coat. The gestures of familiarity and domesticity similarly indicate the diminishment of the large into the small.

Minoration comprises Keaton's means of injecting the large form with components of the small form, but it also assists in the development of recursion series. The disconnection and equivocity of minoration combine with the recursion function. The operational aesthetic, in other words, extends from the machine gag to the trajectory gag and finally to the narrative. The machine in *The General* is of course the train, and the film ceremoniously and comically explores the spectrum of its operational capabilities. The train is derailed, diverted, has its cars uncoupled, is broken into, destroyed, conjoined, refueled, collided with, shown in forward and reverse motion. But it is also an adaptable machine; it can be used to destroy railway tracks and pull down telegraph wires. It is thereby transformed from a cumbersome vehicle lacking the velocity and maneuverability required to make a good chase element to an extension of Keaton's own nimble body.

The train-machine, which includes the railway, also constitutes the film's narrative trajectory, giving the clearest and fullest expression of the trajectory gag. As Moews writes:

> [T]he narrative line of the film is also the spatial line of the film, the distance traveled; and both are none other than the actual railroad line itself. Its rails become a visual embodiment of a comic fatality controlling characters and events. Restricted to them, excluded from other directions and other possibilities of action, the northerners and Johnnie are held in conflict.[38]

While the editing of Keaton's film might appear to conform to the conventional chase sequence, significantly this trajectory has no breaks. The first half of the film inscribes a line that moves from right to left (geographically from south to north and figuratively from good to evil); the second half is simply a reversal of this trajectory. Keaton's dogged pursuit of the Yankees in the first half is matched by the Yankee's determination to run him down in the second.

The recursion function emerges whenever the Keaton character makes piecemeal attempts to further himself along a trajectory, and it impacts on the orientation of the action of the protagonist. Johnnie, for example, divested of his beloved train, pursues the thieves on foot. A handcart aids him and then, when it is derailed, he happens upon a penny-farthing that appears from nowhere (the very terrain of this shot is utterly discontinuous with the shots before and after it: a house is suddenly inserted between shots of a railway cutting). The penny-farthing is in turn upgraded to a train engine. While Johnnie certainly has a goal here, he is without a plan or a schema of how to achieve it. Rather than develop psychologically, Johnnie functions recursively. At best his actions have only tenuous relations to the end, but usually none at all. Values and events are linked not because of their direct relation to either the problem or its resolution, but because they can be related to other values or events.

Even in the absence of the machine, the operational aesthetic still structures the narrative through minoration and recursion. For instance, recursion is apparent in the manner in which Keaton's athleticism allows him to save the girl in *College*, in Willie's confrontation with the cyclone in *Steamboat Bill, Jr.*, where he is literally swept along from one encounter to the next, and in the montage sequence in *Sherlock Jr*. Recursion and minoration are the alternative "mechanical" means to the logic of immanent causality of the dialectic. They are essential components of the structure of comic narrative that Keaton brings to cinema.

In Keaton's cinema the recursion series does not go on ad infinitum; but nor is it brought to an end organically. The organic force that conventionally structures narrative is replaced by the pure mechanical teleology of the trajectory. Through the combination of recursion and minoration, the trajectories and machines of Keaton's films weave contiguous pathways until a solution is at last happened upon. Resolution is due to fortuitous circumstance and divine intervention. In this sense, the rendering of narrative form by inserting the recursive function suggests that Keaton's contribution to the large form of the action-image, which Deleuze deems to be an expression of the American ethos, counters the very basis of its claim to organicism and, therefore, naturality.

Deleuze attributes an ethical dimension to Keaton's deployment of the machine, "a secret higher finality" to it, suggesting that embedded in the strategy of minoration is the notion that the grandest schemas can still be made pertinent to the single individual (C1, 175). The Keaton character, like Rollo Treadway forebearingly trying to tow the ocean liner with a rowboat, persists as the little man struggling with the elemental forces of the universe. Certainly, Keaton's character's stoicism illustrates an ethical determination to live by individual ideals and the recursion function provides a means of expressing this stoical character, but the comic formulation of this idea impacts the presentation of such an ethics. Far from degrading that character, as the comic wants to do, the stoic ethic here takes on a sacred or beatific grace, yet one that nevertheless permits the audience some distance from it.

From the machines and apparatuses for which Keaton is famous to Gunning's operational aesthetic and Deleuze's concepts of minoration and recursion, we thus see the logic that underpins the driving force of Keaton's comic aesthetic. In short, Keaton formulates a single logic for the narrative, the trajectory, the machine, and the gag. The importance of Gunning's work for understanding Keaton's cinema is that he draws attention, perhaps for the first time, to the significance of the coincidence of narrative, gag, and machine. In Deleuze's work we find all the components necessary for a full and clear articulation of the operational aesthetic—the machine, recursion, minoration, and the trajectory. The mechanical imitation of organic narrative that we see in Keaton's work can doubtless be understood in terms of Bergson's conceptualization of the comic as *la mécanisation de la vie*, but I argue, along with Gunning, that the comic lays bare the mechanics of narrative ordering.[39] Narrative is thereby made into a subset of the machine, becomes simply one machine among many, and narrative meaning becomes an effect of basic operationality. Is this not evidence of a certain complicity between restricted and general economy, a doubling of the restricted economy of narrative by the general economy of the comic? To be sure, one of the largest claims that can be made for Keaton's comedy, and for his as no other, is that it exposes the nonsense that lies at the heart of all (cinematic) narrative.

CHAPTER 4

Fool's Gold

Metamorphoses in *Sherlock Jr.*

> *Laughter alone exceeds dialectics and the dialectician: it bursts out only on the basis of an absolute renunciation of meaning, ... And the word "laughter" itself must be read in a burst, as its nucleus of meaning bursts in the direction of the system of the sovereign operation.*
> —Jacques Derrida, "From Restricted to General Economy"

In his dissertation, "An In-Depth Analysis of Buster Keaton's *The General*," Noël Carroll outlines one of the major thematics of Keaton's epic masterpiece as the relation between intelligence and undertaking tasks. Like many other Keaton commentators, Carroll makes his point of departure the nature of the protagonist's subjectivity and the relation to objects that his actions reveal. Viewing the Keaton character as the last vestige of the skilled worker in early-twentieth-century industrial capitalism, he argues that the film explores the thematic of intelligence through gags structured on the basis of the character's success and failure at undertaking tasks.[1] He writes:

> Structurally, Keaton seems to counterpoint the ineptness of his character's performance of some physical tasks with moments of resourcefulness and quickly calculated judgment that seem to establish new levels of precisioned human activity.... Insofar as a task is an amalgam of thought and action, an intentional arc, the formal opposition of successfully executed tasks with failures presupposes an opposition of two different aspects of intellectual activity—fixation versus insight.[2]

Even though Carroll's characterization of Keaton's films centers on the performance of the Keaton character, he interprets this performance in a strictly functional or instrumental manner. This is not to say that considering the thematics of Keaton's films by way of an analysis of his character's relation to his various milieus and specifically to the objects that he encounters therein (precisely the reading that Carroll gives and which is to a degree consonant with the one proposed by Deleuze in *Cinema 1*) is inappropriate. Yet, one could argue that Carroll's focus on the "adaptive" performance of the Keaton character as subject lies within a classical articulation of the subject-object relation, conceiving the fundamental ontological relationship between "man" and the world of objects in strictly humanist and dialectical terms. Although Carroll relates his functional instrumental interpretation of the Keaton character's behavior to the comic—fixation is theorized by Bergson's notion of comic automatism, insight by the less known configurational theory of humor—his analysis nevertheless contains the comic by inscribing it within such paradigms. His interpretation of the film thereby stands as another example of the tendency to assuage the tension between restricted and general economy by unwittingly subordinating the latter to the former.

Without suggesting here that Carroll's reading is in fact wrong, I nevertheless want to question whether it accounts sufficiently for the complexity of representation that occurs in the genre of comedian comedy, whether it enables us to envisage the sovereignty of the operation of the comic that we have been discussing in the last three chapters, particularly its capacity to inscribe the tension between restricted and general economy. To do this, we might initially think further about the status of the Keaton character in his films, the kind of identity he embodies, his relation to the fictional world in which he exists, to other characters in the film, and to conventional articulations of subject-object relations. In conceiving the comicality of Keaton's cinema in terms of automatism and insight, Carroll suggests that his character is alternately stupid and intelligent, that he evinces two distinct kinds of behavior. On the contrary, one could argue that his character's behavior emanates from a single comic disposition and that his personality traits need to be examined with reference to the behavioral paradigm embodied by the fool.

In the history of the occidental arts, the figure of the fool is among the most complex of performers, enigmatically embodying both sense and nonsense: whether the foolishness of the fool is simulated or dissimulated, or whether the fool feigns to know the truth or feigns not to know it, is not clear. In this sense, the fool is one of our mythological archetypes for hiding and revealing. Keaton, like the character he plays in his films, presents this very enigma of the fool. As a comic "type," Keaton maintains a consistency not only in his physical decorum and demeanor, but also in his attitude to objects. We will see that this attitude itself implies a specific conception of the status of the object that departs markedly from the one implied in Carroll's articulation of it along thematic lines.³ We could also say that Carroll's interpretation of the comicality of the Keaton character's performance fails to engage with the specific qualities of the fool and the manner in which so much cinematic comedy—Keaton's included—complicates the relationship between character and performance.

First we should remember that the genre of comedian comedy is identified precisely by the comic doubling of character by performer. Seidman, who gave the genre its name, provides a complex articulation of the relationship between the fictional character and the comic type, identifying two contradictory impulses in this genre of films:

> (1) the maintenance of the comedian's position as an already recognizable performer with a clearly defined extrafictional personality....; and (2) the depiction of the comedian as a comic figure who inhabits a fictional universe where certain problems must be confronted and resolved.⁴

Seidman understands the comic dimension of the character to emanate from his or her aberrant behavior, and as a result, he interprets the narrative function of comedian comedies as the resolution of this contradiction: the extrafictional comic performer is in narrative terms either assimilated and cured of his or her aberrant behavior or expelled from the society of the diegesis. The theory assumes that the genre functions ideologically to subordinate anarchic performance to narrative teleology and thus to restricted economy. In other words, the genre is understood to function ideologically to give vent to the effects of general economy for a limited time before restraining them again by restricted economy. Consequently, the genre of comedian comedy is understood to manifest the confrontation between restricted and general economy, this time in a duel between narrative teleology and the anarchic performance of the comedian. One could argue that the genre is even more subtle than this. The impulses of the genre are contradictory in so far as the first inserts an established and fully recognizable personality whose behavior must satisfy the audience by remaining consistent, and the second envisages that personality as situated in a diegetic context that has the capacity to change it. What Seidman is on the brink of elaborating here is a kind of comic tension generated by the audience's desire for the same, for the performance and identity traits with which they are familiar and admire in the comic performer, and the insertion of that performer into a situation that challenges that identity, but in a manner very different from conventional realist narrative. In the latter, the expectation is that the challenge to the character will result in psychological development and difference. In comedian comedies, by contrast, comic success depends at least on the maintenance of identity and a

Figure 10. The performer's challenge to the concept of identity in *The Playhouse* (1921).

consistency of performance under such conditions, but more often on their capacity to flourish.

In *Acting in the Cinema*, James Naremore distinguishes between realist and comic acting and characterization, suggesting that realist actors showcase their acting abilities by convincing the audience of the unity of the subject while nevertheless performing certain incoherencies or duplicities at the level of character,[5] whereas comic actors make character division (such as that which Carroll elaborates) a central criterion of their performance and a gauge of their virtuosity as performers. In other words, comic performance takes such duplicities and incoherencies to the point that they manifest divisions within the character.[6] Naremore analyzes the complexity of character and its relation to performance in the case of Chaplin in *The Gold Rush* (1925):

> [i]n one sense, he is Charles Chaplin "himself"—an exquisite personality spotlighted and set apart from the onward movement of the narrative, showing off for the audience of the film. In another sense he is a clownish character who is playing a dancer, sometimes glancing upward with graceful aplomb, sometimes peering down with childlike concentration. Still again he is a shy, slightly nervous young man, looking wan and ethereal in his shabby garb, who is seeking the approval of the film's diegetic audience.[7]

Naremore thus draws our attention to three distinct levels of performance in Chaplin's comedy: star performance, clown performance, and character performance.

Much like Naremore, my own approach hinges on the "difference" between character and performer, but it develops along different (and indeed sometimes opposed) lines to those Seidman proffers. My aim is to reverse the more commonplace thematic, rational, and subjectivist treatments of Keaton by providing a reading of his work through a philosophy that is itself concerned with the irrational. I suggest that his comedy goes beyond the success and failure of the character's adaptive strategies that an action-oriented reading of his work envisages. In this kind of reading, the demonic capacity (the general economy) of the comic is never fully articulated. A key point of focus here is how Keaton's comic performance inscribes the object with a diabolical power. More than either a tool to be used or a vehicle for the expression of character, Keaton understands the object's intrinsically comic capacity. As such, locating the dynamic of Keaton's comedy within the logic of the object rather than that of the subject is crucial. In so doing, I still attend to the nature of his character's engagement with the world around him, but I examine the performative dimension of this engagement, one that is unique to the genre of comedian comedy. Baudrillard's delineation of the fatal strategies of the object in this regard offers an alternative means of understanding subject-object relations. Even though his theory of the object is not specifically articulated as being in itself comic, he nevertheless makes clear that the comic demonstrates a particular capacity to deploy objects in a manner consistent with his theory. There is doubtless also something comic in the way he envisages the object reversing Marxist, humanist, and psychoanalytic conceptions of subject-object relations.

THE COMIC OBJECT

The comic logic of the object can be accounted for by extending Baudrillard's theory of the demonic, seductive object to the behavior of the Keaton character. Baudrillard's conception of the object is devised to dispose of the humanist conception of desiring subjectivity, to oppose, that is, the traditional interpretation of the object as either an alienated representation of the subject or the focus of the subject's desire.

The object strategy is best understood through Baudrillard's elaboration of the manner in which the subject is seduced by the object. This is because the object is not that which is reflected in the mirror of the subject, but the mirror itself. As mirror, the object "can fascinate and seduce the subject...because it radiates no substance or meaning of its own. The pure object is sovereign because it is what breaks up the sovereignty of the other and catches it in its own trap."[8] The essential quality of the object that makes such a manifestation possible and that makes the object sovereign is that it has no qualities, and because of this the object professes to be this or that for the subject. It tricks the subject into thinking he is master, thereby seducing the subject and allowing him to assume his position at the center of a world divided into subjects and objects.

Baudrillard's articulation of the sovereign object and its seductive capacities constitutes a specific intervention into dialectical and restricted economic philosophies of culture. It can also be used to think through the logic underpinning comic performance. The performance given by Keaton in his films, for example, has more to do with this Baudrillardian conception of the object than the humanist, subject-oriented performances that usually characterize action cinema. Instead of considering the way that the Keaton character manipulates objects to his own ends, putting them to work by a kind of mastery, Keaton's actions toward objects, comprehended as specific articulations of comic performance, can be understood in accordance with Baudrillard's mirror. Keaton's actions must be seen as an effect of those objects' own transformational capability, their metamorphosability. This interpretation of Keaton's character's behavior and his relation to objects displaces the conventional emphasis on the psychological development of Keaton's character (as subject) from idiot to expert —which has to date been the predominant interpretation[9]—toward the pure sovereignty of the objects he encounters. The nature of these encounters with objects in turn reflects his own sovereignty. An elaboration of this proposition is precisely what we see in *Sherlock Jr.* It accounts for the protagonist's contact with objects and the various dimensions of Keaton's comic performance as manifest in the interrelation between his roles as character and comedian.

Baudrillard provides an example of what he means by the object strategy in *Fatal Strategies*, where he recounts the story of a man who, enamored of a woman, writes her a passionate letter. She replies in turn with the question, "What part of me seduced you the most?" The day after he answers the question with the words "your eyes," he literally receives one of her eyes in the post.[10] Baudrillard in this instance is interested in not just the limitation of a certain kind of subjectivity but also of metaphor. The man replies "your eyes" because they are a metaphor for the soul, "exactly the metaphor," Baudrillard says, "that the woman chooses to repudiate, which privileges her absolutely. He, as subject, can play only the game of metaphor. She, abjuring all metaphor, becomes the fatal object which drags the subject down to annihilation."[11] In sending the man, whose heart she holds, her eye, the woman explicitly avows her object status. The woman's strategy is "the object strategy," which consists in this case, according to Baudrillard, in putting a stop to the metaphorical displacement of discourse. In refusing the man's attempt at metaphor, the strategy of the woman as object is the "liquidation of metaphor," the "precipitation of the sign into brute, senseless matter."[12] According to Baudrillard's account, then, the object has two sides: on the one hand, its reflective capacity and its initiation of the endless circulation of meaning; on the other, its brute senseless materiality and its ability to stop communication dead.

In the instance of the gift of the eye, the object strategy manifests itself as literalization, as an engagement between verbal representation and object presentation, a short-circuiting of verbal discourse by presentation. The object, like a gift that cannot be reciprocated, is inserted into the system of exchange, but cannot itself be exchanged. It has also been proposed, and not only by Baudrillard, that literalization is a technique of comic performance, in which case the recoiling horror that surely must be the man's response to the gift of the eye is replaced by a burst of laughter.[13]

As an operation of the comic, the object strategy, the short-circuiting of discourse, abounds in Keaton's gags. During his gag writing for the Marx Brothers' film *At the Circus* (1939), Keaton devised what he thought would be an ingenious gag. He describes this gag in his autobiography:

> [At the circus] Harpo walks past a camel. It has two baskets hanging on its back. A man with a pitchfork is filling these with straw. Harpo can see this but not the keeper on the other side of the camel who holds the reins attached to the animal's halter.
>
> Some of the straw falls out of the basket nearest Harpo. He picks the straw up and throws it back into the basket. Meanwhile the keeper he cannot see is looking in his pockets for a match. Harpo finds a single straw on the ground and throws this into the basket just as the keeper bends over to strike the match on his trousers, accidentally pulling on the halter and causing the camel to sink on his knees.
>
> Amazed at this apparent proof that there is a last straw that breaks the camel's back, Harpo takes back the single straw just as the keeper straightens up, loosening the rein on the camel who rises to his feet. Now Harpo is delighted: the ancient aphorism is based on truth.[14]

Literalization as it occurs here is a restoration of literal meaning, a cinematic rendition of a linguistic metaphor. Although the cinematic image in this instance negates the figurative, short-circuits linguistic metaphoricity, stops short the system of exchange, it does so for comic effect. One could appeal to Bergson here and invoke the comicality of redundancy and specifically the redundancy of the contingent world in the face of a language that has already accounted for each of its possible manifestations.[15] In this gag, an age-old aphorism, once again a figurative expression, is literalized (literally "objectified") by being cinematically rendered. Language becomes truly prophetic: the world absurdly conforms to it. Baudrillard would call this a fatal gesture because it announces the logic of Manichaeism, conjuring a world "governed solely through the power of the *mind*."[16] Keaton's gag for the Marx Brothers epitomizes an aspect of his comedy that aims to obliterate the distinction between the figurative and the literal.

Other instances of literalization occur in Keaton's third feature, *Sherlock Jr.* The film tells the story of a young cinema projectionist—who in his spare time aspires to be a detective—in the midst of wooing a woman (Kathryn McGuire) for whose attention he must compete with the film's villain (Ward Crane). The Keaton character has the same comic disposition he does in other films: his clothes are slightly undersized, yet his movement is eloquent; his behavior ranges between beatific innocence and comic naïveté. He is a dreamer who conceives the world as his oyster, but in imagining himself able to meet any challenge demonstrates a beguiling ineptitude for defining the level at which to engage that challenge. The character's world of small-town quiescence is perturbed when his rival steals a watch from his girlfriend's father and engineers the ensuing situation so that Keaton himself is accused of the crime. Keaton, exhausting his abilities to rectify the situation by assuming the role of detective, dejectedly returns to the cinema to project a film into which he can project himself and therein overcome the obstacles he has been unequal to in real life. In the meantime, his girlfriend embarks on some proper detective work and establishes his innocence.

An early example of the condensation of the figurative and the literal occurs when the Keaton character's rival dupes him; the rival has not only successfully won over the girl, but also has recast himself as a sleuth of sorts and Keaton as a thief. Ousted from the house of his now ex-girlfriend, the young projectionist consults his detective manual, which instructs him to "shadow his man." A worn metaphor becomes comic hyperbole in Keaton's literal and physical shadowing of Crane. In a series of long shots, he trots along behind Crane, doubling the movements of his rival with combined mechanical precision and balletic grace. When his rival bends forward to pick up a cigarette butt, Keaton simultaneously arcs his own pelvis back, both accommodating the movement and providing a graphic echo of it. Tossing the cigarette over his shoulder after having a few puffs, Crane unwittingly passes it on to his shadow, who likewise puffs at it before tossing it to the ground. Together they perform a pas de deux. When Crane trips on the footpath, so does Keaton; and when Crane stops abruptly to avoid a collision with oncoming traffic, Keaton follows suit. As well as literalizing the notion of "shadowing" through comic performance, Keaton is simultaneously figured as "the shadow of a man," the shadow of the man he once was, following his own identity, trying to become it once again by sticking as close to the other as possible.

This gag also allows the attenuation of character by comic performance. Keaton's literalization takes his character's trait of naïveté as its initial justification but pushes it to the limit of plausibility. In the meantime, the excess that characterizes his performance explores the vicissitudes of the object. The object here is not merely some accessory that Keaton uses to express himself. The subject/self/body is an object for comic deployment and as such its destiny lies beyond the bounds of realist, sensible, or meaningful articulation. By becoming the shadow, Keaton partakes of the strategy of the object: he short-circuits language, transforms it into performance, and literalizes it. His films therefore redeploy this object strategy as a technique of the comic. Whether Keaton replaces the figurative with the literal, or obliterates the distinction between the two so that one metamorphoses into the other and vice versa, his comedy undertakes a thoroughgoing transgression of the boundaries that separate the cinema, verbal discourse, and the world of objects. Indeed metamorphosis in Keaton's comedy involves the realms of cinema, verbal discourse, and the world of objects interpenetrating one another to the point where the logical operations of each lose their specificity.

Chaplin, too, uses the specific performance license of comedian comedy to submit conceptual difference to vertiginous spiraling effects. Consider his audition for a job as a clown in his film *The Circus* (1928). The Tramp's comic potential is first realized within the film's diegesis when his attempts to abscond from the law lead him into the circus arena, resulting in a slapstick performance for the circus audience and a bounty of mutual interference gags for the film audience.[17] The circus audience's appreciation of the Tramp's shenanigans prompts the circus owner to audition the Tramp for permanent employment as a clown. During the Tramp's performance, however, it soon becomes apparent that he can only make people laugh inadvertently. Although the diegetic audience is nonplussed by his performance, the film's audience doubles over at the doubling of the Tramp's diegetic performance by Chaplin's performance. As the sequence progresses, the audience is increasingly less able to determine what they are laughing at. The sequence thus condenses the questioning of the ethics of the comic that seems to take place throughout the entirety of the film, which asks the audience to consider two concepts of the comic, embodied in the distinction between "laughing at" (the comic as it is found, comic naïveté) and "laughing with" (the comic as it is made, comic artifice). The possibility of innocent comicality (the comic as it is found) would exist only at the level of the diegesis, but this, as Chaplin so convincingly demonstrates in the sequence, is always an utterly contaminated level. In a sense, then, Chaplin's questioning of the morality of "laughing at" as opposed to "laughing with" can never be adequately posed because there is no comicality outside of performance. If Chaplin here seems to want to engage the audience in a debate about the ethics of comic degradation, he also seems to have (either reflexively or surreptitiously) abnegated any responsibility for his exploitation of the Tramp for comic ends.

THE SOVEREIGN DISPOSITION OF THE COMIC PERFORMER

For Keaton, words operate like objects and images, images and objects like words, and so forth.[18] Comic performativity transmutes the logic of various realms. Keaton's performance in *Sherlock Jr.* exemplifies such comic performativity. Among all the characters in the film, Keaton alone has a privileged capacity in the utilization of object strategies. His character not only switches signs and dons disguises, but the film's access to his character's realm of fantasy also sees him undergo metamorphoses and transform objects. The character himself operates in a "space" where the boundaries separating language, cinema, and the world of objects no longer exist. Crane conversely exists within a realist cinematic diegesis and remains within an economy of mere fraudulence. Although both Keaton and Crane play with appearance, where Crane in his petty thieving only tampers with the location of objects, Keaton indulges in a full-scale metamorphosis (he becomes Sherlock Jr.). Keaton's particular affinity with the object is attributable to his special status as fool. Seidman argues that this kind of liberty of performance is in fact one of the distinguishing features of comedian comedy. The central comic performer has "idiosyncratic control of his environment by virtue of his special powers of imagination, perception, and logic, pleasurable forms of fantasy (which are visualised in the films), and the presence of magic or fate, which allows the transcendence of normal physicality."[19]

One could argue that Keaton's difference is contained within the dreamworld of the film and therefore does not impact the rational basis of the action cinema that brackets the dream sequence. True, Keaton's metamorphoses are predominantly in the dream within the film, where the logic of condensation and displacement is legitimate. The tendency of the Keaton character to take things literally in the real world of the diegesis stands as the inverse of his metamorphic capability in the dreamworld. This is evident not only in his shadowing of Crane, which happens in the real world, but also in the lost money episode when Keaton sweeps up candy wrappers littering the floor of the cinema. Dubious about a woman's right to reclaim the lost dollar bill that he has just found and pocketed, Keaton asks her to describe it. Keaton's demand that something whose appearance is as universal as the letters of the alphabet be described as though it were singular or unique exemplifies comic literalization and testifies to a universe of absolute contingency.

Figure 11. Keaton playing the detective in *Sherlock Jr.* (1924). Courtesy of BFI Stills.

Keaton's special disposition can be more incisively related to the notion of sovereignty as Bataille understands it. And here my departure from Seidman's views is pronounced. Whereas he appeals to the presence of another identity, such as the extrafictional comic performer, the star or personality, whose existence outside the text underwrites the comic performance within the narrative, considered as an operation of sovereignty, the doubling of character by performer would elude both presence and identity.

Bataille, we have seen, articulates what is at stake in sovereignty by specifying its relationship with the comic and with laughter. For Bataille, the sovereign operation is synonymous with the comic operation. Sovereignty is a doubling of Hegelian mastery but it upsets the dialectical trajectory inscribed by mastery. When sovereignty performs as simulacrum of mastery, it does not, Derrida tells us, "govern in general: it governs neither others, nor things, nor discourses in order to produce meaning."[20] The sovereign operation is neither "subordinate to anything," nor subordinates anything to itself. With sovereignty the notion of identity disappears: "For sovereignty has no identity, is not *self, for itself, toward itself, near itself* . . . it must expend itself without reserve, lose itself, lose consciousness, lose all memory of itself and all the interiority of itself."[21] By doubling mastery, sovereignty opens discourse to the effects of the comic. Derrida says it is the "burst of laughter" that "makes the difference between lordship and sovereignty shine, without *showing it* however and, above all, without saying it."[22]

This doubling of mastery by sovereignty describes the relationship between the Keaton character and the comic performer. The character is the conventional hero, caught in an ordinary kind of dialectic, a duel with another character that will produce a winner and a loser. The duel is rendered comic by the fact that it is not Crane's recognition that Keaton seeks, but the girl's and her father's, and because the duel itself (Keaton putting his life at stake to save the girl and establish his self-identity) takes place in the realm of fantasy. It is not Keaton's fantasized performance, however, that I am arguing for as sovereign, but his comic performance. What I mean is that the Keaton who shadows Crane and fails at mastery is not simply the dolt that the delineation of his character by the plot would seem to suggest; there is also the shadow of the shadow—the Keaton whose primary purpose it is to get a laugh, the performer who is constituted at the moments at which we laugh. The sovereignty of comic performance thereby involves the performer doubling the character, but dissolves the identity of that character in this performance. As such, Keaton's sovereignty as performer is nothing like an attribute; it is by no means equivalent to anything like a character trait. We cannot use it to characterize his being, either at the level of performer or character. Sovereignty is indicative of the utter elusiveness of that being. The performer Keaton only exists momentarily as a doubling of the character he plays, and this doubling arises only at the point at which we laugh. This is why laughter for Bataille comprises the "instant" at which sovereignty emerges, which is constitutive of sovereignty "without *showing* it however and, above all, without saying it."[23]

Compared with the character-extrafictional comic performer relation in Seidman's theory of comedian comedy, the understanding of the fool foregrounded here binds the performativity of Keaton to the sovereignty of the comic and in turn affords the possibility of the operation of general economy. That Seidman's theory of the extrafictional comic performer has little claim to the specificity of the comic is apparent in Krutnik's retheorization of the relationship between character and extrafictional performer in terms of the more pervasive relationship between character and star.[24] Furthermore, Seidman's theory of performance in comedian comedy partakes of a notion of restricted economy in terms of both its emphasis on the presence of the extrafictional comic performer and its contention (reemphasized by Kramer) that the comic performer's behavior constitutes an unsanctionable countercultural drive that the narrative works to resolve by transforming the comic figure into a conventional hero.[25]

The doubling of the character by the performer likewise gives Keaton a sovereign relation to objects.[26] In Baudrillard's terms, this sovereign relation entails engaging the metamorphosability of objects, which is their sovereignty. Keaton's comic performance, for example, does not distinguish between the "essential" properties of objects and the ends he wants such objects to serve. His character perceives objects only in terms of the same and in accordance with this peculiar kind of recognition he makes the object conform to his perception of it and in the process makes it function as other to itself. The metamorphosis of a car into a sailing boat is *Sherlock Jr.*'s most obvious instance of this. The secret "intelligence" of the fool is bound up with his understanding of the sovereignty of objects. There is the sovereignty of the object on the one hand, and the sovereignty of the character-performer on the other, but the imbrication of the two is such that object and subject as they are conventionally understood disappear.

Take, for example, a trajectory gag generated by the object strategies of no less than three Keatons in *Sherlock Jr.*—the character, the performer, and the metteur-en-scène (the director who literally choreographs the scene). In the dream sequence, Crane, playing the same villainous part that he does in the film's real world, diverts Sherlock Jr. and traps him on the roof of a building. To free himself, young Sherlock takes a vertical boomgate and transforms himself into a weight on the end of it. In so doing, he also transforms the boomgate itself from a barrier into a vehicle for transportation. As a mechanism, the boomgate is also an element of scenography, of mise-en-scène, but its essential mechanism—as a boomgate—is, narratively speaking, redundant. The character is a genius mastering the objects in the world around him by the insightful interpretation of their capacities and the dissolution and reconstitution of their properties. The detective, however, is also the cinema projectionist, the projectionist's ideal ego, and the dignity of his escape from the roof is an inversion of real entrapment on top of the train carriage at an earlier point in the film. Sherlock's mastery is therefore the dolt's wish fulfilment. Our laughter at the gag emerges on the basis of the metamorphosability of the one into the other and vice versa. The extrafictional Keaton performs both parts. But a third Keaton, the metteur-en-scéne likewise plays a significant part in the orchestration of both incidents. The gag is cinematically expressed in the geometrical perfection of the downward swoop of the boomgate's arc, the grace of which is constituted in its subtle resistance to the gravitational pull of Sherlock Jr. toward the ground. As the boomgate carries Keaton downward, the arc it describes is met by the tangential line of the trajectory of the villain's car. Keaton, thus dropped to the ground below, is fortuitously deposited in the backseat of the villain's car.

The interplay between the Keaton character, performer, and the metteur-en-scène gives the gag its geometrical precision. In this sense, cinema, for Keaton, presents the possibility of creating a perfect contingency between time and space effected by the hand of the director as metteur-en-scène, who literally puts himself into the scene.[27] The "presence" of a third hand operates as God the Father did to Jesus (where Jesus sacrifices his life on the cross only to be resurrected by his father). It also resonates with the master asserting his "independence" both by risking life and necessarily staying alive. The geometrical precision of the gag, its perfect contingency, is also the technical basis for much cinematic slapstick. Although it is perhaps less important in the most rudimentary slapstick where emphasis is on the violence of its perpetration rather than the spatiotemporal contingency that allowed the violence to be perpetrated (Judy walloping Punch with a baton and vice versa) and remains absent from much buffoonery and rough-and-tumble comedy. Keaton develops the contingency of time and space to express (doubtless among other things) the literal in as much as the fictional world of the film's diegesis literally conforms to narrative necessity and the comic is deployed to reveal this manipulation. Indeed, Keaton's gag for the Marx Brothers (the literal doubling of the aphorism about the straw that broke the camel's back) is likewise achieved through this very orchestration of time and space by the metteur-en-scène. Chaplin takes slapstick even further in the direction of choreography, using it to shift "real" time and space into poetic rhythm (think of the boxing match in *City Lights*), while forty odd years later Jean-Luc Godard makes his slapstick distinctive precisely by eradicating this kind of perfect contingency between time and space. As such, the fight scenes at the garage in *Pierrot le fou* (1965) are characterized by clumsiness and misconnection.

The hand of the metteur-en-scène calls into question Carroll's conceptualization of Keaton's comedy in terms of the success and failure of his character's adaptive strategies, and particularly the idea that success and failure are premised on the internal teleology of rational causality and actually emanate from the character's intelligence or ineptitude. Kramer, on the other hand, discusses the function of the metteur-en-scéne in terms of authorial agency. Yet he contends that the purpose of this agency is to disrupt the narrative, and further claims that in *The Blacksmith* Keaton's authorial agency, like the comic performer's, is dissolved by the film's narrative reordering.[28] The inappropriateness of this proposition to the gags of *Sherlock Jr.* that I have just described as well as to the endings of several of Keaton's other films (think, for example, of the deus ex machina in *The Navigator*—the submarine emerging from the depths of the ocean to save the drowning couple) is indicative of a larger problem in the theorization of comedian comedy. Seidman and Kramer both consider sovereign performativity as disruptive of normative social conditions and set out to examine the extent to which the narrative is able to subordinate this disruptiveness. Thus Seidman and Kramer see the narrative trajectory working to dissolve unruly comic effects, while Krutnik argues that this is not a universal feature of comedian comedy. More recently, Geoff King has argued that although the narratives of such films set the central comic performer "against formal institutions," comedian comedy (like comedy in general) aims to transgress established norms. Comedy is committed to asserting "the value of creative individuality in the face of dehumanizing abstraction."[29] To illustrate this point, King considers how the theme of creative individuality works in the cycle of comedian comedies with a military subtext, finally concluding, against Seidman, that "[i]n ideological terms, comedian comedy can be read as a celebration of the individual in opposition to restrictive social or collective institutions."[30] And, as I have suggested, the very proposition that narrativity dominates the comic or vice versa is based on a misconception of the way narrative and the comic relate to the hierarchy between restricted and general economy. The "purpose" of the comic is not intrinsically to disrupt the narrative but to get laughs. As such, comicality does not preclude narrative resolution. Although the two might partake in different economies, one economy does not dominate the other. Both operate at the same time.

For example, narrative and comic destiny pursue the same path in the trajectory gag culminating in Sherlock saving his damsel in distress. Here cinematic contingency exceeds itself and gives way to the surreal logic of the dream. The sequence begins with Sherlock riding on the handlebars of Watson's motorbike. A large puddle floods their path and jolts Watson from the driver's seat. While Sherlock remains ignorant of this mishap, the metteur-en-scène magnanimously directs him along his way while horizontal obstacles and lacunae threaten the continuity of his trajectory. Each gag in this running gag arises from the chance coincidence of spatial and temporal factors. The obstacles or objects that Sherlock encounters might seem to be spatial—vectors that cross his path or gaps that open his trajectory onto the abyss—but they are just as fundamentally temporal. The contingency of time and space one minute threatens Sherlock and the next becomes the source of his salvation. Despite the improbability of these gags (an improbability that relates precisely to the contingency of time and space), most of them are almost plausible. Thus Sherlock alone on the bike sails unscathed through three busy intersections, avoids colliding with a loaded-up pedestrian, withstands being pelted with shovels of earth by roadside workers, and survives crossing a breached bridge because of the fortuitous intervention of not one but two trucks. However unlikely, each of these events—abridgments and near misses—remain within the realm of plausibility. The regime of cinematic representation shifts from the improbable to the implausible when a tractor cutting a horizontal line across the screen and threatening to unmake Sherlock is rotated by ninety degrees to reveal itself, in depth, as a surrealist

Figure 12. *Sherlock Jr.* (1924). Courtesy of The Academy of Motion Picture Arts and Sciences.

grotesquerie, a tractor with legs up to its armpits, a hybrid engine-tunnel that will unexpectedly provide passage for him.[31] Here the contingency of time and space, which the metteur-en-scène has orchestrated repeatedly and consistently, now alters the world of objects to produce a reversal of causality, a fatal causality. It is as though Keaton's narrative destiny to save his girl has finally contaminated every last element of the mise-en-scène of his dream to make possible his achievement of that goal.

Lest we are tempted to argue, along with Carroll and others, that the Keaton who fails in the real world succeeds in the dreamworld, we should observe that while the young projectionist enters the dreamworld to achieve the mastery he is incapable of in the real world, his character is not convincingly transformed from a state of maladaptation to one of supreme adroitness. As a detective he in fact deduces nothing; it is largely fate that rewards him. Even if Sherlock is goal-oriented, arguing that he accomplishes anything through his own prowess is impossible. He is not masterful. In the performance of the comic, sovereignty replaces mastery. The fool's harnessing of the secret "power" of the object through his performance makes him sovereign and, it is this that he, like all those apprenticed in the "order" of seduction, simultaneously seems to conceal and reveal.

Fool's Gold 103

Figure 13. Photograph by Arthur Rice, 1921. Courtesy of The Academy of Motion Picture Arts and Sciences.

The comic (sovereign) moments "captured" here all relate to aspects of performance, the performance of character, the performance of objects, of the metteur-en-scène and of causality. Whereas orthodox film theory focuses on these as sites of the inscription of cinematic meaning, (for example, on the meaning of the Keaton character's behavior in terms of intelligence or stupidity, or on the narrative's work to correct aberrant antisocial drives) their reconfiguration in the light of the sovereignty allows us to think through the comic's complex relation to meaning. In accordance with the conditions of general economy—sacrifice, waste, play, excess, and expenditure without return—the sparkle of the comic is glimpsed only at fleeting moments within restricted economy and is easily dulled by it.

CHAPTER 5

Jokes and Their Relation to...

To read Bataille's theory of comic sovereignty—the method relating restricted economy to the effects of general economy—in tandem with Freud's discussion of the joke's relation to the unconscious suggests a constitutive break in the history of the philosophy of the comic. Where Bataille postulates the effects of comic sovereignty on determinate discourse, and opens the system of knowledge to unknowability, Freud provides us with a mechanism, indeed a veritable apparatus, for the production of these effects. In distinguishing the joke from the broader category of the comic, and by arguing that the joke is formed by the unconscious, Freud envisages how the operations of the primary process act on a preconscious thought (discursive meaning) and transform it to the point that what is said articulates something altogether different from what was intended. The unconscious can thus be conceived as the means of turning sense into nonsense—a psychical structure the very function of which is to carry out the "inner ruination" that Bataille seeks to invoke with his notion of comic sovereignty. The originality of Freud's contribution to the theorization of the comic is that he opens the comic itself up to the effects of general economy in a manner that is unparalleled, perhaps even in Bataille's writing. In so doing, he departs from a philosophical tradition that has limited the conceptualization of the aesthetic of the comic to mimetic degradation. Freud offers instead a conception of the joke that comes into being through transformation, that is, by subjecting meaning to a radical indeterminacy.

Bataille's claim that a philosophy of laughter takes the unknown as its ground does not mean that the comic, its themes and devices are indefinable. He also insists that laughter "in no way eludes the clarity of knowledge or of methodological investigation" and in as much as comic technique is a transmittable skill, "knowing means knowing how."[1] In the second half of this study, Freud's analysis of the joke becomes the principle means for inquiring further into comic techniques, although not without some qualification for the study of cinematic comedy. My first aim is to produce a reading of Freud's delineation of these techniques, the psychical processes they entail and their communicative status, which relates them to Bataille's concepts of restricted and general economy as well as to comic sovereignty. My second is to seek evidence of the existence of these techniques in early cinematic comedy to examine the way they impact on the pictorial and thematic conditions of cinema.

In the last twenty years Freud's study of the joke has effected three specific areas of philosophical and aesthetic inquiry. The first is primarily poststructuralist and includes the work of writers such as Jeffrey Mehlman, Weber, and Jean-Luc Nancy.[2] The second largely appropriated the work of the first group of writers and adapted their insights to the study of cinematic comedy. It includes the work of Neale, Eaton and Mellencamp.[3] The third took up Freud's work not so much in the name of poststructuralism as postmodernism, and its object was literary rather than cinematic. Here the aesthetics of the comic were identified with the aesthetics of postmodernism and Freud's work on the joke became a means of articulating this aesthetic.[4]

My purpose here is not to give an overview of these theoretical "advancements" and appropriations, but to develop further some of the points at which Freud's work on the joke might be useful for understanding the aesthetics of the comic. His work is of interest to an understanding of a general conception of the comic because he delineates several techniques that produce comic effects. The tenets of the comic that have so far emerged in this study are polysemy, the simulation of both the operation of the dialectic and the risk of death (laughter, in other words, humiliating the pretensions of reason), the proliferation of trajectories, the graphic excess of slapstick, the narrative excess of the gag, the sovereignty of the comedian comic, and the comic divinity of the metteur-en-scène. And we have seen that these are all broadly encompassed by the imbrication of sense and nonsense. Even more importantly, Freud provides a formal theory of the imbrication of sense and nonsense, which he uses to account for the comicality of incidents and events. Freud's work on the comic is significant to a philosophy of laughter that establishes the relation between the unknown and the known because it hypothesizes the existence of specific psychical conditions that explain why we laugh.

Freud's commitment of 300 odd pages to a discussion and theorization of the *witz* makes his book one of the most extensive treatments of the aesthetics of the comic. His professed interest in the comic is not philosophical but psychological. As Weber has noted, he developed his theory of the joke to prove to his colleague Wilhelm Fliess that the witty nature of dreams was not a projection on his part but results from the peculiar structure of the psyche.[5] The joke, like other compromise formations such as the dream, the slip of the tongue and the hysterical symptom, emerges from the unconscious strata of the psyche. Indeed, the peculiarity of the operation of the primary processes and the energetics of the unconscious coming up against the censorship barrier both explains the origin and emergence of the joke and allows Freud to distinguish it from the comic.

Those of Freud's commentators interested in his work on the joke have tended to overlook the importance of his theorization of the comic, both as an aesthetic form with its own essential characteristics and as he uses it to assist in the determination of the joke. Freud theorizes the joke first by extracting it from the comic in general, and then by opposing it to the comic point for point. Two separate concepts of the comic thus seem to be implied by the development of Freud's argument: on the one hand, a broad genre of funny instances, on the other, a specific aesthetic technique distinct from the joke. Freud maintains, however, that the joke also functions in accordance with the conditions he specifies for the comic.

Given that one of the major themes of this analysis is the relation of the comic to meaning, Freud's intra-comic distinction between the joke and the comic demands some attention to how each relates to the question of meaning. The techniques of the comic and the joke, as Freud elaborates, can be analyzed in terms of their peculiar methods of relating sense and nonsense, and ultimately in terms of the relation between restricted and general economy. What follows, therefore, is not simply an explication of Freud's means of differentiating between the formal techniques of the joke and the comic, but a consideration of how these "techniques" produce "meaning" and "nonmeaning" in fundamentally different ways. Freud's theses are represented here more abstractly and less tentatively than in his own text because I render them in the sharpest possible focus to concentrate on both the difference between the joke and the comic, and the implications of this difference for the mechanics of meaning.

FROM MIMESIS TO METAMORPHOSIS: ARISTOTLE, BERGSON, AND FREUD

Freud's theory of the joke breaks with the historically dominant conception of the comic as a form of "mimetic degradation," a view of the comic that can be found as long ago as Aristotle and as recently as Bergson. Whereas Freud conceptualizes the joke from his findings regarding the dream and the unconscious and draws on the work of the philosophers Theodor Vischer, Kuno Fischer, and Theodor Lipps, his theory of the comic is derived from Bergson's treatise on "Laughter." From our vantage at least, Bergson's work falls within the purview of the Aristotelian conception of comedy, to the point that his essay might even be considered an extended or updated elaboration of that view.

Aristotle deals with the comic somewhat summarily in the *Poetics*. Comedy or the ridiculous is a species of the ugly, "the *imitation* of men worse than average."[6] The Aristotelian point of view implies a norm or an ideal against which comedy, as "mistake and deformity," can be judged. In *Laughing Matter: An Essay on the Comic*, Marcel Gutwirth argues that the Aristotelian definition of the comic established a tradition of "undervaluing the one art [comedy] and disparaging ordinary humankind."[7] The laughter induced by the comic is henceforward interpreted in terms of its social utility. It served society as a cleansing and controlling agent in so far as it "sanitizes... the forbidden" and manages the offensive.[8]

Bergson's theorization of the comic as "*la mécanisation de la vie*," as the mechanical encrusted on the living, and laughter as the means of correcting this aberration lies within this tradition.[9] The comic for Bergson is associated with mechanical inelasticity, absent-mindedness, automatism, repetition, rigidity, imitable deformity, ugliness, the stereotype, and so on. Bergson's theory of the comic, and the laughter that responds to it, is in fact a justification for his philosophy as a whole. This philosophy aims to redress the inadequacy of mechanistic concepts such as spatialized or chronometric time for understanding the human organism and its relation to the world. This is nowhere more evident than in Bergson's characterization of the distinction between the comic and the dramatic and their correspondence to the two opposed forces—tension and elasticity—that life brings into play.[10] The comic constitutes a form of rigidity, whereas drama gives rise to flexibility.[11]

Bergson proposes, for example, that repetition is funny because it is the opposite of life "which is the complete negation of repetition" (L, 34) and that the comic illustrates "a certain rigidity of body, mind and character that society would still like to get rid of in order to obtain from its members the greatest possible degree of elasticity and sociability" (L, 24). So, where the comic for Aristotle was constituted by the degradation of the average, for Bergson it is the degradation of the essence and vitality of life in its unique and inimitable heterogeneity. The main limitation of these models of the comic as mimetic degradation is that they conceive the comic to be less than, rather than other to, the real or ideal.

The argument put forward by Freud in his book on the joke takes Bergson's theory of the comic as its starting point. However, Freud finds within his empirical experience of the comic something that operates quite differently from the way Bergson describes it. This is the joke. Through the joke, Freud extends the predominantly mimetic conception of the comic to an aesthetic with a transformative capacity. While Freud still conceives some aspects of the comic in terms of mimetic degradation, his theory of the joke constitutes a fundamental shift away from this tradition.

The special case of the joke as Freud theorizes it has its counterpart in Bergson's "comic of words," but Freud breaks significantly with Bergson precisely at this point. Bergson distinguishes between "the comic of words" and wit. Whereas "the comic of words" makes us laugh at the person who utters them and uses the techniques of the comic in general (which Bergson generalizes into the three operations of repetition, inversion, and reciprocal interference), wit makes us laugh at a third person or at ourselves and is closer to the poetic (L, 97). Wit is distinguished from the "comic of words" because of its propensity to make words and symbols communicate with themselves by putting them on stage (L, 98). Paraphrasing Victor Hugo, a wit, Bergson contends, is a poet who lets "his ideas hold converse with one another 'for nothing, for the mere joy of the thing!'" (L, 99).[12] Bergson, however, abandons his pursuit of this notion of wit, which he argues is, in any case, dramatic rather than comic because the animism it entails is precisely the opposite of the automatism that essentially defines the comic.[13]

We will see that for Freud the joke will free at least some instances of what Bergson calls "the comic of words" from the comic as such. On the one hand, Freud amplifies the comparative or mimetic aspect implicit in Bergson's definition of the comic so that degradation will become much more explicitly and systematically its defining characteristic.[14] On the other hand, Freud theorizes the joke as a form with a duplicitous double structure, a form that necessarily reveals something *other* rather than *less*, and is in this process liberated (if only momentarily) from the identity of meaning. In so far as it is constituted through transformation (elasticity and animism), Freud's conception of the joke is closer to Bergson's broad definition of wit, which Bergson dismisses as lacking in pertinence to his study of laughter. A crucial distinction, however, is that the unconscious plays the animating role in Freud's conception of the joke.

THE SCENARIOS AND THE PLAYERS

For Freud both the joke and the comic are for the most part social acts. They involve people in specific relations with one another. Yet the joke and the comic are considered to be not so much intentionally communicated utterances, as situations or scenarios in which something humorous or amusing is put into process. Freud distinguishes the two scenarios according to the number of participants. Yet, underlying this headcount is Freud's attempt to clarify the specificity of the performative dimension, the inter- and intrasubjective nature, of both processes.

The joke scenario according to Freud involves three people: the joke teller, the person to whom the joke is told, and the object, or butt, of the joke. The comic, on the other hand, need only involve the person who finds something comic, but usually involves two people: the person who finds something comic and the person who is found to be comic. The second person can just as easily be an object or situation and is equivalent to the butt of the joke.[15]

In theorizing the positions of the players and the nature of their psychical involvement in the processes of the joke and the comic, Freud differentiates between the conditions of production and reception. These conditions show the limits that both the joke and the comic present to the logic of communication. While both present scenarios that conventional theories of communication cannot fully comprehend, they nevertheless articulate meaning in very specific ways. They present two modes of the relationship between meaning and nonmeaning. By attending to the participants involved in both processes we can begin to understand this relationship in each case.

Let us consider first the processes of production. While the joke is undoubtedly an act of communication, a mode of address, a message or signal transmitted from a sender to a receiver, the criterion of intentionality presupposed by communication theory is not met by the joke process. Freud argues that the production of the joke is involuntary (*JTRU*, 209):

> What happens is not that we know a moment beforehand what joke we are going to make, and that all it then needs is to be clothed in words. We have an indefinable feeling, rather, which I can best compare with an *"absence,"* a sudden release of intellectual tension, and then all at once the joke is there—as a rule ready-clothed in words. (*JTRU*, 224–25)

The conditions of the joke's reception similarly make placing it in terms of communication theory difficult. In his chapter "The Purposes of Jokes," Freud's example of the smutty joke describes a scenario in which a man has been rebuked when he has introduced sexual innuendo into his conversation with a woman as a means of sexual foreplay. Trying to salvage something from his failed attempt at seduction, the man finds himself making a joke of the woman to a second man who has witnessed the embarrassing incident (*JTRU*, 142–43). Many of Freud's commentators have argued that the case of smut is paradigmatic for the inter- and intrapsychical relations that contribute to the production of the joke in general. The smutty joke clearly illustrates how the third person's role as witness and the second person's role as repudiator compel the joke to be told. The teller's relation to "the other" is responsible for the joke's emergence. Weber has emphasized, in this regard, the unusual manner in which the third person gets the joke.

Far from simply decoding a message, the listener, assisted by the joke, abandons his moral and critical judgment, and finds himself laughing without being quite aware of what he is laughing at. Just as the joke had emerged from the depths of the teller's unconscious, its first and foremost audience is the unconscious of the listener.[16]

Unlike the joke, Freud discusses the comic in the first place in terms of observation rather than as a communicative act. The comic that is intentionally produced in art and literature is, according to Freud, simply an "evocation of the comic," whereas the "pure comic" is found (JTRU, 240). Although the comic emerges as a result of observation, understanding it in terms of perception or apprehension is not altogether correct. Freud uses the words *apperception* and *ideation* to indicate the distance between the feeling of the comic and conscious attention to what causes its production. The actual mechanics of the comic involve a process of comparison that lacks "the cathexis of attention with which consciousness is linked" (JTRU, 283–84). Importantly, the person who finds something comic does not recognize it as comic. This is also the case in the evocation of the comic; even when the comic is intentionally produced the audience does not decode it as it might an informational message. The comic as code must not be recognized because recognition entails an evaporation in advance of the feeling of comic pleasure.

For Freud then, the apprehension of the comic belongs, like the joke, to the condition of unknowing. Emerging from the preconscious system, comic pleasure, just like the pleasure one experiences upon hearing a joke, takes place without conscious attention to its cause.

TECHNIQUES

In Freud's discussions of the techniques of the joke and those of the comic, he elaborates significant differences between the two forms. The joke uses the same devices that he discovered five years earlier in his theorization of the dream. Like the dream, the joke relies on the techniques of condensation and displacement. The comic, however, uses a method of degradation. (Freud himself uses this term intermittently in his analysis of the comic. I have emphasized it here as *the essential method* of the comic in accordance with Freud's own argumentation although not his explicit address.) That the joke is still a subspecies of the comic, however, is evident in Freud's method of deducing the technique of condensation by analyzing the thought or the meaningful content of a joke and comparing it with its form of expression.[17]

To explain the technique of condensation, Freud recalls a joke made by one of the poet Heine's character's, Hirsch-Hyacinth, "the lottery-agent and extractor of corns," "who boasts to the poet of his relations with the wealthy Baron Rothschild, and finally says: 'And, as true as God shall grant me all good things, Doctor, I sat beside Salomon Rothschild and he treated me quite as his equal—quite famillionairely'" (*JTRU*, 47). According to Freud, the meaningful content of the joke comprises its comment on the condescending attitude the rich take to the poor: "'Rothschild treated me quite as his equal, quite familiarly—that is, so far as a millionaire can.' 'A rich man's condescension,' we should add, 'always involves something not quite pleasant for whoever experiences it'" (*JTRU*, 48).

The economy of expression, compared with the extended intricacy of the thought it conveys, catches Freud's attention. He explains it by way of a mechanical operation, a compressing force, that must have been brought to bear on the thoughts that were intended to be expressed. More specifically, one thought, less resistant to compression than the other, disappears in the process but nevertheless leaves behind a trace that is fused with the resistant thought. Strictly speaking, the technique here is "condensation, accompanied by the formation of a substitute" but Freud in fact uses *condensation* to account for the technique of a dozen kinds of jokes that are produced specifically by playing with verbal expression (*JTRU*, 51).

Displacement jokes are distinctive because of the manner in which they divert a train of thought from its anticipated trajectory. Freud says, "I propose to describe it as 'displacement,' since its essence lies in the division of the train of thought, the displacement of the psychical emphasis on to a topic other than the opening one" (*JTRU*, 88). The subsidiary techniques of displacement jokes involve indirect representation and include things such as representation by something small, by the opposite, allusion, analogy, and omission. Here is one of Freud's examples of a displacement joke:

> An impoverished individual borrowed 25 florins from a prosperous acquaintance, with many asseverations of his necessitous circumstances. The very same day his benefactor met him again in a restaurant with a plate of salmon mayonnaise in front of him. The benefactor reproached him: "What? You borrow money from me and then order yourself salmon mayonnaise? Is that what you've used my money for?" "I don't understand you," replied the object of the attack: "if I haven't any money I can't eat salmon mayonnaise, and if I have some money I mustn't eat salmon mayonnaise. Well, then, when am I to eat salmon mayonnaise?" (*JTRU*, 86).

Freud differentiates between condensation and displacement jokes according to the "material" they work with. Condensation jokes are verbal, they treat words as "a plastic material with which one can do all kinds of things," whereas displacement jokes are conceptual. To understand more precisely what the condensation joke does with the plastic material, we need only look to the Saussurean conception of the sign (*JTRU*, 68). Ferdinand de Saussure's sign has two inseparable components: a sound-image, which is a material signifier, and a concept, or immaterial signified. The function of the sign depends on the arbitrary connection between the signifier and the signified, and the signifier's operation as a transparent vehicle for the signified concept.[18]

The joke, however, perturbs this logic of signification. We can see, for instance, that the word *famillionairely* does not use a transparent signifier that remains subordinate to its concept, but rather makes the signifier opaque and puts the process of signification on display. In other contexts this would be called drawing attention to the materiality of the signifier. But the joke goes further than this expression suggests, undermining the structural rules that ground the operation of signification. The joke in this example emerges from a *resemblance* between two signifiers; yet other kinds of condensation jokes—double meaning jokes in particular—work by compressing two concepts into one signifier. (They work, in other words, precisely in accordance with the polysemy central to Bataille's reading of Hegel.) Still other jokes function by making multiple use of the same material, whether it is the double meaning of a name and the thing denoted by it or the double meaning of the literal and the metaphorical.

Whereas condensation jokes work by meddling with the means of signification, in displacement jokes the integrity of the sign remains intact. Even so, displacement jokes can and often do take polysemy as their point of departure. Freud recounts the following Jewish joke: "Two Jews met in the neighbourhood of the bathhouse. 'Have you taken a bath?' asked one of them. 'What?' asked the other in return, 'is there one missing?'" (*JTRU*, 85). The displacement in this joke obviously originates in the two senses in which "taken" is understood, but continues in the diversion of the train of thought (*JTRU*, 90). Sometimes now described as "kettle logic,"[19] the displacement joke works by setting in play a series of chain reactions that cause meaning to depart from its intended purpose and thereby undermine the logic of reason (*JTRU*, 244).

Freud understands the comic, on the other hand, to be brought about by a process of comparison from which a method of degradation can be deduced. He includes the following as techniques of the comic: one can make oneself comic (by being clumsy or stupid); one can make other people comic by putting them in comic situations (practical jokes, convincing them that something nonsensical is true by exploiting their credulity, or simulation of their speech and mannerisms); or by mimicry, caricature, parody, travesty, and unmasking. Freud argues that caricature, parody, and travesty all work by diminishing the power of the sublime. They are all directed against people and objects that are exalted, have authority, or are in one way or another sublime (JTRU, 260–61).[20] We find something to be comic when we undertake a preconscious comparison between the comic object and its standard. Degradation is tied to this comparative process in so far as it spares the observer the necessary expenditure for the usual maintenance of "solemn restraint" and this surplus is discharged by laughter. Caricature degrades the object by representing a general impression by a single trait; parody and travesty by destroying the unity of something (for example, "people's characters as we know them and their speeches and actions") by replacing something superior with something inferior; and so on (JTRU, 262).

Freud's identification of comparison as an essential aspect of the comic means that his theory of the comic complies with the tradition Aristotle established and Bergson followed. For all three theorists the comic is mimetic. By inflecting this characteristic back on to the joke, we see that no such quality inheres in the latter's techniques of condensation and displacement. Condensation and displacement have a transformative capacity rather than a comparative one.

One of the most important formal properties of the joke is its double structure, which Freud describes in terms of both a Janus head and a relation between kernel and envelope. This double structure accounts for the distinctive relationship between sense and nonsense embodied in the joke and allows us to differentiate further between the joke and the comic. The *Janus head* is first of all Freud's term for the dual purpose of the joke: on the one hand, the joke has to express some meaning that the first person is prohibited (by social mores) and inhibited (by his own psychical makeup) from communicating in a semiotically/rationally conventional way; on the other hand, it must also bribe the listener not to object by giving him or her pleasure. In James Strachey's translation of *Jokes and Their Relation to the Unconscious* this distinction is carried over into another between the kernel of thought and the joke envelope, or the meaning of the joke and its expressive technique (JTRU, 182).

Weber, however, has taken Strachey to task for misattributing the terms of Freud's analogy in this regard, contending that Strachey inverts the relation of form and thought. In his reading of Freud, Weber argues that the thought constitutes the envelope and the witty form lies at the heart of the joke.[21] Meaning seduces the listener, allowing him or her to think that the joke has substance when in fact the joke is an indulgence of the unconscious. Weber argues:

> What Strachey has difficulty in accepting is precisely the point Freud, in his study of jokes (and indeed, in his entire psychoanalytic theory) is striving to make: that "the most substantial thoughts," products of con-

scious intentionality, are used by the unconscious as a foil, "envelope," or guise (*Einkleidung*), to disguise and conceal its operations.[22]

Weber insists that in the dual structure of the joke, its Janus head, meaning and play, sense and nonsense, occur at the same time. Meaning constitutes the palatable exterior that momentarily hides the forbidden interior—the playful adventure and the release of repressed desire. The envelope engages our attention so that the relief from inhibition occurs without our conscious attention—as Weber says, "in the meanwhile."[23]

Weber's primary concern here is with the temporality of the joke. The simultaneous expression of sense and nonsense catches the listener in a trap and distracts him or her from what is going on. Certainly we see a tension between play and meaning throughout Strachey's translation of Freud's text. At times it appears that the antisocial meaning that is forbidden in ordinary expression lies at the heart of the joke and at other times it seems that the operation of the primary processes—the "playful" techniques of condensation and displacement—constitute its essence. This is not the first time that a confusion between the inside and the outside is significant in Freud's work. Lyotard observes, for instance, that according to Freud the dream "wear[s] its heart on his sleeve,"[24] which suggests that Freud's conceptualization of space is as inexplicable and awkward as his (dis)articulation of time. Weber's argument, nevertheless, draws our attention to the fact that not a single antisocial impulse is being indulged but two: the aggressive, antisocial thought mobilized against someone or something *and* the use of methods outside the parameters of conventional signification for communicating ideas. As we will see, this double aspect of the joke also structures Freud's distinction between its tendentious and innocent manifestations.

In the meantime, perhaps the best way to understand the significance of Freud's point about the joke's Janus head is by examining his articulation of this property's relation to the comic because the comic exhibits no such double structure. Freud demonstrates this point by way of an analysis of the witty letters of a Berlin journalist named Julius Stettenheim, who wrote under the pseudonym "Wippchen" the Correspondent from Bernau (*JTRU*, 275). Freud identifies the prevalence of condensation in his writings, which gives them the appearance of the joke (*JTRU*, 277). "'Turkey has money *wie Heu am Meere* [like hay by the sea].' This is made up of the two expressions: 'Money *wie Heu* [like hay]' and 'Money *wie Sand am Meere* [like sand by the sea]'" (*JTRU*, 276). But he proposes:

> one face of the joke is blank, as though it were rudimentary: a Janus head but with only one face developed on it. If we allow the technique to lure us into the unconscious, we come upon nothing. *The amalgamations lead*

> us to no instance in which the two things that are amalgamated really yield a new meaning; if we attempt an analysis, they fall completely apart. The modifications and substitutions lead, as they do in jokes, to a usual and familiar wording; but the modification or substitution itself tells us nothing fresh and as a rule, indeed, nothing possible or serviceable. So that only the one view of these "jokes" is left over—that they are nonsense. (JTRU, 278, my emphasis)

Because one face is left blank, because the thought is itself nonsense, Freud argues that it cannot be considered a joke. This does not, however, prevent him from considering it comic:

> Rudimentary jokes of this kind undoubtedly produce a comic effect, which we can account for in more than one way. Either the comic arises from the uncovering of the modes of thought of the unconscious,... or the pleasure comes from the comparison with a complete joke. (JTRU, 278)

The distinction between the joke and the comic is thus made clearer for us. That Wippchen's examples use the unconscious technique of condensation, but in such a manner as to "tell us nothing fresh and as a rule, indeed, nothing possible or serviceable," implies that the joke must tell us something new or serviceable. The comic likewise plays with words, but only to the extent that such play produces no new meaning. Although the comic can use the techniques of the unconscious, it does so without the transformative impact of the joke. The joke makes a dual presentation of sense and nonsense, whereas in comic words we see just nonsense.

As I have suggested, in Freud's theorization of the impact of the unconscious on the relation of meaning and nonmeaning in the joke, he also distinguishes between innocent and tendentious jokes. Tendentious jokes are those that express antisocial impulses in their content. They might be aggressive or sexually suggestive, or they might express extreme cases of cynicism or skepticism. Freud suggests that in these kinds of jokes the unconscious processes have managed to transform not just the form in which the thought is expressed, but the thought itself. The transformation of the thought distinguishes the tendentious joke from its innocent counterpart. Heine's "famillionairely" joke cited earlier is one such example.

Freud classifies the following as an example of an innocent joke: "'How are you getting along?' the blind man asked the lame man. 'As you see,' the lame man replied to the blind man" (JTRU, 68). Freud says that the most innocent jokes of all are verbal jokes, such as spoonerisms, which make use of condensation purely for reasons of technique: the preconscious thought is retained and only its form is worked over by the unconscious. Freud is also quick to point out that innocent jokes are not necessarily trivial or without substance; rather the substance or value comes from the thought itself (as compared with the case of comic nonsense, in which there is no thought at all).

He explains the "motive force" of the innocent joke as exhibitionism or the desire to "show one's cleverness" (*JTRU*, 194). Making innocent jokes is the talent only of those people who have a "special *personal aptitude*" for exchanging a preconscious cathexis for an unconscious one (*JTRU*, 237). In the case of the tendentious joke, on the other hand, the pressure of the unconscious itself and the strength of antisocial impulses (aggressive, sexual, cynical, and skeptical) are credited with its production.

And yet, if we acknowledge that the innocent joke is in a certain sense destructive of signification and the institution of the rules of language, then we find nothing innocent in the innocent joke. Freud touches on this point repeatedly throughout his work but never as strongly as he might. Innocent jokes can be considered tendentious to the extent that they undermine or destroy the operation of language and its articulation of meaning as it is conventionally understood.

Despite the shifting representation of Freud's classification of jokes from the unconscious techniques that produce them to the material on which they operate and to their purposes, the techniques of condensation and displacement need to be remembered. The unconscious source of these techniques and the fact that they are bound up with the primary process, not in a merely coincidental way but in a manner essential to the particular function of its economy, is crucial to Freud's overall argument. These techniques are responsible for transforming the preconscious thought. They also serve Freud's distinction between the joke and the comic in as much as the latter is understood as relying on a process of degradation and comparison.

THE JOKE AND THE UNCONSCIOUS

The specificity of Freud's differentiation between the joke and the comic must be understood not only in terms of the techniques that each uses—condensation and displacement in the joke and degradation in the comic—but also in terms of the places in the psychical topography from which they respectively emerge and the economic regimes that give these places their character. Although the techniques of the joke and the comic articulate relations between sense and nonsense, these relations can themselves be specified further by recourse to the operations that constitute them.

What distinguishes the joke from the comic is precisely the "psychical scene of action" in which each originates. The joke emerges from the depths of the unconscious, the comic from the preconscious. Traversing the topographical sites of the joke and the comic are the different operations of the primary and secondary processes, which are governed respectively by the pleasure principle and the reality principle. The joke's emergence from the unconscious connects it overwhelmingly to the dream—both the joke-work and the dream-work are dominated by the primary process and the pleasure principle. By contrast, the mechanics of comic pleasure take place in the preconscious strata of the psyche.

In the Freudian schema, the unconscious comprises the repressed contents of the preconscious-conscious system. These repressed contents (ideas) are representatives or delegates of instincts that cannot be satisfied by the subject (or wishes that cannot be fulfilled) because satisfaction would, for one reason or another, result in unpleasure.[25] Within the confines of the unconscious, however, the primary process governs the circulation of energy in accordance with the pleasure principle. This means that energy is characteristically unhampered and flows freely from one idea to another. Condensation and displacement, in particular, assist this free circulation of energy. As mechanisms of the primary process, they enable ideas to be reunited (recathected) to the satisfying experiences of unconscious wishes.[26] Due to the freeflow of energy in the unconscious, these repressed wishes and contents are strongly cathected and seek reentry into the preconscious-conscious system. However, the distorting impulse of the censorship barrier, which operates between the unconscious and the preconscious system, means that repressed contents only enter the preconscious or conscious systems in compromise formations such as jokes, dreams, and slips of the tongue.

In proposing that the distinctive nature of the joke results from its unconscious origin, Freud makes a forceful connection between the joke and the dream. In the very same manner that the day's residue and bodily sensations are dragged down into the unconscious to be transformed by the dream-work into the dream-content, when a joke is made an as yet unarticulated thought drops down to this deeper level of the unconscious for a moment, and afterward emerges in the form of the joke (JTRU, 224–25).

Even so, a distinct point occurs in Freud's work where the constitution of the joke parts company with the dream. The primary factor responsible for the difference between the two forms is the condition of intelligibility. Lyotard has argued that the dream is not an intelligible object or that the intelligibility it maintains is a façade constructed to deceive us.[27] To the extent that the joke, on the other hand, is a communicative act, it must have a degree of intelligibility.

In the dream, condensation and displacement are two of four operations responsible for the transformation of the latent dream-thoughts (which are themselves meaningful) into the manifest content. Their job is to reduce a meaningful discourse into a jumble of images that requires an elaborate process of interpretation to have its sense restored. Condensation is the same in both jokes and dreams whereas the operation of displacement varies. Condensation abbreviates or compresses the material of the dream and the joke. Some objects are preserved whereas others are lost; the ones that remain combine with the traces of those that are lost and become overdetermined (JTRU, 226). In the dream, the action of displacement works to level the varying psychical intensity of the unconscious dream-thoughts so that what is significant in them is trivialized in the manifest content. Freud writes:

> things that lie on the periphery of the dream-thoughts and are of minor importance occupy a central position and appear with great sensory intensity in the manifest dream, and *vice versa*. This gives the dream the appearance of being displaced in relation to the dream-thoughts, and this displacement is precisely what brings it about that the dream confronts waking mental life as something alien and incomprehensible. (JTRU, 220)

Displacement in the joke also involves the leveling of psychical intensity. The variation of displacement between the joke and the dream comes into play because in the dream-work displacement "exaggerates" the "method of indirect expression beyond all bounds," whereas in the joke-work such methods remain subordinate to the *"limits imposed on their employment by conscious thinking"* (JTRU, 230). These are limits of *intelligibility*. Despite the condition of "unknowing" that contributes to the joke, if it is to be successful and met by the laughter it seeks, the listener still has to get it. Although the difference seems to be only a question of degree, something more fundamental results: in jokes the nonsense must also have an intelligible or meaningful aspect, whereas this condition is not binding in the dream. (In this respect, the dream is more like comic nonsense.)

THE PRECONSCIOUS AND THE COMIC

Whereas Freud's attribution of the joke to the unconscious firstly concerns the psychical scene of action in the joke teller, he locates the emergence of comic pleasure in the psychical conditions of the audience or finder. According to Freud, the specificity of the apprehension of the comic can be accounted for by the operation of the audience's preconscious. The preconscious system is distinct from both the conscious and the unconscious systems. Jean Laplanche and J. B. Pontalis tell us that because the operations and contents of the preconscious are not present in the conscious system, they are said to be "unconscious" in the descriptive sense of the term. But they are by no means synonymous with the contents of the unconscious system. That they are in principle accessible to consciousness distinguishes them from the contents of the unconscious. The contents of the preconscious system comprise knowledge and memories that are simply not present to consciousness at a given moment.[28] The system is governed by the secondary process that operates in accordance with the reality principle. This means that energy in the preconscious is bound and "movement towards discharge is checked and controlled."[29] The cathexis of ideas is undertaken in a stable fashion and the satisfaction of desire is postponed while different paths leading to satisfaction are explored.[30] In other words, pleasure seeking is held in check by the subject's engagement with and understanding of reality.

PLEASURE AND LAUGHTER

Freud's emphasis on laughter as a necessary part of the joke process and his desire to account for it leads him to theorize the different distribution of energy in the psychical scene from which it emerges. Certainly laughter immediately unites the joke and the comic, yet Freud's general inference is that laughter at the joke is much more intense than at the comic. For example, he says, "the *explosive* laugh...signalizes a good joke" and the joke's intensity is evidenced in the hearer's "*burst* of laughter" (JTRU, 123, 197, my emphasis). Laughter at the comic is discussed in much more subdued terms and is framed in an account of pleasure. Whereas the joke is only a joke in so far as the third person laughs at it, Freud puts forward no such criterion for the comic.

The difference between the laughter that responds to the joke and the laughter that responds to the comic might be conceived as a difference of degree and hence a quantitative difference, but it is also arguable that it is a qualitative one. This is because the surpluses of cathectic energy discharged as laughter are released for completely different reasons. The joke and the comic differ to the extent that they access different sources of pleasure. We will see that pleasure from the joke comes from the decathexis of inhibition whereas pleasure in the comic results from a release of an excess of cathectic energy expended on ideation.[31]

Freud conceives the unconscious as something like a seething mass of banished ideas and brute energy that will resort to any means to return to consciousness and the censorship barrier as a counterforce that works to inhibit the entry of repressed ideas to consciousness, a filter that deactivates some of the potential tension of the unconscious by breaking it up and rearranging it to make it incomprehensible to consciousness. He argues that both the erection and maintenance of this inhibitive barrier requires psychical expenditure (JTRU, 166). The purpose of the joke is to remove this barrier so that the psychical expenditure that was being used to maintain it is discharged in laughter:

> Relief from psychical expenditure that is already there and economizing in psychical expenditure that is only about to be called for—from these two principles all the techniques of jokes, and accordingly all pleasure from these techniques, are derived. (JTRU, 177)

Weber points out that this ultramobility of cathexis in the unconscious makes the establishment of meaning impossible.[32] Only when cathexis is controlled or bound (as in the secondary process), when its freedom is limited, do we have enough stability of representation to make meaning possible. That the joke simultaneously produces sense and nonsense, therefore, also demands the simultaneous binding and discharging of cathexis in the psyche of the listener who obtains pleasure from it.

Freud notes that both the teller and the listener have a similar inhibitory cathexis or anticathexis, which the joke frees up. In the case of the smutty joke, if the lifting of the inhibitory cathexis does not take place, the listener will not be seduced by the joke but join forces with the butt and rebuke its teller. Freud thus lists the following as the conditions necessary for the joke's success:

> (1) It must be ensured that the third person is really making this cathectic expenditure. (2) It is necessary to guard against the cathectic expenditure, when it is liberated, finding some other psychical use instead of offering itself for motor discharge. (3) It cannot but be an advantage if the cathexis which is to be liberated in the third person is intensified before-hand, raised to a greater height. (JTRU, 203)

Freud expands on these conditions, noting not only the necessity of psychical accord between the teller and the listener, but also a whole range of techniques that detach the hearer's attention from the joking process so that it can run its course automatically (JTRU, 204). Thus Freud considers brevity of expression, easy intelligibility, omissions in the joke's wording, and syllogistic façades auxiliary techniques. Significantly, Freud still calls the condensation and displacement discussed earlier the techniques proper. As I suggested then, condensation and displacement thereby simultaneously serve to undertake the work of the transformation of meaning and to distract us from that work.

Freud defines the comic as a means of obtaining pleasure from an economy in expenditure on what he calls ideation. The mechanics of this process are apparent in his example of the comic of movement. Freud says that to understand (apperceive) a movement undertaken by someone else, the best method is to imitate it and then through comparison (of one's movement with the other person's) determine which requires the greater expenditure.[33] Of course, imitation does not have to be literally carried out because memory-traces make an idea of movement available. This process of ideation differs from acting or performing "above all in the fact that it displaces far smaller cathectic energies and holds back the main expenditure from discharge" (JTRU, 251). The comic process begins when the object of our attention moves clumsily or inexpediently. In such cases we:

> *simultaneously or in rapid succession,* ... apply to one and the same act of ideation two different ideational methods, between which the "comparison" is then made and the comic difference emerges. Differences in expenditure of this kind arise between what belongs to someone else and to oneself, between what is usual and what has been changed, between what is expected and what happens.[34]

Consequently, Freud theorizes the origin of comic pleasure in "the difference between our own psychical expenditure and the other person's as estimated by empathy" (JTRU, 256). Because of this empathy, we undertake a comparison between two cathectic expenditures, one on the person, the other on our idea of what the action should be (JTRU, 256). The surplus between these two expenditures and its discharge results in comic pleasure.[35] Clearly, there is no explosive character to the laughter that might result.

※

Freud's analysis in his book moves toward the tendentious joke to justify his argument of the joke's relation to the unconscious because at its most extreme the joke is constituted not simply by the lifting of inhibitions but also by the liberation of repressed contents. The trajectory of Freud's discussion thus appears to relinquish gradually the initial emphasis he places on the techniques of condensation and displacement. Yet they remain of the greatest significance. If we maintain, for instance, that the joke techniques of condensation and displacement are the same techniques that enable the free circulation of energy in the unconscious, then they themselves are responsible for bringing together sense and nonsense. Although Freud refers only to displacement jokes as nonsense jokes (attributing the pleasure obtained from condensation jokes to a saving of psychical expenditure), there is, nevertheless, a sense in which condensation jokes introduce an element of nonsense into their technique. This is their flagrant disregard for the arbitrary nature of signification that underpins the system of language. Similarly, displacement jokes seem to disrespect the laws of syntactic arrangement, even while appearing to maintain them. Both condensation and displacement jokes thus introduce elements of nonsense into sense.

While the joke is produced by the unconscious transformation of a preconscious thought by the primary processes, the comic is produced by the degradation of "the ought" by "the is." Freud's conceptualization of the joke and the comic makes reference to two distinct economies of exchange that work on several levels—their operation can be examined through semiotic, social, and psychical concepts. The joke is a communicative act underpinned by a tripartite structure. An unconscious complicity between two people and an excluded third person make the exchange possible. The techniques of the joke are psychical techniques that involve the condensation and displacement of the processes and meaning of signification. Condensation and displacement are operations capable of undertaking a transformation of sense. The joke belongs to general economy to the extent that this transformation is not dialectical. Such transformation means that the initial meaning is not interiorized in the same way that it is in sublative negation. Furthermore, the joke involves a destruction of the conventions of signification and the logic of reason. But the complicity between the teller and the listener and their exclusion of the middle person (or institution) might also be understood within the terms of restricted economy in as much as the joke process serves to salvage communication at the level of the unconscious.

The comic, by contrast, is not necessarily communicated at all and, according to Freud, derives its structure from being found rather than made. It is social to the extent that it involves two people, but the belittling laughter that the comic gives rise to does not establish a complicity between the person who is comic and the person who laughs, but a distance and even a repudiation of the former by the latter. In psychical terms the comic produces a surplus of energy available for understanding in the person who finds something comic. In terms of technique the comic is produced by a kind of degradation. The comic is a mistake or a bad copy of something that creates a feeling of amusement rather than a desire to correct it. It might be thought to embody the conditions of general economy to the extent that it involves minor transgression, but restricted economy is still operative in so far as the comic relies on "the ought" (whether it be convention or law) to operate.

CHAPTER 6

The Comic

Degradation and Refinement in 1920s' Cinematic Slapstick

In the final chapter of his book on the joke, Freud deduces a conceptual basis for various manifestations of the comic. For him, all instances of the comic involve ideation, normativity, comparison, and degradation. His deduction also holds for preceding historical and philosophical formulations of the comic. Aristotle, for example, conceives the comic as partaking in the Ugly, whereas Bergson makes it the negative outcome of a contamination of *élan vital* (life force) by the mechanical. Given the pejorative connotations of the notion of degradation, Freud's evaluation of the comic holds with traditional treatments of comedy as a lesser form of art than tragedy and, indeed, with the an unwillingness to grant it a place in aesthetic sensibility.[1] This chapter interrogates the conceptual efficacy of the formulation of the comic by Aristotle, Bergson, and Freud for understanding the cinematic comedy of the 1910s and 1920s, particularly the films of Sennett, Keaton, Lloyd, and Chaplin.

Although Freud's conception of the comic remains effectively correct in its generality for examples of the comic considered in isolation, an examination of the dynamic operation of the comic within the films' overall performative, textual, and formal registers suggests that the comic has a rather more complex set of allegiances than the psychical, social, and implicitly moral functions that Freud envisages for it. Impacting the nature of the comic within these films is an intricate convergence of changing pictorial conditions, aesthetic tendencies, communicative strategies, moral imperatives, and cinematic developments. These factors are most acutely manifest in the differences between the Keystone comedies of the 1910s and the refined slapstick of the 1920s. Their impact on the development of cinematic comedy in the 1920s caused some of Keaton's critics to reject a notion of comic degradation as an appropriate description of his comic aesthetic. I argue here that the refinement of the comic in the cinema of Keaton and others is consistent with changes to the conventions of caricature in the early twentieth century, which Ernst Kris and Rudolf Arnheim noted. Whereas Arnheim argues that pictorial caricature was a necessary stage in modernist art's movement toward abstraction, 1920s slapstick introduced a perceptual clarity and visual intelligibility necessary for the development of sight gags distinguished by their use of the operations of the primary process.

DEGRADATION

For Aristotle, Bergson, and Freud, the comic involves degradation of one kind or another. Degradation for Aristotle is a ridiculous kind of ugliness, a mistake, or a deformity. The comic for him concerns:

> an imitation of men worse than average; worse, however, not as regards any and every sort of fault, but only as regards one particular kind, the Ridiculous, which is a species of the Ugly. The Ridiculous may be defined as a mistake or deformity not productive of pain or harm to others; the mask, for instance, that excites laughter, is something ugly and distorted without causing pain.[2]

Bergson, on the contrary, argues that the comic "partakes rather of the unsprightly than the unsightly, or rigidness rather than the ugly."[3] Seeing it only as an imitable deformity, rather than a deformity as such, he concurs with Aristotle that the comic that produces laughter causes no pain. But Bergson departs from the Aristotelian view of the comic when he attributes characteristics to it that have come to predominate in the modern industrialized world. His notions of the mechanical encrusted on the living, *la mécanisation de la vie*, inelasticity, repetition, and automatism are the tropes of modernity. The operation of the comic partakes in a more general imposition of the mechanical on the living, and it is always less than (rather than other to) the vital forces that constitute life. Bergson's view of the comic as the deformation of the essentiality of life in its unique and inimitable heterogeneity is therefore also a theory of degradation.

In his discussion of the comic, Freud frequently uses the word *Herabsetzung*, which is German for *degradation*, and means to lower, reduce, belittle, and disparage.[4] Whereas Freud makes no explicit association between degradation and the procedure of the comic in general, degradation can be seen to operate in the three subcategories of the comic that he distinguishes: (1) making oneself comic; (2) making other people comic by inserting them into comic situations; and (3) making things comic by mimicry, caricature, parody, travesty, and unmasking.[5] It is in explaining the third of these categories that Freud explicitly considers degradation. Caricature, parody, travesty, and unmasking all use the technique of degradation "against people and objects which lay claim to authority and respect, which are in some sense '*sublime*'" (*JTRU*, 261). In addition, Freud writes of mimicry as a case of imitating the inimitable (*JTRU*, 271), of unmasking as bringing to light the deception of a person or thing that has authority under false pretences, and of parody and travesty as destroying the unity of the thing (*JTRU*, 262). But degradation is evident in the other two to the extent that making oneself comic involves being clumsy or stupid, hence degrading oneself; and putting other people into comic situations in Freud's estimation makes them inferior and degrades them by making them seem clumsy, stupid, incredulous, and so forth[6] (*JTRU*, 260).

This notion of degradation is underpinned in Freud's schema by psychical comparison. In such comparison the object itself does not give rise to the comic, but rather the object as a point of comparison. Comparison is thus essential to the psychical process of the comic. Freud defines comic comparison as occurring when "something serious and unfamiliar, especially if it is of an intellectual or moral nature, is brought into comparison with something commonplace and inferior" (*JTRU*, 273). An object, person, or situation is not therefore comic in itself but only in relation to what it ought to be. The comic is a relational concept—it inscribes a relation not, however, between two objects, but between a perceived object and an ideation of it.

The quantitative measure implicit in Freud's theorization of the comic is apparent in his discussion of the role of ideation in the apprehension of comic movement. We laugh at someone's inexpedient movement because we make a comparison between the movement we see and the movement we would have carried out ourselves were we in the same position. We thus have a standard (which is quantitatively expressed in a psychical expenditure on innervation) to which we compare the behavior of others.[7] Freud writes, "[i]deation or 'thinking' differs from acting or performing above all in the fact that it displaces far smaller cathectic energies and holds back the main expenditure from discharge" (*JTRU*, 251). As such, watching someone move involves an empathetic expenditure of psychical energy. When a person's movement is comic (exaggerated, clumsy, or inexpedient), the comparison I make between their movement and what my own would be produces a surplus of psychical energy that is discharged in laughter[8] (*JTRU*, 250, 254).

SUPERIORITY

The theory of the comic as degradation has gone hand in hand with an idea of audience superiority. This alignment is often associated with Thomas

Hobbes who, writing in the seventeenth century, is the first modern proponent of what is commonly known as the superiority theory of the comic,[9] but it is implicit in earlier as well as more recent views on the matter. In Plato's *Philebus*, for example, the comic pertains to self-delusion and self-ignorance. Those who are found comic suffer from "the illusory conceit of knowledge."[10] And in Bergson's writing, the superior disposition of the audience is implicit in his view of laughter as a corrective to the comic exemplification of rigidity and mechanism. Society is generally:

> suspicious of all *inelasticity* of character, of mind and even of body, because it is the possible sign of a slumbering activity with separatist tendencies, that inclines to swerve from the common center around which society gravitates: in short because it is the sign of an eccentricity.... Laughter... [is] a sort of social gesture. By the fear which it inspires, it restrains eccentricity, keeps constantly awake and in mutual contact certain activities of a secondary order which might retire into their shell and go to sleep, and, in short, softens down whatever the surface of the social body may retain in mechanical elasticity.[11]

Laughter thus constitutes a moral rectification by society over its occasionally recalcitrant manifestations.

Although Freud's line of argument on comic pleasure relies less overtly on moral rectification, his contention that such pleasure arises from "the difference between our own psychical expenditure and the other person's as estimated by empathy" (*JTRU*, 256), has led theorists to presume that his view of the comic implies the superiority of the finder or audience. Neale and Krutnik argue, for example, that the Freudian theory of the comic produces pleasure "from a process of comparison, in which the difference between the superior position and capacities of the observer and the inferior position and capacities of the observed results in an economy of psychic energy in the observer which is discharged in laughter."[12] This is in spite of numerous qualifications that Freud makes. Although he initially admits that "a uniform explanation" of the comic is found in laughter's expression of "a pleasurable sense of superiority which we feel" (*JTRU*, 256), he subsequently observes that "[t]he feeling of the superiority does not arise in the other person if he knows that one has only been pretending; and this affords fresh evidence of the fundamental *independence* of the comic from the feeling of superiority" (*JTRU*, 260, my emphasis) and that "when we have a clear judgment of our own superiority, we merely smile instead of laughing, or, if we laugh, we can nevertheless distinguish this becoming conscious of our superiority from the comic that makes us laugh" (*JTRU*, 288), Therefore, that Freud's view of comic pleasure arises from feeling of superiority is not quite correct.

DEGRADATION IN CINEMATIC COMEDY

Nevertheless, the idea that the comic involves the degradation of a person or a thing and serves to give the person who finds something comic a sense of superiority has certainly played a significant part in the development of cinematic comedy between the 1910s and the 1920s. Indeed, a perception of the comic as a kind of degradation has proven more useful for detractors who incorporated it as part of a rhetorical strategy to rail against comic aesthetics than for those who wished to celebrate it. Mast and Riblet, both rather dispassionate in their description of the comedy of the Keystone studio, nevertheless use terms that legitimate a pejorative view of the comic. Mast views Sennett films as "the culmination of fifteen years of comic primitivism,"[13] and Riblet describes the iconography and cinematic characteristics of Sennett's cinema in terms of degradation, exaggeration, anarchic buffoonery, violent knockabout, and burlesque.[14]

Sennett films are primarily known for their preoccupation with motion, their reliance on caricature and stereotypes, their deployment of "characterless jest[s]" and their flagrant use of extremely violent slapstick.[15] Jay Leyda coined the term *California slapstick* to describe the comedy produced predominantly at Keystone, as well as other U.S. studios.[16] What made it distinctive was its incorporation of a variety of cinematic and performance traditions such as vaudeville, burlesque, the circus, early chase films, French and Italian comedies, and Griffith's melodramas. And it stood in stark contrast to the genteel comedy that was becoming increasingly popular at this time.

Riblet notes that whereas Sennett films were extremely appealing to audiences in the teens, the industry generally considered them to be an embarrassment because of their vulgar, immoral, and unrefined sensibility, as well as the way they reveled in bad taste and sexually suggestive situations, relying on grotesque makeup and plots constructed around misunderstandings and racist and barbaric pranks. The popular press of the late 1910s and 1920s was rife with the specifications of puritanical moralists who clearly thought this kind of comedy was degrading, belittling, and disparaging. The September 1919 edition of *Moving Picture World* advocated that "[s]lapstick must be taboo.... Instead, a more subtle, clean-cut production, with at least some semblance of a story, is the current demand in the comedy line."[17] Charles Maland notes that representatives of the National Board of Censorship actually visited Chaplin to convince him that his comic sensibility needed refinement.[18] Kerr is probably the most recent exponent of the view of comic degradation. In his book *The Silent Clowns* he likens Sennett's comedy to the playful behavior of monkeys:

> learning by rude and random and utterly amoral behavior what the universe and his fellow creatures will tolerate,... this *is* play, but it is

primeval play, play in the treetops before mores were heard of, play without cause or consequence or social feeling. It erupted volcanically, as though from the bowels of the earth....[19]

Whether the success of Sennett's films was due to their capacity to give audiences a sense of superiority is debatable, however. Riblet, for example, considers the views of Umberto Eco and T. G. A. Nelson on the issue of sympathy and superiority in regard to Sennett's films. Eco contends that whereas audiences may well feel superior to unsympathetic comic characters, they nevertheless enjoy their capacity to violate or transgress social norms. Nelson goes even further, arguing that the audience often unashamedly admires the antisocial behavior of comic protagonists. Riblet himself suggests that characters vary in their efforts to arouse sympathy, seeing the positions represented by Eco and Nelson as "poles on a continuum of possible forms of comic representation and audience address," from "admirable comic roguery" to "reprehensible barbarity."[20]

But the judgment that these films operated through degradation was without doubt upheld by those who felt superior enough to both abstain from the popular indulgence and actively sought to have the cinema industry clean up its act. A sense of superiority *and* a lack of a certain kind of humor (at the least) clearly combines to celebrate 1920s slapstick more readily than the cinematic comedy that immediately preceded it.

THE COMIC IN KEATON'S OEUVRE

Not surprisingly, then, Keaton's commentators go to great lengths to distance his comedy from degradation. Robert Benayoun rejects the claims French journalists made following the retrospective of Keaton's work in 1966 that Keaton was a "stonefaced man from Mars."[21] Such a claim is so far from his own view that in his book *The Look of Buster Keaton*, Benayoun situates Keaton's work in relation to several twentieth-century avant-garde aesthetic movements, drawing comparisons between Keaton's accomplishments and those of Dada and Surrealist artists, and the literary achievements of Franz Kafka, Eugène Ionesco, and Jorge Luis Borges. Lebel too explicitly opposes the idea that Keaton's work partakes in the genre of the ugly or is correctly understood in terms of an aesthetic of degradation. Although Lebel acknowledges a relationship between the comic and degradation, he insists on the uniqueness of Keaton's contribution to the comic on these very grounds. He differentiates Keaton's beauty from what he calls the ugly nudity and overall buffoonery of Laurel and Hardy, applauding the grace and elegance of Keaton's sartorial style—"Keaton does not 'bring out' clothing so much as clothing 'brings out' Keaton"²²—and proposing that "[o]f all the great cinema comics, Keaton alone comes off to advantage when clad only in shorts."²³ To this he contrasts the comic indignity of Laurel and Hardy: "their more or less relative nakedness is turned into a 'comic situation,' and a generally degrading one."²⁴

Both Lebel and Benayoun take issue with a critical tendency to characterize Keaton's behavioral disposition as a kind of impassivity, consonant with phlegmatic, recalcitrant, and sluggish behavior.²⁵ Lebel's issue is with the allegiance that the connotations of impassivity have with "comic reduction" or degradation.²⁶ He contends that those critics who reduce Keaton's comedy along such lines are simply without an adequate appreciation of the comic. The supposedly "enlightened" audiences who held comedy to be antithetical to the higher, in fact, supreme, art of the sublime, he writes, "could only conceive of this expressive impenetrability as being something anti-artistic, something incapable of expressing the sacrosanct human emotions, and thus as a rather coarse and schematic comic artifice."²⁷

Lebel argues, to the contrary, that what makes Keaton's rendition of the comic distinctive is its supreme elegance. This elegance emanates form the performer's statuesque beauty and exquisitely accented facial features. Far from suggesting an impenetrable mask, his features enhance the subtlety of his expressivity. A contrast can be drawn here between the grotesque caricatures of Sennett films and the physical refinement of Keaton. The former, Riblet notes, wore "ill-fitting costumes," had "extreme body types," "exaggerated and ugly"..."facial features," and "bizarre facial hair."²⁸ And Mast writes that the extras in Sennett's film *Tango Tangles* (1914) comprised "the oddest assortment of couples in the most bizarre masquerade costumes, wearing the silliest expressions, dancing with partners who are horrendously mismatched in size, shape, type and sex."²⁹ Keaton, on the other hand, wore only slightly undersized clothes, which served to accentuate his athleticism and the movement of his body in space. One could even argue that Keaton's beauty radiates outward from movement and his actions, his physical agility and athleticism, and extends into the director's use of mise-en-scène, image composition, choreography, and his orchestration of the gag.

Sennett's knockabout style of comedy was one where characters were barely individuated, where they were distinguished only to the point of being crude stereotypes rather than psychological beings. Mast describes their acting as "demonstrative, excessive, ridiculous burlesques of human attitudes and emotions."³⁰ Speed was added to the action by undercranking the camera with the result that movement sometimes seems to jolt between frames. The reconfiguration of the natural rhythm by the mechanical tempo of the camera worked in tandem with grossly exaggerated gestures and awkward, frenetic, even frenzied movements. The multiple collisions of bodies in space and a heightened level of physical abuse went without saying. Again we can draw a contrast between all of this and the grace of Keaton's characters' movement, his precision and rhythm, the deliberateness of his actions, the balletic quality of his walk (the pas de deux in *Sherlock Jr.*, for example) and the acrobatic quality of his falls.

Establishing a persona was a distinctive feature of all the silent comedians of the 1920s and is conventionally discussed in terms of the development of cinematic comedy in relation to the institutional emergence of the star system and narrative-based character-oriented cinema. It is the means by which the mute clowns differentiated themselves from each other and explains the distinctive quality of their aesthetic and its contrast with the Sennett comedies of the 1910s. Keaton's character has clearly articulated behavioral traits, such as his tenacity and forbearance, his self-conscious disavowal of the need for recognition,[31] and a singularly focused and encompassing vision relayed through a gaze forever training itself on the horizon.[32]

Kerr claims that Sennett was largely insensitive to the quality of the performers he employed and that although he selected hugely creative people to work for him, his style of cinematography, such as his favoring of long shots over closeups, made no effort to establish identificatory relations between the audience and character and prevented performers developing the kind of acting techniques that were to dominate 1920s slapstick. He writes that "[t]hough Sennett could detect talent, it was enormously difficult for that talent to ripen under him in any personal, idiosyncratic way."[33] Riblet, however, has a more nuanced view, admitting that although Sennett's films were always billed as having "all-star casts" where the company of performers were generally conceived as an ensemble or troupe, the "top comedians [also] developed their own idiosyncrasies of performance and comic business."[34] He thereby implies some continuity between the two approaches to cinematic comedy, even while he concedes that the development of comedian comedy "requires not only a recognizable star but also a consistent comic persona from film to film."[35] Seidman also stresses that iconicity, "the instant identifiability of these comedians—their cultural significance—as much as their performing talents" was necessary to the success of the 1920s (and subsequent) comedians.[36]

GENTEEL COMEDY AND *SAFETY LAST!*

Experts generally contend that the appropriation of the conventions of the emergent genre of genteel comedy meant comic performers such as Keaton, Chaplin, and others became less caricatured in the late 1910s and early 1920s than in earlier Keystone slapstick. Even though Keaton himself performed in only one genteel comedy—*The Saphead* (1920)—which he made between his last two-reeler and his first feature-length film, the conventions of the genre nevertheless assisted the 1920s directors to make successful feature-length comedies.

Genteel comedy is like Romantic comedy in contemporary cinema. It grew up alongside the extreme slapstick of the Sennett and Hal Roach studios. Neale and Krutnik define the genre in terms of plausible situation comedy and polite comedy.[37] These comedies eschewed the broad physical comedy of the likes of Sennett and produced highly sentimental films with greater emphasis on narrative development and realism. The comedy in such films had to be motivated by the narrative and could not be gratuitous. It emerged from situations rather than the peculiar traits of comic personae. Indeed, the films placed much greater emphasis on character, particularly characters that were psychological entities with whom the audience could identify, than on caricature.

Along with Keaton, Chaplin, and Langdon, Lloyd is considered one of the four great comedian comics of the silent era. Unlike the other three, Lloyd did not come to the cinema from vaudeville or the music hall and therefore could not draw on an already developed comic repertoire. Lloyd worked initially as a dramatic actor with the producer Roach (who was Sennett's major competitor during the 1910s), and when Roach lost his "comedy man" he passed the role on to Lloyd. Critics and historians place much emphasis on the idea that Lloyd was not a natural comic (as were the other three) and that he labored to make people laugh. Indeed, in terms of short films, he was far more prolific than any of his peers, making more than 200 one- and two-reel films before turning to feature-length comedies.[38] Lloyd's comedy is worthy of closer examination because it is the straightest of the four performers and it sets the stage for a discussion of what is distinctive about the comic in the slapstick of the post-Keystone era. Because Lloyd's deployment of the comic is the most restrained, he provides the most extreme example of the refined aspect of the comic that I am concerned with here. Indeed, the straightness of Lloyd's character derives from his appropriation of the conventions of genteel comedy. Donald McCaffrey argues that Lloyd drew much more heavily on "both the story material and the characterizations of genteel comedy than his slapstick contemporaries."[39]

Lloyd was considered to have made it only once he established his comic persona, known as the "glasses character" due to his horn-rimmed spectacles.[40] He derived his persona from contemporary genteel performers such as Charles Ray, Douglas McLean, and Johnny Hines.[41] John Belton claims that Lloyd's screen character presents a quintessentially American contradiction: "He wants to be average, yet competitively strives to best those around him...to *win* the Average American Boy contest."[42] As the best average

American, Lloyd, unlike the other clowns of the silent screen, personified the ordinary and the normative rather than the eccentric.[43] As Mast writes, "Harold is the affable boy next door, anxious to get ahead, not very good at anything, but willing to compensate with energy for his lack of talent. He is the American Dream of what a mediocre man can accomplish with a lot of hard work."[44]

Lloyd's glasses character was therefore far less downtrodden than the characters Chaplin and Langdon and even, to some extent, Keaton, played. While his persona clearly could be identified by his visual distinctiveness and by consistent behavioral traits, the enunciative register of his comedy manifests much less of a tension between the diegetic and the extradiegetic (fictional and extrafictional) realms than that of his peers. Indeed, the diegesis was more closely bound to the representational conventions of melodramatic realism than the presentational mode of performative comedy. Part of this was no doubt due to the fact that Lloyd did not have a previously established comedic repertoire to draw on, and the audience did not have a previous investment in him that would give him the license to behave in ways that pushed the improbable to the point of the implausible or that allowed him to move from story mode to performance mode. Even so that Seidman considered Lloyd as working within the genre of comedian comedy is telling.[45]

In *Safety Last!* Lloyd's character embodies all of the virtues and vices of the go-getter stereotype he appropriated from genteel comedy. The breach in the narrative results from the character's combination of ambitiousness, boastfulness, and bad luck. Lloyd's character, Harold, has left his sweetheart (Mildred Davis) back in the small town where he grew up to make something of himself in the city. It turns out, however, that opportunities for success are not quite as abundant as he had hoped and a humble sales clerk in the haberdashery section of a department store is the best position he can find. He nevertheless writes to his girlfriend every day enclosing tokens that he can barely afford that support his exaggerated tales of success. The girl takes him at his word and decides to join him. Forced by circumstance, Harold pretends to be the store manager to his girlfriend while arranging for his best friend to perform a death defying stunt that entails scaling the façade of a twelve-story building to obtain funds that are, to some degree, equal to his boasting. A previous altercation between his friend and a policeman (itself the result of an innocently misplaced prank) interferes with the plan and Harold has to perform the stunt himself.

Lloyd's character is not particularly comic in himself but certain aspects of his personality push him toward extreme kinds of behavior from which comedy emerges. In addition to scaling the building—the film's comic clincher—other situational stresses give rise to inventiveness on Harold's part and hence to comic performance. When Harold, for all his diligence, arrives late to work, he pretends first of all to be a mannequin so that he can be transported discreetly onto the store floor and then, as circumstance demands, a frog. More generally though, Lloyd pursues an extreme kind of physical comedy known as thrill comedy, risk comedy, or sure-fire comedy. Even though his films are peppered with sight gags, their ultimate success results from his character becoming enmeshed in situations of extreme physical danger. And once he gets into them, he works them to the hilt. Scaling the façade in *Safety Last!*, for example, takes approximately nineteen minutes of screen time. After indicating Lloyd's lack of physical coordination and thereby clearly establishing that he is not up to the task, the sequence develops through two parallel series of images. One series depicts Lloyd climbing the outside wall of the Bolton building and is punctuated at various points by horizontal pauses that interrupt, divert, or threaten to extinguish the vertical or "ascending series."[46] The other series comprises the lines of a chase, one line (inscribed by the cop) threatening to catch up with another (inscribed by Harold's friend) that seeks to elude it. The point is though that the two ascending series (one on the inside, the other on the outside of the building) are meant to converge; the two series are meant to meet at an apex so that Lloyd and his friend can exchange places, the lower the better from Harold's point of view. The gags work by clear delineation of, and the audience identification with, the excessive physical punishments to which Lloyd's own body is subjected. As if having to climb the building in a three-piece suit, dress shoes, and boater hat were not enough, at every floor the danger of the feat is ramped up by different factors intervening. Lloyd is covered in birdseed, becomes a beacon for pigeons, is ensnared by a net, suspended from the second hand of a clock, then from its face, electrocuted by it, and finally entangled in its mechanism. At one point a mouse crawls up the leg of his trousers; at another he is temporarily blinded by a puff of smoke from a photographer's flash. Lloyd scales the face of the building like a crab, hangs from its edge by his fingertips, then by a rope, pounds his head again and again on a ledge, and so it goes on.

Despite the fact that Lloyd appropriated many of the conventions of genteel comedy, his work clearly did not give up on slapstick or violence. His comedy still relies on audience identification with his plight and the kind of bodily identification that Sennett's slapstick reveled in (and very close to the one exploited by the horror genre). The concentration of his comic efforts in terms of sure-fire comedy, however, meant that critics judged Lloyd to have a shallower comic persona than his contemporaries, Keaton and Chaplin. Mast, for instance, makes comments such as, "Lloyd was a great comic of the surface, with very little beneath," and:

> There is something very deliberate, cold-blooded, and detached about Lloyd's hiding inside this box of literary conventions. Lloyd's character,

his makeup, his goals, and his problems are intentionally superficial. The same is true of his gags. Many of them are brilliantly funny and often serve as perfect models for how to set up a gag, develop it, twist it, scramble it, then redevelop it, twist it again, and top it. They are constructed to achieve certain effects, and they succeed. But instead of coming from inside Lloyd's emotions and intellect—as Chaplin's and Keaton's do—they are cunningly plotted and built from the outside.[47]

That Lloyd should be criticized for being superficial, two-dimensional or depthless when this is exactly the idea that his film very explicitly thematizes is not without irony. Many critics have noted that Lloyd's climb to the top of the building emblematizes the "climbing to success" plotline—Lloyd literally rises to the top—produced in numerous genteel comedies of the day. The relentless complication of the situation gives the audience time to consider the figurative dimension of the image—that Lloyd himself is maintaining a façade. Although Harold gets to the top, even his best efforts do not get him inside. And he climbs the building only as a *stand in* for the character who should have performed the feat. So Mast is right: Lloyd is a façade. Lloyd draws on this notion of the façade to develop the story line and produce comedy. His conceit allows the film to play with the relationship between representation, truth, and knowledge. The opening gag of the film, for example, deceives us into thinking that Lloyd is about to be hung until a reverse-shot gives us the full picture and evidently the truth—he is at a train station about to leave small-town life to make his fortune in the big smoke. (We see also something prescient or fatal in the image of the noose. It isn't just an isolated gag but poses a question to the narrative that follows: Will Harold hang himself?) Lloyd's character in the film also operates in terms of deceitful appearances: he presents a sham to his girlfriend, hides from his landlady, steals his friend's phonograph, and so forth. At its most potent, the film subjects the notion of the smooth surface of the American Dream to comic exposition.

The motif of the façade that surfaces in multiple ways in relation to Lloyd's comedy provides an interesting segue into a deeper consideration of what is entailed by the concept of the comic. For the distinctiveness of the deployment of the comic in 1920s slapstick concerns all that is entailed by the façade: that is, it concerns not just the face of an edifice, but putting a face on things, a front, something established for the sake of appearances, an outward show of respectability or virtue, a pretence or a mask.[48]

CARICATURE

Although feature length comedies by Keaton, Chaplin, Lloyd, and Langdon gave their characters somewhat more psychological depth than performers had in Sennett films, we nevertheless see a sense in which these characters emerge from a set of clearly identifiable and consistent traits. And certainly when compared with dramatic performance styles, personality, and psychology simply exemplify traits. In Keaton's films, his traits extend from persona to film form in the simplicity of the narrative structure, the use of an extremely pared down mise-en-scène and the tendency toward a limited profilmic space. The linear trajectory of the train in *The General*, for example, travels from right to left and back again, whereas in *The Navigator*, the mise-en-scène is reduced to the ocean liner on which the Keaton character and the girl are stranded.

Although Keaton's films without doubt refine the grotesqueries of Sennett slapstick to a considerable degree, indications of the comic in Keaton's cinema nonetheless remain consonant with the Freudian definition of the comic. As a means of developing this question about the efficacy of Freud's conception of the comic for understanding the aesthetic of Keaton's comedy, I want to consider comic caricature, not only as Freud understands it, but also as art historians subsequently developed it, and as it is manifest in the cinema under consideration. Through the differentiation between different kinds of caricature (simple and complex) and various techniques (exaggeration, conjuration, and accentuation), we can understand what is pictorially distinctive in Keaton's comedy and indeed how the comic operates through pictorial means.

Freud opens his discussion of caricature by citing Fischer's definition of it as uncovering or accentuating the ugly: "If it [what is ugly] is concealed, it must be uncovered in the light of the comic way of looking at things; if it is noticed only a little or scarcely at all, it must be brought forward and made obvious, so that it lies clear and open to the light of day."[49] Freud also contends that caricature can produce ugliness independently of how the object looks in reality. In his definition, caricature is obtained by two separate means, one of revealing what is hidden, the other of conjuration: on the one hand, "caricature...brings about degradation by emphasizing in the general impression given by the exalted object a single trait which is comic in itself but was bound to be overlooked"; and on the other, "[i]f a comic trait of this kind that has been overlooked is lacking in reality, a caricature will unhesitatingly create it by exaggerating one that is not comic in itself" (*JTRU*, 262).

Drawing on Freud's work, Kris, in his chapter "The Psychology of Caricature" in *Psychoanalytic Explorations in Art*, notes that caricature means to charge or overcharge with distinctive features:

> the Italian *caricare* and the French *charger* (charge = caricature) convey the same idea: to charge or to overcharge; we would add, with distinctive features. Thus a human countenance may have a single trait accentuated so that the representation is "overcharged" with it.[50]

On this basis, Kris distinguishes between two forms of caricature—simple and complex. For him, simple caricature is found in the figure of the clown and accords with the terms of Freud's definition of the comic. Kris says that the pleasure we obtain from such caricature originates in the preconscious and results from a comparison between reality and a distorted reproduction of it, which gives rise to a saving of expenditure on thought.[51] Simple caricature ranges from accentuation to exaggeration. We might think of it as the inscription of a trait in the undifferentiated field of the visible or the exaggeration of a trait that is already present. The former causes distinction to emerge from indeterminacy. Were the iconic force of accentuation to fail to give rise to comic pleasure, the image would simply form a hieroglyph. By contrast, the overcharging of complex caricature produces overdetermination. Complex caricature is tendentious and, at least when it is aimed at an individual or type, exaggerates individual features and thereby reveals "a contrast in the personality between looks and character."[52] Chaplin's Tramp is an excellent example of this contrast: visually he represents urban poverty but he behaves as an aristocratic gentleman. When exaggeration goes too far, it becomes independent of the appearance of the object it is representing and moves from degradation to transformation. Tendentious or complex caricature, Kris suggests, can be theorized in terms of the joke. He describes it as a "graphic form of wit" and locates its origin in the primary process.[53]

Examination of the shifting representational practices between Sennett's comedies and the 1920s films, of which Keaton's work is exemplary, indicates a polarization of exaggeration. On one hand, the exaggeration that tended toward the ugly in Sennett slapstick is refined—it becomes accentuation. On the other hand, some traits are exaggerated to the point that they express a duality in the representation. Keaton, one could argue, refined the pictorial qualities of cinematic comedy by shifting from a caricature of exaggeration to one of accentuation.

Rather than simply attributing the changing nature of cinematic comedy in the 1920s to the increasing influence of the conventions of genteel comedy and as just another instance of the recurrent displacement of Old Comedy by New Comedy,[54] the shift in the nature of caricature from exaggeration to accentuation resonates with changes to pictorial aesthetics under way at the time. Arnheim, for example, claims that by the twentieth century caricature was no longer used merely for either comedy or expressionism but presented the possibility of breaking from mimetic representation at a much more fundamental level and even assisted in the movement toward abstraction in art generally.

Arnheim argues that whereas Paul Klee could only understand the tendency toward abstraction evident in Auguste Rodin's drawings in terms of caricature: "[t]oday, almost a century later, it would not occur to anybody to describe Rodin's quick figure sketches as caricatures."[55] Klee's own exploration of the border between caricature and abstraction stood as an example of so much of what was modern in modern art, its drive for self-sufficiency, its determination to seek independence from the world it had historically endeavored to represent. According to Arnheim, this growing independence is expressed in the trajectory that developed from the satirical cartoons of Honoré Daumier, through the deformation of reality evidenced in expressionism, to a true independence from reality in abstraction.

My intention here is not to claim a direct link between a popular cinema, which was undoubtedly moving toward classicism, and the modernist interrogation of the nature of representation, and certainly not to conflate the two. Yet, viewed from the perspective of the present, when the project of modernism in the arts has to a large extent played itself out, it seems plausible that the growing restraint in the nature of caricature (and I'm thinking here of Lloyd's cinema as much as Keaton's) was an artistic tendency, the implications of which deserve to be considered in their own right. Thus in the work of Lloyd and Keaton—and to a lesser extent Chaplin and Langdon—caricature shifts from being something concerned purely with exaggeration and excess to something altogether different.

SLAPSTICK

We have seen how slapstick developed from a stage prop, to an aural device used to cue the audience to laugh, to violent physical comedy dependent on expert timing. In Sennett's comedy, slapstick functioned as physical violence, mechanical repetition, speed, and excessive movement. Narratives in early cinematic comedy were not narratives of meaning but expositions of the relation between cause and effect and detailed the new technological ability of cinema to manipulate these relationships. The body was a material substance that demonstrated or disavowed the laws of the physical universe. This slapstick has also been discussed as tending toward a kind of stylization. With the further development of stylized slapstick came a tendency toward elemental decomposition, the exchange of one thing for another, the joining and separation of matter, and the emphasis on encounters and altercations (attraction and repulsion) between bodies and objects. Deleuze observes in this regard that cinematic comedy began "with an enormous exaltation of sensory-motor situations, where the links of each of them were enlarged and brought forward, indefinitely extended; where the junctures and shocks between their independent causal series were multiplied, forming a proliferating whole."[56]

Keaton's contribution to the development of slapstick was to take both stylization and elemental decomposition further. Deleuze writes of the second age of the burlesque in terms of the survival of the Sennett element "with enrichments and purifications."[57] For Keaton's part we have seen that he develops an operational aesthetic that relies on the slowing down of the camera and a decomposition of the mise-en-scène into elements. The ocean liner in *The Navigator*, for example, is not itself simply a ship but an assemblage of objects, a compendium of mechanical, poetic, figural, even actual, possibilities that can be and in fact are used by the characters on board. The most comic elaboration of Keaton's elemental mise-en-scène is given in the galley sequences and the contrast between them. In the first sequence, the couple has to contend with implements and utensils designed for catering for masses of people; in the second the couple have inserted miniaturizing machines in them to diminish their productive capacity to a more appropriate scale. But other elements of the mise-en-scène are just as significant: for instance, the animistic deck chairs and phonograph, the storage hulls in which the characters sleep, the funnels, flags, firecrackers, and so forth.

Keaton had a well-known, deep fascination with technology. He conceived the cinematic apparatus not only in the narrow sense of filming and projecting, but also like any mechanical apparatus, as something that both relies on decomposition and can itself be decomposed. Keaton's gags work by apprehending specific elements within the apparatus—elements such as mise-en-scène, editing, composition, framing, scale—and exploring their comic potential. Keaton thus always reconstituted the phenomenal world in a technological manner and in so doing his films approach the kind of abstraction that Arnheim notes but at a physical level.

Take Keaton's approach to editing as a case in point. While slapstick revels in violence, what makes it comic is more often derived from the logic of cause and effect, which is illustrated through action and reaction. Keaton's slapstick is most cinematic when it produces unexpected occurrences from the relationship between editing and the codes of continuity within the shot (the continuity of action, space, lighting, subject matter, and so forth). We see this in an extended gag in *The General*, where Johnnie (Keaton) simultaneously demonstrates his combative deficiency (degradation) and stabs a sniper in the back. After a series of extreme long shots detailing the battle between the Yankees and the Confederates where the bridge is engulfed by flames and the riverbanks are under siege, the camera cuts to a long shot of Johnnie standing before two of the Southern army's generals. While Johnnie's inferiority is conveyed in the contrast between his diminutive stature in the bottom left hand corner of the frame and the generals' lofty position perched on their horses above him, he nevertheless tries to equal them by mimicking their authoritative gestures. When he attempts to imitate one general drawing his sword, Johnnie's sword's handle detaches from the blade, which remains sheathed in its holster. The faulty sword occasions several gags, which are orchestrated through editing together a succession of shots. When Johnnie uses his sword to point to an offscreen space, the blade flies off to the left. His retrieval of it places him and the camera in front of some ballistically active cannons, while a cutaway shot of a sniper, lying on the upward incline of an embankment firing his rifle off-screen to the right, introduces a new line of action. A match on action between the shooting sniper and a space adjacent to him shows the soldiers dropping like flies. Johnnie stands amidst them and is of course oblivious to the cause of the ongoing devastation. In desperation he draws his sword for a third time and once again the blade detaches from the handle. This time it flies out of the frame and delivers a fatal blow to the sniper (which we see in the following shot).

We could undoubtedly analyze this sequence of events in terms of comic degradation: the gag in its entirety is about Johnnie's militaristic ineptitude; the faulty sword is also an object subjected to comic degradation; the restriction of Keaton's point of view in comparison to ours implies degradation; and the comic solution to the problem entails "the is"—the relative unlikelihood of such an event being compared with "the ought"—a less implausible narrative contrivance. Yet the complexity of orchestration relies on clearly delineated objects and spaces, and the meticulous organization of audience attention.

As well as developing slapstick through editing and the dynamics of composition, Keaton produces the comic through performance, using his body as just another element in the technological apparatus. In this regard, Lebel cites André Martin's notion of "perfect geometry" to describe this facet of Keaton's comic aesthetic.[58] Stills and publicity shots from his films illustrate how Keaton positions his body to inscribe oblique lines across the surface of his images. Keaton's attention to balance, according to Lebel, is not just an example of comic reduction but evidences the development of a conceptual basis to the image:

> Buster Keaton's oblique stance is an expression of tenacity, openness toward great spaces, and intensity, both in tension and attention.
>
> These poses are pauses (the oblique position is without doubt the most perfect and expressive pause imaginable) and, as such, are static sketches of Keaton's dynamic attitude towards the world.[59]

Keaton suspends his body within mechanicophysical structures in a way that acknowledges gravity by renouncing the precariousness and fragility of such feats. In the boomgate gag in *Sherlock Jr.* discussed earlier, Keaton escapes from the rooftop by taking hold of the boomgate and transforming himself into a weight on the end of it. Rather than showing Keaton violently crashing to the ground, the sequence details how a counterbalancing force ensures the grace of the movement.

Figure 14. *Go West* (1925). Courtesy of The Academy of Motion Picture Arts and Sciences.

Figure 15. *The Love Nest* (1923). Courtesy of The Academy of Motion Picture Arts and Sciences.

As metteur-en-scène, Keaton coordinates composition and editing with his character's performance to produce gags. In the "bombarder-mortar-cannon" gag discussed in chapter 2, the tool that had been Johnnie's ally turns against him by lowering its aim and making him its target. But at the moment it takes fire, a bend in the track removes Johnnie and his train from its line of fire to present a clear path to the cannon's original target. Gags such as this can be considered as the degradation of probable reality, but they are ultimately achieved through the orchestration of a perfect contingency between time and space.

This refinement of slapstick, geometrification of the image and careful choreography recalls Bergson's conception of the comic as the imposition of the mechanical on the living, demanding a reexamination of his work in light of these observations about the distinctive qualities of 1920s slapstick. Chaplin's conception of the machine in Modern Times (1936) is textbook Bergsonism. The film takes issue with all the components of the Taylorist philosophy of scientific management devised to increase the output of workers: the standardization of tools, implements and work methods, task allocation, assembly line production, the division of labor, functional or specialized supervision, time and motion studies, and so forth. Bergson's notion of the mechanical encrusted on the living provides an explanation for the factory scenes, where the workers are subordinated to a mechanistic mode of production and the repetitive operating processes of the machine resonate in the convulsive spasms of Charlie's body long after he leaves the production line. Think, for example, of the gag in which his character confuses the buttons positioned like a double set of nipples on a woman's dress with the bolts on the conveyor belt.

In Modern Times, laughter comes to the rescue—just as it does for Bergson. The moralizing of the film is also Bergsonian to the extent that comic contrasts between the vital and the mechanical, and between human beings and abstract relations (such as employment and the law), deny the needs of individuals and turn people against each other. In the comic comparisons that take place "the ought" is without doubt, for the most part, the élan vital and "the is" is the mechanical encrusted on the living.

Whether the comic emerges from the mechanical encrusted on the living or from contingent reality that messes up the operation of the mechanical is a moot point, however. Certainly we see the former in Charlie's convulsive, machinelike movements and in the constraint of his vision to a world comprised of nuts and bolts. The meal-dispensing machine is likewise comic because it shows the mechanical to be incompatible with the human need for sustenance. And yet the logic of the machine has become so pervasive that it is contingent reality, what Bergson calls élan vital (life force), that upsets the functioning of the assembly line: the fly on Chaplin's face, his need to go to the bathroom or to stop work to eat lunch.

So it is not simply a case of contingent reality being subordinated to the mechanical or vice versa; rather the comic emerges in many instances from the imbrication of the mechanistic and the vital. The tension between the two forces is what gives rise to laughter.

Similarly, in Keaton's films, Keaton's movement is balletic and acrobatic rather than mechanical and seems to emanate more directly from a desire to play on *cinema's* capacity to engage with chance and the contingent than from an idea of purely mechanical repetition. In a *Steamboat Bill, Jr.*, gag, young Willie's life is spared when the façade of a building descends on him because his body is precisely situated in the space cut out by the window frame. While a certain facility with technology undoubtedly contributes to the success of the gag, technology here is deployed creatively rather than reductively.[60]

Between Keystone's and Keaton's slapstick everything is toned down. The camera is no longer undercranked, the movement of physical bodies in space is much more systematically organized, and plot lines are more carefully delineated. The custard pie throwing and Punch-and-Judy violence does not disappear, but rather the orchestration of the gag is made visible. Slapstick's priority is no longer the transgression of physical laws or the expression of aggressive, violent, antisocial tendencies, but its own virtuosity; not the ends it serves, but its own aesthetic triumph.

Carroll has described Keaton's comedy as working with an "aesthetic of intelligibility" by linking visual intelligibility to the structure of Keaton's gags. He demonstrates the way Keaton's shot compositions and editing techniques authenticate the action and serve the purpose of comic functionality. They also emphasize the *visual* construction of the gags, giving the audience the experience of *seeing* the event rather than simply inferring it. Such visual construction in turn assists causal construction by showing *how* the event occurs.[61] Although Carroll eventually reunites this notion of visual intelligibility with the theme of concrete intelligence that he had previously developed in his doctoral thesis, an alternative interpretation of Keaton's predilection for visual intelligibility can be made solely from considerations pertaining to the comic. The refinement of cinematic slapstick—the shift in caricature toward the iconic construction of the façade, Keaton's pared down mise-en-scène, his isolation and delineation of props, even the care he takes in his choreographing of the gag—are indeed part of an effort to ensure that the visual is intelligible. An intelligible (or perceptually unequivocal) mise-en-scène and structure are necessary preconditions for further developments in the comic. Although visual ambiguity is the stuff of dreams and poetry, we will see in the chapters that follow, that it is antithetical to the comic as well as to jokes and gags. Freud, we must remember, distinguishes between the joke and the dream on the grounds of such intelligibility. Intelligibility is just as necessary for the gag's success. As will become increasingly clear, in Keaton's work an excessively pared down mise-en-scène is vital to ensuring that the audience gets the equivocity produced by condensation in the same way that the listener gets the joke.

CHAPTER 7

From Words to Images (Gagging)

Gag, *sb.*[1] **1.** Something thrust into the mouth to keep it open and prevent speech or outcry. **b.** *fig.* (Now often applied to the "closure" in parliamentary proceedings.) **c.** *School slang.* **2.** *Theatr.* Matter interpolated in a written piece by the actor.
Gag, *sb.*[2] *slang.* A made up story; an imposture, a lie. **b.** *U.S.* A laughing stock.
Gag, *v.*[1] ME. [perh. imit. of the sound made by a choking person, though a poss. Scand. origin may be seen in ON *gagháls* with the neck thrown back.] **1.** *trans.* To strangle. ME only. **b.** *intr.* To choke (*lit.* and *fig.*) Also, to retch. Also *trans.* (*causatively*). **2.** *trans.* To stop up the mouth of (a person) with a gag in order to prevent speech or outcry; spec. in *surg.* **b.** *transf.* and *fig.* esp. to deprive of power or freedom of speech. **3.** To apply a gag-bit to (a horse); to obstruct the working of (a valve); to stop up the valves of (an engine). **4.** *Theatr. intr.* To introduce "gag" into a piece; *trans.* to fill *up* with "gag."
Gag, *v.*[2] **1.** *trans.* To jerk. Also, to toss *up* (the head). **2.** *intr.* To make thrusts or pricks (*at*); *trans.* to prick. **3.** *intr.* To stick out.
Gag, *v.*[3] *slang.* [perh. fig. use of GAG *v.*[1] with the notion of thrusting something "down the throat" of a credulous person.] *trans.* To impose upon (a person), to "stuff"; *intr.* to practice imposture.[1]

Derived most immediately from the theatrical comedy or burlesque that graced the vaudeville stage in North America and the music halls of Europe, the cinematic gag, we have seen, is a loose term that covers a variety of comic actions and effects, the parameters of which are succinctly, yet rather benignly, set by Neale and Krutnik in their definition of it as a nonlinguistic piece of funny business.² The *OED* definition cited earlier provides more elaborate and often less mirthful conceptions of the term, adding considerable nuance to the way we can think about it here. The substantive form of the theatrical term, from which the cinematic one is derived, is less innocuous than film theorists would have us believe, being that which *interrupts* a *written* piece, while the infinitive *to gag* involves imposition, stuffing, and imposture. Even the apparently dry, mechanical practice of gagging "to stop up the valves of (an engine)" anticipates some kind of emission of energy. Much more violent, however, are the jerks and pricks it involves, to say nothing of "thrusting something 'down the throat' of a credulous person," or strangling someone. Of course, one can gag by oneself, but only involuntarily, as in choking, retching or, indeed, laughing. Laughter here gives the term some levity, such as when to gag means only to imitate the sound of a choking person "with the neck thrown back." The favored site for gagging is the oral cavity; the purpose, in nearly all cases, being the prevention of "speech or outcry." The etymology of the term thus bears within it the traces of two contradictory imperatives: suppression on one side, transgression on the other.

This very suggestive etymology might also define the admittedly less obvious operational parameters of the cinematic gag. My aim here is to investigate how the psychical terrain Freud mapped out in his study of the *witz* allows us to understand the cinematic gag. Certainly, film theorists have previously sought to test and expose the limits of the relevance of Freud's hypotheses regarding the joke to the study cinematic comedy. My purpose is to work through some of these perceived limitations by establishing a broader psychoanalytic terrain for film comedy than that strictly circumscribed by the study of the joke and by reexamining Keaton's deployment of literalization gags in relation to this broader context. To do this, I consider Carroll's emphasis on the *visual* nature of the sight gag³ in the light of what Freud in his work on the dream calls considerations of representability. Such representability concerns the relationship between *pictorial* images and verbal thoughts. It articulates not only how different parts of the psychical apparatus favor some kinds of presentations over others, but also, more importantly, it shows that *visual* regression is both an unconscious process in its own right and a facilitator of other unconscious processes such as condensation and displacement.

FREUD AND THE THEORY OF CINEMATIC COMEDY

Freud's theory of the joke has been surprisingly underutilized in the Anglophone theorization of cinematic comedy. As I mentioned in the introduction, only a handful of film theorists, writing in the 1970s and 1980s, have attempted to consider what Freud's work on the joke has to offer the study of cinematic comedy. By taking Weber's essay "The Divaricator: Remarks on Freud's *Witz*" as their major reference, these theorists sometimes limited their approach to Freud's work.[4] Certainly they focused on those aspects of it that interested Weber himself. The result is that not enough emphasis is given to the crucial point, indeed, one that arguably motivated Freud to take the joke as an object of study; namely, that the joke evidenced the *unconscious processes* that he had already discovered in the dream. We will see, too, that in some cases Freud's work is too readily dismissed or subordinated to what seemed to be more compelling theoretical issues at the time of writing.

Eaton's discussion of the pertinence of Freud's study of the joke to the analysis of cinematic and (in his case) televisual comedy focuses on the tension between the joke's playful and meaningful dimensions, or as he puts it, its "formal and...semantic components."[5] Eaton argues that the tension is manifest in the numerous contradictions that have concerned scholars seeking to understand how comedy impacts on and indeed perturbs the conventions of televisual and cinematic fiction. The contradiction between narrative and gag is the most obvious of these, but he professes as well that we need to pay attention to the constraints and allowances the institutional structures of film and television imposed. Hence, he turns to Freud's work to determine whether the seemingly transgressive capacities of comedy and laughter allow for a critical distance from, and fresh perspective on, the stereotypes and prejudices they appear to deride or simply reinforce them. The pleasure obtained from the *playful* aspect of the joke derives first from the recognition of the familiar as Freud accounts for it in his discussion of the jest,[6] and second from rebellion against authority as he characterizes it in his account of the fort-da game in "Beyond the Pleasure Principle."[7] The *meaningful* component of the joke contributes knowledge and provides the possibility of reflection and critical distance by "seeing familiar things, familiar people, familiar institutions in a new light."[8]

In fact, not merely the tension between play and meaning concerns Eaton, but also the manner in which play exposes our acceptance of the conventional signification of meaning and assists in an unconventional articulation of new meaning. Eaton thus deems comedy to contribute positively to cinematic and televisual culture in that it adds to meaning and to our understanding of meaning. At the same time, he envisages limits to this, insisting that illumination only takes place on the basis of prior recognition. As such, the transgression of codes "paradoxically serves only to reinforce the immediacy of the television image as a constant source of reference and plenitude—'our window on the world.'"[9] A Brechtianism, particularly in the joke's capacity to de-familiarize, pervades his reading of Freud and leads him to judge cinematic and televisual comedy with some ambivalence. Indeed, ambivalence about comedy's capacity to either generate or accommodate a politicized spectator gives way to a kind of despair—Eaton laments that although comedy can be directed against anything it constitutes analysis of nothing.[10]

Acknowledging the contribution to the joke made by the unconscious and retaining the strictly psychoanalytic emphasis of Freud's theory, Neale delineates the differences between the comic and the joke, their appeal to distinctive and irreducible components of the psyche, and the kinds of psychical energy released in the pleasure they afford. Using the interpretations of Freud's work Weber and Mehlman provide, he speculates, for example, that the pleasure obtained from the comic could well signal the triumph of the narcissistic ego, whereas the pleasure from the joke results in a bursting forth of the id, and hence an overcoming of the ego.[11] Because cinematic comedy embraces both comic and jokelike expressions, Neale argues that it results in "a complex articulation of narcissism and aggression across the instances of the ego and the unconscious" respectively.[12] Neale's work therefore points to important instances in Freud's study of the joke and considers their implications for cinematic comedy. He attends, for example, to the multimodal status of film comedy, its contradictory and paradoxical structures of figuration, and the difficulty of ascribing any particularity to the subject these structures constitute.

Neale, however, addresses this complexity by giving preeminence first to the comic over the joke and then to narrative form over both of them. Concerning the disparity between the subject positions made available to the audience by the comic and the joke and, indeed, the menace of the ego by the joke, he claims that "the comic aspect of comedy works to some extent to counteract the threat that the joke-like aspects of comedy may involve, the position of superiority inscribed there working to restore the ego's position."[13] If the comic fails here, narrative itself will come to the rescue, because comedy as such falls within its dominion: "comedy is a string, a sequence, a *narration* of jokes and joke-like structures (i.e., gags, comic segments)," and this ultimately means that the complexity of interpsychical relations encapsulated in its components will be subordinated to narration itself.[14] In the last instance, narration transforms the status and meaning of gags, jokes, and comic segments "by acting as the agent of their articulation and by providing the context of significance in relation to which they are read."[15] Accordingly, "any disturbance or disruption of the ego's position would ultimately be contained by the narration itself, order restored by the story precisely for the ego of the viewer."[16]

So although Neale goes to great lengths to point out the differences between the joke and the comic, their respective modes of address and their ability to inscribe subject positions, in the end he subscribes to the view that the comic, the joke and, indeed, the gag, all occur within the parameters of comedy—which for him is indisputably a "mode of signification"[17]—and this comedy in turn falls within the parameters of narrativity. Rather than concluding from his evidence the existence of a dynamic subject, bearing the heterogeneity of the two topographies (the unconscious, preconscious, and conscious systems on the one hand, and the three agencies on the other), Neale proffers instead a subject isomorphic with a particular agency or one governed by a hierarchy of the agencies.

Both Neale's and Eaton's analyses and their deployment of Freud's work for the study of cinematic comedy undoubtedly bear on the arguments developed in the first half of this book regarding the problematic status of the comic in discourses concerned with signification and meaning. As with the other theorists discussed there, they want to resolve the tension between the comic and meaning by posing an implicit confrontation between restricted and general economy. Eaton does not really distinguish between comedy, the comic, and the joke, but his elevation of the status of meaning within his general discussion of them suggests an orientation toward the dialectical structure of restricted economy. The best the comic can do is to transgress familiar meaning to produce new meaning. Neale, on the contrary, seems to imply that the joke alone has the capacity to operate within the terms of reference of general economy, but that the restricted economic functions of both the comic and narrative subordinate its transgressive potential. For Neale and Eaton respectively, both the comic and the joke have to be considered within their narrative and institutional contexts; and such contexts, as outer frames, redefine what lies within them. Cinema for them would seem to be an incontrovertible instance of the corroboration, endorsement, and stabilization of restricted economy. Neale in fact suggests that if the joke is to be truly transgressive, it must exist in a context in which signification, discourse, and narration would themselves be different.[18] The importance of Neale's work lies in its insistence that Freud's book is not just a study of the joke but the comic, its concern with the irreducibility of the joke and the comic, and its emphasis on the complex inter- and intrasubjective relations that comedy entails. Yet, his assimilation of the cinematic gag to a jokelike formation denies the possibility that some gags, such as those we saw in Lloyd's risk comedy, may simply be comic.

Where Neale thinks gags as such can be likened to jokelike formations, Mellencamp, in her examination of the Marx Brothers' comedy, happily takes up Freud's theory of the joke in relation to the tendentious and naïve punning of Groucho and Chico, but this is only because their jokes are *verbal*.[19] Indeed, she aligns Freud's conceptualization of the joke with the auditory mode of cinematic comedy, whereas the visual mode, which is exemplified by the comic antics of Harpo, is, for her, merely comic. "Freud's distinction between the processes of joking and the comic," she writes, "particularly dramatizes our relation to Harpo (and to a degree Chico), often described as a child (but what an evil one).... In the comic our pleasure comes from 'empathy.'"[20] The Marx Brothers' films thus "document the endlessness of language (whose symbolic order Harpo and Chico have never fully entered, and therefore cannot tolerate as a means of power, of authority)."[21]

We should note that Mellencamp's deployment of Freud's work along these lines has more in mind than an explication of the specificity of the comic in Marx Brothers' films. It is intended to indicate that the auditory apprehension of the comic is less ideologically problematic than the visual apprehension of it. Certain propositions that have been made about cinema are consequently advanced to cast the visual/spectatorial apprehension of film as inherently bad and auditory apprehension as good.[22] Contesting classical psychoanalytic film theory's conception of cinema as the by-product of the domination of the look (scopophilia) and "the look of desire as 'identification,'" Mellencamp argues that the "auditory" joke provides a means of problematizing the dominance and mastery of the spectator.[23] Furthermore, the auditory joke gives provision for the possibility of examining "the reciprocal relation between image and enunciation and its effect upon the *position* of the film spectator."[24] Mellencamp's inquiry therefore also aims to displace Christian Metz's conceptualization of the "spatial" position of the subject in favor of its temporal position. The "when" of the subject is none other than "the movement in time of narration" by jokes in the Marx Brothers' films.[25]

Mellencamp's argument implies, however, that unconscious processes impact only on words and not images. To be sure, her distinction between Groucho's use of the joke process through verbal tirades and Harpo's exemplification of the comic through visual means alludes to some rather thorny issues—not just Lacan's infamous declaration that the unconscious is structured like a language,[26] but the more general and no less perplexing question of the role of words and images in the structure and functioning of the psyche. When Freud himself examines the various determinants of the joke and their degree of necessity, he says nothing whatsoever about a linguistic capacity. It is significant for the issues we are concerned with here that he specifically deals with the relationship between the visual and the verbal in his elaboration of the dream-work, and in his discussion of words and images in the unconscious. His comments in both cases are directly pertinent to a study of the cinematic gag.

Whatever similarities exist between the joke and the dream emerge from the fact that both are formed in the unconscious. Both, in other words, are subject to the operational principles of the primary process—condensation and displacement in particular. In his discussion of the joke, the role of the primary process is in fact limited to the operations of condensation and displacement, whereas in the dream two other processes—secondary revision and considerations of representability—play a significant part. The latter process comes into operation specifically because the dream, unlike the joke, comprises pictorial images rather than words. We need to turn to Freud's discussion of considerations of representability to understand the contribution the unconscious makes to visual comedy. The unconscious comprises both pictorial (which Freud sometimes calls visual) contents and processes specifically directed at their pictorial and visual conditions. Therefore, around the notion of representation in the dream, we find a means of bridging Freud's study of the joke to our efforts to understand the gag in cinematic comedy.

When Freud discusses considerations of representability he also refers, at times, to a regression to the visual. He calls it a regression because it reverses the direction of "the course of development of mental complications,"[27] inscribing a path "from thoughts to perceptual images...from the region of thought-structures to that of sensory perceptions."[28] With respect to the dream, the latent dream thoughts are rational, logical, and verbal, but they are transformed by the primary process into a series of relatively nonsensical images. The latent thoughts exchange their verbal form for a pictorial form. Although Freud habitually and somewhat conventionally treats visual communication as a more primitive mode than verbal communication,[29] the manner in which he theorizes the interrelation of the verbal and the pictorial in the interpretation of dreams, suggests that the visual mode, far from being superseded or transcended by the development of a linguistic capacity, continues to play a crucial role in the unconscious processes. Importantly for us, this regression implies that the unconscious is as capable of working on visual material as on verbal material, if not more so. Therefore, not only do we find an absence of justification for assuming that the operation of the primary processes that constitutes the basis of the joke must be confined to verbal material, but also the very fact that cinema is a visual medium makes it incumbent on us to examine how visuality is theorized in psychoanalysis. Whereas a huge amount of work has, of course, been undertaken regarding the pertinence to identificatory processes in film viewing of Lacan's reworking of the fort-da game into the mirror phase, very little has been said about the implications that Freud's theory of the primary process has for our understanding of visual processes and viewing practices.

THE JOKE AND THE SIGHT GAG

Where Mellencamp attempts to limit the interpretative or analytical efficacy of Freud's theory of the joke for cinema to instances of verbal comedy, Carroll's theory of the sight gag is altogether dismissive of the Freudian study (in fact, he never addresses it), seeking at the outset of his essay to distinguish between the visual gag and the verbal joke on the grounds that the joke has to have a punch line whereas the sight gag does not:

> Verbal jokes generally culminate in a punchline that at first glance is incongruous by virtue of its appearing to be nonsense. Once the punchline is delivered, however, the audience has to give it an unexpected, although latently predictable or retrospectively comprehensible, interpretation that makes sense out of the incongruity. Succeeding in this, the audience is amused and the result is standardly laughter.... In order to appreciate this joke, one must reinterpret the riddle in light of the punchline in a way that effectively amounts to retelling the joke material to oneself. One is initially stymied by the incongruity of the punchline, which leads to a reinterpretation of the joke material that makes it comprehensible.[30]

For Carroll, the "interpretations" that the audience makes of the sight gag are afforded to them by its visual nature and are made simultaneously. The distinctive feature of the sight gag is that no punch line is needed to put such "interpretative play in motion."[31] Carroll's argument for the punch line as an essential component of the joke, however, is by no means supported by Freud's exposition of the joke. Although undoubtedly many jokes do have punch lines that act as reinterpretations of material already disclosed, many others do not. Hirsch Hyacinth's joke of being treated "famillionarely" is an example.[32] Puns and condensation jokes often involve simultaneity.[33]

At the same time, however, Carroll puts forward a theory of the sight gag that is completely consistent with the substance of Freud's theory. According to Carroll, a cinema preoccupied with "the transgression of social inhibitions about the proper way in which to treat the human body" was replaced by a cinema of "the sight gag," a cinema of a more "structural" nature.[34] Structural gags are classified into the following species: mutual interpenetrations of events, mimed metaphors, switch images, switch movements, object analogs, and solution gags. Incongruity is the defining structure, arising from the multiple interpretations of an object, event, situation, point of view, or movement.[35]

In spite of his unwillingness to acknowledge the significance of Freud's theorization of the joke for cinematic comedy, one could argue that the operations of condensation and displacement underpin the formal mechanisms of each of the gag types that Carroll specifies. Condensation is the disarticulating process of the gags that rely on an incongruous doubling of the image. Displacement operates in what he calls the solution gag. Indeed, the distinction between these two operations makes sense of Carroll's uncertainty about how to classify the solution gag. He hesitates, for example, over including solution gags under the rubric of the sight gag because they do not involve the incongruity of his other examples. "[R]ather than play with the presentation of visual ambiguities," the solution gag operates through "unexpected, indeed brilliant, reversals based on practical ingenuity."[36] Carroll illustrates this with a gag from *The General* where Johnnie has just managed to avoid the derailment of the train he is driving by lifting a huge tie from the track (strategically placed there by enemy Union spies who have stolen his train). As Johnnie picks up the tie, his encroaching engine, forces him back onto its cowcatcher so that he is pinned beneath the tie. The train is meanwhile about to run into a second tie. Johnnie ingeniously maneuvers the tie he is pinned under, dumping it on the tip of the tie obstructing the track so that it catapults out of the way. Johnnie has thus eliminated two problems with a single action.[37] Carroll says that our humor at this routine comes from:

> the lightning reversal of one interpretation of the situation by means of an unexpected, economical, and effective reconceptualization of the situation. It depends on Johnnie seeing that the beam on his chest is not a burden but a tool. Johnnie sees this, but the standard viewer does not until Johnnie demonstrates it. The reconceptualization of the situation surprises the audience, which also would appear to derive pleasure from the situation by reinterpreting the scene in light of the absolute fitness of Johnnie's action.[38]

Carroll rightly argues that visual ambiguity is not the operative means by which this gag is orchestrated, but this does not mean that another kind of condensation does not play a part. Condensation and displacement come together here to link the gag to Johnnie's capacity to keep his wits about him. Even if it isn't the cinematic image that is primarily being exploited here, Johnnie's "vision"—we might call it insight—allows the transformation of the object to take place. (Stanley Cavell likewise acknowledges the importance of Keaton's gaze, noting his character's specific mode of "perception or apprehension of the things of our world"[39] and a capacity for "sensuous awareness" of "a world that goes essentially beyond the delivery of our senses."[40]) Johnnie's treatment of the object as a *tool* rather than a *burden* involves displacement, yet one that implies that the object is already multiple. The condensation here is virtual then, rather than actual.

Furthermore, Carroll's differentiation between Sennett slapstick and the sight gag could easily be read as a configuration of Freud's distinction between the comic and the joke. We have seen that film historians have generally considered the silent cinematic comedy of the early part of the twentieth century to have undergone a dramatic change between the Keystone era of the 1910s and the beginning of the comedian comedy of the 1920s associated with Chaplin, Lloyd, Keaton, and Langdon. (Neale and Krutnik, we have seen, argue that slapstick or broad physical comedy was refined by genteel comedy to the point where narrative and characterization became important preconditions for getting laughs.⁴¹) Carroll accounts for the transformation in the nature of the comic that occurred in silent cinematic comedy by contrasting roughhouse slapstick to the subsequent cinema of the sight gag. He describes Sennett mayhem thus:

> Buffoons, marked by only slightly disguised clown outfits,... set into exaggerated fisticuffs, discharging pistol shots into each other's behinds, jabbing each other with pitchforks, and clunking each other on the head with bricks. Because these clowns were signalled to be not quite human, they could be pummelled, dragged, hurled, hosed, burned, and stomped with impunity. Their fantastic biologies allowed the free reign of sadism in terms of either comic debacles or sprawling accidents.⁴²

What would the comic be—as a relation between "the is" and "the ought"—if not a transgression of the proper. The physical comedy of Sennett can thereby be understood as celebrating the manner in which the newly emergent medium of cinema demonstrates the capacity of the body to withstand any number of physical abuses. Sennett's comedies, we have also seen, revel in the medium's ability to accelerate reality and to exaggerate or minimize the connection between cause and effect according to whim. They defy the laws of the physical universe and transgress the value of material existence through the ritualistic destruction of objects. The physical order of things is the object of such comedy, but only to be negated by the capabilities of the cinematic medium itself.

If this nonstructural slapstick of Sennett is to be understood within the terms of reference of the comic, the structural gags that Carroll delineates, the gags that define the so-called transition from slapstick to narrative, would most likely signal a transition from a cinema in which the comic predominated to one in which the joke (or something like it) plays an increasingly significant role. The incongruity that Carroll argues distinguishes the slapstick of the 1920s is precisely what Deleuze has called *equivocity* and what Freud labels *condensation*. In as much as the image now mobilizes not one sign, but two, cinematic comedy shifts from a straightforward celebration of the deceit of appearances and the negation of the epistemological connection between vision and truth, to a contemplation and exposition of the manner in which such belief is questioned. The emergence of the sight gag is then a second step in cinema's exploration of its potential to deceive and to make its audiences laugh at the same time. A shift from the physical to the visual is implicit here. It has a familiar ring, demarcating the first stage of a movement from the sensible to the intelligible, from physicality to visuality to language.

CONSIDERATIONS OF REPRESENTABILITY

While the exploitation of the ambiguity of the visual makes Carroll's structural sight gags possible, Freud similarly suggests that a regression to the

Figure 16. Visual condensation in the sight gag: "Buster de Milo." Publicity shot for *College* (1927). Courtesy of BFI Stills.

visual, or the pictorial, means of representation plays a crucial role in facilitating the unconscious processes of condensation and displacement. The transformation of the verbal thought into the pictorial image in the dream is but the first stage in the unconscious operation; regression to the visual is the preliminary operation for condensation and displacement. In Freud's discussion of both the means of representation and considerations of representability, we see evidence of a theory of visual sense and nonsense, a theory, in other words, that is highly relevant to the way we might understand the generation (and destruction) of cinematic meaning. The "primitive" aspect of the visual, the pictorial quality of the manifest content—a content composed of images that, to be sure, are never seen, never apprehended by the physical eye—simultaneously reduces and complicates verbal discourse, and facilitates the operation of the other three mechanisms of the primary process. Even before the operations of condensation and displacement come into play, the precise "meaning" of the representation is compromised.

Indeed, the peculiar pliancy of the pictorial mode of expression means that it simultaneously limits the representation of abstract thought, offers compensation for such limits, and does so by manifesting a propensity to articulate illogical thought. Pictures, Freud notes, lack the capacity to represent abstract relations such as negation, causality, qualification, fine differentiation, subjunctive and conditional articulations, and so forth. He writes, for example, that the:

> incapacity of dreams to express... [logical connections such as "if," "because," "just as," "although," "either-or" and a number of other conjunctions] must lie in the nature of the psychical material out of which dreams are made. The plastic arts of painting and sculpture labour, indeed, under a similar limitation as compared with poetry, which can make use of speech; and here once again the reason for their incapacity lies in the nature of the material which these two forms of art manipulate in their effort to express something.[43]

But whereas dream images lack the capacity for the dexterous articulation of conceptual propositions, retaining only the "substantive content" of the dream-thoughts,[44] in the course of the section on "The Means of Representation in Dreams," over more than thirty pages of his book on the dream, Freud also argues that the images of the manifest content bear decipherable traces of logical relations. The traces of logical relations, which compensate for the lack of logic, are found in aspects of the dream's form and are expressed through processes such as simultaneity, division into parts, transformation, unification (identification and construction of composite figures), reversal, exchange, and substitution. Significantly these processes are demonstrated via the pictorial and temporal form of the dream. Freud writes, for example, of the way the dream compensates for its inability to reproduce logical connections between propositions by representing the component parts simultaneously:

> [D]reams take into account in a general way the connection which undeniably exists between all the portions of the dream-thoughts by

combining the whole material into a single situation or event. They reproduce *logical connection by simultaneity in time*. Here they are acting like the painter who, in a picture of the School of Athens or of Parnassus, represents in one group all the philosophers or all the poets. It is true that they were never in fact assembled in a single hall or on a single mountain-top; but they certainly form a group in the conceptual sense.[45]

The simultaneity of elements thus implies some kind of intimate connection between them. An unrepresentable causal relationship, on the other hand, can be indicated by a division of the dream into parts—a dependent clause will be represented by an introductory dream, the principle clause by the main dream. In the course of the chapter, Freud maps out the extent to which the dream's limited ability to represent articulate thought is compensated through the formal processes mentioned earlier, which in turn impact on its pictorial, temporal, and structural dimensions.

We can easily see the similarity between condensation and simultaneity, transformation and unification, on the one hand, and displacement and reversal, exchange and substitution, on the other. Indeed, we could even to say that condensation is the general process that underpins simultaneity, transformation, and unification, whereas displacement serves an equivalent function with regard to reversal, exchange, and substitution. The limited capacity of the pictorial means of representation to articulate abstract conceptual relations in effect facilitates the play of condensation and displacement. Or put another way, at the same time that the pictorial image is incapable of fully representing manifold logical connections, it demonstrates a propensity to represent illogical ones. Freud says as much in the section "Considerations of Representability" when he confirms the assistance that the pictorial image gives to the mechanisms of the dream-work. "[T]he interests of condensation," he writes, profit by the exchange between the verbal and the pictorial so that "contrasts and identifications of the kind which the dream-work requires, and which it creates if they are not already present, can be established more easily than before between the new form of expression and the remainder of the material underlying the dream."[46] The conversion of the linguistic script into a pictorial script, the conversion of words into concrete visual images, thus gives the unconscious some latitude. In short, the pictorial image assists the characteristically unhampered, free-flowing cathexis from one repressed content of the unconscious to another. Freud confirms this five pages later when he writes:

> This pouring of the content of a thought into another mould may at the same time serve the purposes of the activity of condensation and

may create connections, which might not otherwise have been present, with some other thought; while this second thought itself may already have had its original form of expression changed, with a view to meeting the first one half-way.[47]

Freud says that condensation profits by the pictorial means at the same time that the contrasts and identifications that are part of the dream-work are more easily established between the pictorial means and the dream-thoughts.[48] In effect Freud is suggesting here that no rational means of accounting are found for translating discursive thought into a pictorial image. The exchange between the two forms can find no grounds for equivalence. But at the same time the irreducibility of the difference between them can be expressed through the factor of condensation. Condensation therefore operates as an agent of modification, the impact of which can be determined only retrospectively by the pictorial means on one side of the equation and the dream-thoughts on the other. Condensation is that x that accounts for the lack of equivalence between the dream-thoughts and the pictorial content.

Because the image cannot represent logical thought, it gives an approximate rendition of it. It sketches, literally, what it means to say. This imprecise representation of the dream-thoughts is also the first means of disarticulating their meaning. What is significant here is that the same formal processes that assist in the representation of logical relations in the pictorial image also bring about the destruction of meaning. In facilitating the destruction of the discursive meaning of the dream-thoughts, the means of representation also assist in establishing the manifest content, or the façade, of the dream.

Freud's thesis about the nature of pictorial representation can be extended beyond the dream. Its significance lies in the fact that it hampers a particular verbal and logical mode of the thinking while aiding the expression of desire. Freud's emphasis on the pictorial means of representation as one of the operations of the primary process demonstrates once again that although the book on the joke is almost exclusively concerned with verbal wit, we have no reason to presume that this work is not pertinent to the study of visual comedy.

With this in mind, let us return to Mellencamp's classification of certain aspects of the Marx Brothers' comedy. Whereas Mellencamp argues that Harpo has the status of "a comic" rather than "a joker" and that this status signals a failure on his part to enter the symbolic order, she also considers his comic tendency to literalize "every metaphor, wreaking havoc...on the clichés of language and the mise-en-scène."[49] Harpo's literalization of metaphor is evident when Harpo overhears one man in a speakeasy asking his partner to cut the cards and "produces an ax, and maniacally grinning, does just that."[50] According to Mellencamp:

The arbitrary nature of language, its infinite capacity for substitution, "logically" cascades to meaning less and less; or its circulation as signifier is abruptly stopped, as Harpo produces the "real" referent, the object signified by the signifier. For Harpo, language is never arbitrary, merely ridiculous and completely unnecessary.[51]

Harpo's behavior in this regard is comprehended by Freud's definition of the comic. The comparative aspect of the relation between "the is" and "the ought" can be brought to bear on the literal and abstract dimensions of Harpo's substitution of the referent for the sign. Yet, we saw in chapter 5 that Freud interpreted the literalization of the figurative as a condensation joke. And in his discussion of dreams, literalization is bound with both unconscious regression and displacement. Freud gives an example of an association between a dream-thought that a piece of written work needed editing and the dream image of planing a piece of wood.[52] We have seen too that for Freud jokes can be simultaneously understood as comic. Accordingly, if literalization were only funny because it entailed a comparison between the concrete and the abstract, it would remain within the confines of the comic, but if it involved giving the object another sense, then it could be considered a joke. The literalization Harpo undertakes that Mellencamp cites can be understood within the terms of reference of the joke as well as those of the comic because Harpo's behavior transforms the meaning of the instruction to cut the cards to give vent precisely to those socially unacceptable maniacal tendencies to which Mellencamp refers. Harpo, after all, is not just cutting the cards; he is wielding an axe.

Mellencamp's contention that Harpo has not entered the realm of the symbolic is called into question in so far as his literalization also entails the revivification of figurative meaning that occurs with worn metaphors. Whereas Mellencamp distinguishes between elements of visual and auditory humor in the Marx Brothers' films, her failure to examine the basis of this distinction between the pictorial and the auditory in Freud's work means that she cannot adequately tease out the implications of Freud's theory of the joke for her assessment of the Marx Brothers. Harpo, in fact, symbolizes the unconscious as such, all the while substituting thing presentations for word presentations. And in this sense he gives a perfect illustration of the access that silent cinema had to that *other* scene of the unconscious.

In his essay "The Unconscious," Freud argues that different parts of the psychical topography favor different kinds of presentations. The preconscious-conscious system permits the presentation of words and things whereas the unconscious system consists entirely of thing presentations. Although we may well find words in the unconscious, they are treated there only as things. In other words, they are acted on by the primary processes as things and not in terms of their signification. As Freud writes, the difference between a conscious and unconscious presentation is not the "different registrations of the same content in different psychical localities, nor yet different functional states of cathexis in the same locality; but the conscious presentation comprises the presentation of the thing plus the presentation of the word belonging to it, while the unconscious presentation is the presentation of the thing alone."[53]

Mellencamp's characterization of Harpo's gags as literalizing the figurative also has a general applicability to the strategies of other silent clowns. In Keaton's films, the literalization of words or phrases is conceptually developed through a complex of gags scattered throughout a given film. In many films, the word denoting the profession of the character that Keaton plays both encompasses his general strategies of behavior and occasions multiple transformational gags. We see, for example, the many gags relating to projection and framing in *Sherlock Jr.*, to navigation in *The Navigator*, and engineering in *The General*. These literalizations, far from constituting a coherent meaning for the story, serve to dismantle the film's thematics at the same time as they construct them.

In respect of literalization, then, or the pictographic script as Freud calls it in his discussion of the dream, we are dealing with something closer to the rebus. As we see in the following quotation, for Freud the pictographic script of the dream is not to be understood in accordance with conventional pictorial composition—this, he contends, would make it seem "non-sensical and worthless"—but as a rebus "whose characters and syntactic laws" must be discovered by comparing the dream-thoughts to the dream-content, that is "by comparing the original and the translation":[54]

> If we attempted to read these characters according to their pictorial value instead of according to their symbolic relation, we would clearly be lead into error.... A dream is a picture puzzle of this sort and our predecessors in the field of dream-interpretation have made the mistake of treating the rebus as a pictorial composition: and as such it has seemed to them non-sensical and worthless.[55]

Importantly Freud's recommendation against interpreting the dream-images in terms of pictorial composition is not intended to suggest that the interpreter ignore the specificity of pictographic qualities of the dream-image, but that they should not be judged by recourse to realist pictographic representation. Cinema, on the contrary, is capable of eliciting both kinds of readings. If the rebus is a particular kind of cinematic signifier, it works differently from the conventional cinematic image. Here it is neither a question of the image being the signifier for some referential object nor of the image operating in connotative symbolic terms. Rather in the rebus the image is the signifier whose signified is a word. A verbal sign is substituted for a pictorial one, an absence for a presence; something sticks out in the text, and because it so protrudes must be subject to attracting cathectic energy. It is both comprised by cathexis and will demand more cathexis.

In *Sherlock Jr.*, Keaton, as the projectionist, makes several attempts to project himself into various situations. In one example projection involves spatial insertion. Both the Keaton character and Crane, the rival for girl's affections, arrive at her house bearing gifts of chocolates, Keaton first, then Crane. Keaton's is a modest gift but he has inflated the price by turning the one dollar sign on the price tag into a four. The monetary value, however, becomes irrelevant when Crane arrives with a box three times the size. The parlor of Keaton's girlfriend's house is, not completely surprisingly, the space that is made available for projection. Shown in a long shot, Keaton, Crane, and the girl fill the right side of the tableau. The left side is empty apart from a wide door frame dressed with curtains that close off a deeper interior space from view. Keaton is still seated on the lounge where a few minutes before he has proposed marriage, given the girl a ring with a minuscule diamond, and a magnifying glass with which to find it. But Crane, winning his bid for the girl, lures her to an adjoining dining room, which is framed by curtains. This framing—the widened doorway to the room filling the screen and the curtains on either side—produces a visual harmony with the cinema screen. The shot is also composed so that Keaton, momentarily flummoxed by the ease with which Crane has sidelined him, is seated in the anteroom as though watching a film. But as in a nightmare image or surrealist conceit, he is positioned with his back to the screen. Keaton determines to do something about the situation, rises and redraws the curtain, revealing Crane and the girl somewhat intimately engaged with one another. He tries to intervene, but Crane condescendingly pats him on the back and sends him on his way with a banana. Keaton peels the banana, positions the skin strategically on the floor and calls Crane over but these attempts to cause Crane to *slip up* end with Keaton on the floor, the victim of his own contrivance. Keaton's various attempts to either get *into the picture* or draw his rival out of it ensure that the scene directly impacts on an even more literal manifestation of projection later in the montage sequence that begins Keaton's dream. Not only does Keaton project the circumstances of his own real-life situation onto the narrative unfolding on the screen before him by identifying with the story, but he also literally projects himself into the film *Hearts and Pearls* by leaping into the screen space. The "motif" of projection (and identification) also resurfaces at the end of the film when the callow Keaton looks to the characters on the screen as romantic role models and mimics the male character's lead in courtship, gesture for gesture.

Similar to this literalization of projection, the concept of the frame is also figured as a significant visual component of the film. The most dramatic instance of this occurs when Keaton has been framed by his rival for stealing his girlfriend's father's watch and is subsequently visually framed by the mise-en-scène. Keaton has been caught out *shadowing* his man and to avoid a confrontation with Crane, Keaton nonchalantly boards a nearby train as if his intention had always been so. Once Keaton climbs on board the carriage, however, Crane quickly barricades him inside. As the train begins to roll out of frame, Keaton pops out of the top of the carriage and runs along the roof in the opposite direction to the one the train is taking. Rather than emphasizing the movement of the train and Keaton in opposite directions, however, the squareness of the camera angle immobilizes Keaton in a statically framed two-dimensional image, thereby keeping him perpetually in the same position. The imminent departure of the train from the station platform can be attributed to the orchestration of the metteur-en-scène, the director Keaton, challenging the character, and attempting to expel him from the frame by driving out the train which supports him. In this way, the image also echoes the previous expulsion of the character from his girlfriend's house by her father. Whether the director of the film is literally visualizing the conceptual framing of Keaton, attempting to set him free or remove him from the picture altogether, cannot, however, be determined unequivocally. Similarly, the two ideas of Keaton wanting to be *in the picture* and the frame as signifier of entrapment conflict with one another. Duplicitous frames also appear in Sherlock Jr.'s abode—what appears to be a mirror is in fact a doorway, while a safe door conceals the direct point of entry to the outside world. From these examples we can see the manner in which the contaminating force of literalization prevents the delineation of themes. The frame is not a motif that serves to unify the threads of the story but an image that obliterates meaning by being subjected to comic proliferation.

The effects of framing are complicated further at the beginning of the famous dream sequence. Garrett Stewart has acknowledged the deployment of literalization in this sequence in his essay "Keaton Through the Looking Glass," in the following quotation with regard to the montage sequence:

> Latent verbal translations refine this arbitrary blitz of split-second visual settings into a punning continuity which links them analogically to dream. The figure of speech of a door slammed in one's face is, for instance, quite blatantly visualised at the opening of the sequence, and is followed in the pummeling rush of locales by a number of symbolic fortuities which suggest, especially knowing what we do of Keaton's verbal imagination, a visual graveyard of dead metaphors jostled and joked into action.[56]

The sequence begins with Keaton falling asleep while at work in the cinema projecting a film. As he dreams of entering the fictional world of the film he screens, he transmigrates from his sleeping body, walks down to the screen and tries to enter the world of the film, and indeed the house in which a surrogate for his girlfriend is about to be ravaged by a villainous thief. Undeterred by having had the door slammed in his face the first time, Keaton stands poised to knock at the door again when the shot changes and he finds himself balanced precariously on a narrow garden bench. He responds to this new situation by moving to sit on the bench, but again the scene changes and he reclines unceremoniously onto a busy street. Heeding this new environment, he walks back and forth, only to nearly topple off the edge of a precipice when the film cuts to a mountain top. When he bends over to inspect the abyss that has been laid out before him, he finds himself face to face with a lion. And so it goes on. Every attempt he makes to adapt to his new situation meets with a brutal cut to another situation. The character attempts in vain to ground himself in a world whose fictionality is premised on a constant destabilizing of diegetic spatiotemporal coordinates. The humor—and the horror—of the sequence arises from the double edge of the gag that, on the one hand, innocently mixes the realms of diegetic reality and diegetic fiction (a real man experiencing the disconcerting effects of representation) and, on the other, advances a much more serious contemplation of the existential crisis resulting from a person being reduced to a component part of a technological apparatus he no longer controls. Keaton's meditation is a lucid articulation of what becomes of subjectivity in a world where film doubles reality (and vice versa).

The psychoanalytic rationale for these examples of literalization refers us to the unconscious operations of regression, and condensation and displacement. What is less than clear is whether the verbal concepts preexist their pictorial rendering or whether they emerge from the rendering as such. In either case the comic potential of the concepts seems to be unconditionally exploited. Unlike metaphors, which remain subordinate to the imperatives of reason and meaning, these literalizations are in the order of general economy, they are expenditures without return. Sylvain du Pasquier aptly sums up Keaton's talent in this regard, writing that the gag in Keaton's oeuvre is "like a parasite, [it] corrupts the plot, and a corollary is that the multiple meanings hidden in normal or realistic discourse are exposed, unmasked, laid bare."[57]

Beyond the analysis of Keaton's comedy that I have undertaken here, Freud's comments on the operation of regression present much more to contemplate regarding the impact of the primary processes on cinematic comedy. His insistence that the transformation of the rational dream-thoughts into hallucinatory representations entails both a loss of logical relations between these thoughts and a compensation for this loss is an important point. His

Figure 17. The Keaton character trying to adapt to rapid scene changes in *Sherlock Jr.* (1924).

argument about considerations of representability hold the promise of a visual semiotics of cinema; not a semiotics limited to thinking about the relationship between signs and meaning, but one that anticipates the construction of meaning through irrational rather than arbitrary processes. It suggests that the very logic that the image uses to articulate thought is also capable of dismantling it. The last two chapters of this book address these issues specifically as they are dealt with by cinematic comedy, making reference not only to Keaton's work, but also to the films of Chaplin and the Marx Brothers.

So where in the terrain Freud maps out as the province of the joke are we to place the cinematic gag? We saw in the previous chapter that Lloyd's thrill comedy and Keaton's causality gags could both be comprehended within the terms set out for the comic. These are physical gags, gags about movement and about the contingency of time and space. Clearly then the gag in general cannot be understood as a simple equivalent to the joke. On the other hand, if we take the defining characteristic of the joke to be the contribution made to the articulation of meaning by unconscious processes then some cinematic gags take on the features of the joke. Moreover, cinema is a convenient medium for the intervention of such processes because of its visual means. The kind of preliminary regression that occurs to enable the working over of preconscious material by the unconscious is not necessary here. Literalization gags nevertheless involve an engagement with verbal signification, and we could from one perspective—as in the case of Harpo—see the gag as the interruption or transgression of verbal discourse. Literalization gags are thus comic engagements between words and things or words and images. In Keaton's films he uses literalization slightly differently to overdetermine the visual aspects of the mise-en-scène. Literalization here is a figure readily exploited by the cinematic medium. Vision is not something simply implied or given by the medium; it is foregrounded in the structure of "communication."

CHAPTER 8

Figural Vision

Freud, Lyotard, and *City Lights*

> *It is not only the author's text which is cut, superimposed, scrambled, it is also the face of the actors, the place where they stand, their clothing, their identity; as to the sets, they change in the middle of the action without warning. Action itself has no unity.*
>
> —Lyotard, "Connivances"

In his essay "Cinema and Psychoanalysis: Parallel Histories," Stephen Heath remarks on the ability of cinema to figure the unconscious processes formulated in Freudian psychoanalysis, suggesting that this very much depends on how one conceives of the cinema and particularly the role of visuality in the cinema. When Freud was approached by his colleagues Hanns Sachs and Karl Abraham to become involved in a film about psychoanalysis, *Secrets of the Soul* (1926) (*Geheimnisse einer Seele*), at the time being envisaged by G. W. Pabst and Ufa (Universum Film AG), he refused to entertain the notion that cinema could figure the unconscious or any of the concepts that pertained to it.[1] Pontalis, slightly less than forty years later, expressed similar reservations in his introduction to Jean-Paul Sartre's scenario for John Huston's 1962 film *Freud*: "the unconscious does not present itself to be seen, fall into sight; the image does not receive, entertain, quite simply get the unconscious."[2]

Yet, Freud undoubtedly attaches great significance to the role of visuality in the dream. The regression to the visual, also known as "considerations of representability," is one of the four operations of the dream-work, and hence of the primary process. For Freud, the difficulty encountered in a cinematic appropriation of this operation emerges from the fact that, as Heath puts it, "in cinema considerations of representability are everything: the nonfigurative collapses into the figurative, the symbolic becomes a matter of symbols, cinema *holds to* the visual."[3] Heath explains, "'Freud's psychoanalysis... interrupts the vision of images, challenges the sufficiency of the representations they make, where cinema aims to sustain vision, to entertain—to bind in—the spectator with images."[4] Heath, however, argues that such reservations might apply only to specific kinds of cinema. He contrasts, for example, the views of Kafka and Virginia Woolf. Kafka's conception of the limitation of cinema is consonant with Freud's: he dislikes the medium's containment of vision, and "pulls away from cinema as surface continuity of images, urg[ing] an excess in seeing, a more-visual of vision."[5] And Woolf sees in cinema the possibility of exactly what Kafka urges, something "radically *obscene*."[6] Heath's demand for an examination of cinematic specificity here is a legitimate response to Freud's reservations about cinema's ability to figure unconscious concepts and processes.

Indeed, whereas the cinematic apparatus has often been called the dream-machine, one could argue that what is really at stake in the Freudian conception of the dream has not been fully brought to bear on our understanding of the processes of cinema. Lyotard's reading of Freud is, in this regard, profound. His development of an understanding of figurality as bound up with the specificity of the operation of the primary process as a force or energetics quite distinct from the figurative, and his examination of the impact such figurality has on signification and meaning, stand in stark contrast to the way film theory has used psychoanalysis to give meaning to films in terms of such Freudian scenarios as the Oedipus complex, the fort-da game, and the concept of wish fulfilment. Even the theorization of cinema as a projection of an imaginary plenitude, which affords the viewer the opportunity to regress to a state of narcissistic identification with the screen, neglects the pertinence that the psychoanalytic conception of the primary process has for the visual and figural operations of the cinema.

A rereading of Freud's theory of the dream and the joke and indeed the operations of the primary process that connects them through Lyotard's study of figurality is crucial to further our understanding of the processes of cinematic comedy. Lyotard's poststructuralist reconfiguration of psychoanalysis, his use of the concepts of discourse and figure to schematize the operation of the primary process and the function of the dream-work as both destructive and transformative of meaning are reoriented here to consider the aesthetic of transformation that prevails in Freud's understanding of the joke. This framework provides a means of theorizing cinema's access to the figural vision that Freud supposes is specific to the unconscious, which I argue is evident in the sight gags that made the slapstick in the latter part of the silent era distinctive. I examine this figural vision in Chaplin's film *City Lights* to show how the comic can be conceived as a relation between sense and nonsense.

DISCOURS, FIGURE

Lyotard's book *Discours, Figure* has been understood as an intervention into the debates around signification and subjectivity that were prevalent in France in the late 1960s and early 1970s, and somewhat later in Anglophone countries.[7] The book, like so many of the theoretical projects with which it was contemporaneous, attempts to move beyond both structuralism and Saussurean semiotics and the kind of textual analysis that the two together engendered. What still makes it worthy of attention is the way its poststructuralist position is produced by opening up the discourses of linguistics and psychoanalysis to aesthetic considerations.

Central to Lyotard's project are the eponymous "concepts" of discourse and figure, although precisely what they entail is not easily encapsulated. Throughout the book they are mobile terms that designate different things in different places. Considered as oppositional, commentators have noted the alignment of discourse with the word, reading, intelligibility, surface, the law, systematicity, and the code, and the figure with the image, seeing, depth, desire, transgression, difference, and instability.[8] Yet, both the meaning of the terms and the success of any such efforts to oppose them are complicated by the imbricated relation between them. Mary Lydon qualifies this relation by noting:

> discourse and figure are given together. Not sequentially, not in juxtaposition, but together, at once, one on top of the other like two superimposed photographic images, or like the representations of the unconscious. This is a spatial relationship that language in its linearity does not permit, hence the imperative to write "Discourse, figure," where the comma...represents graphically, but mutely, as a pause, a blank, a hesitation, one might say, that which cannot be verbalised.[9]

Discourse and figure considered in this manner are not orders of meaning that preside over separate or exclusive domains, rather the realm of each inhabits the other. Lyotard suggests, rather enigmatically, that "the figure dwells in discourse like a phantasm while discourse dwells in the figure like a dream."[10] In some instances of "textual production," discourse will dominate; in others, the figure takes hold of the text. Although discourse and figure at times have distinct methods of operation and are geared toward particular ends, the precise form of a given "text" is based on the specificity of the relation between discourse and figure in that text. Lyotard's book stages the various imbrications of discourse and figure in the separate fields of linguistics, phenomenology, aesthetics, and psychoanalysis. Discourse and figure together are responsible for linguistic, pictorial, plastic, poetic, rhythmic, and oneiric form; the text's transparent, intelligible, meaningful, rhetorical, deconstructive, destructive, and comic posturing.

As well as demonstrating such imbrications, Lyotard charts a sliding scale from discourse to figurality, from the transparent signification of the written word, which is exemplary of discourse, through to the space of language, the phenomenology of the senses and of the body in space, the pictorial dimensions of the visual image, the figurality of the poetic, until ultimately one arrives at the nonsensory destructive figurality of the unconscious. Is this trajectory a movement from the restricted economy of discourse to the general economy of figurality, where restricted economy is an economy of the production of meaning, of investment and return, where surplus is incessantly reinvested, while general economy is an economy of absolute expenditure, of waste, entailing the destruction of meaning without reserve? Certainly, once the figure liaises with the unconscious and "connives" with desire, as Lyotard puts it, it takes hold of the operations of discourse and transforms them to the point where sense becomes nonsense.[11] In *Discours, Figure*, Lyotard might thus be understood to be pursuing a Nietzschean-Bataillian reading of psychoanalysis wherein the unconscious is the source and arena of the destructive Dionysian tendencies of general economy, while the conscious-preconscious system effectuates the formative strategies of an Apollonian restricted economy.[12]

THE FIGURALITY OF THE DREAM

We can see how the imbrication of discourse and figure inscribes a relation between restricted and general economy, and how the figural operates in accordance with Dionysian destruction, in Lyotard's revision of the Freudian dream-work. Lyotard grafts the concepts of discourse and figurality onto the components of the dream to account for the dream's sense and nonsense. This elaboration of the relation between sense and nonsense is pertinent not just as a starting point for understanding the dream but for all that psychoanalysis concerns itself with—hysterical and neurotic symptoms, instances of parapraxis, and jokes as well. Indeed, Lyotard wants to show that the figural operations of the unconscious exist independently of the privileged subject matter of psychoanalysis, exist, that is, as the means of aesthetic production. "Considerations of beauty aside," he writes at the beginning of the chapter on the dream-work, "art begins here."[13]

The general orientation of Lyotard's reading of chapter six of *The Interpretation of Dreams* is directed toward his dispute with Lacan over whether the unconscious is structured like a language. Lyotard is motivated simultaneously by his conviction that the unconscious should not under any circumstances be understood as an agency capable of intelligent thought and volitional activity and by his determination to show that the operations of the primary process are not reducible to rhetorical operations (as Lacan deems them to be when, in "The Agency of the Letter in the Unconscious or Reason since Freud," he argues that condensation and displacement coincide respectively with metaphor and metonymy).[14]

Having no truck with Lacan's idea that the unconscious is structured like a language, Lyotard seems to conceive the unconscious as a prelinguistic formation that comes into existence as a result of the simultaneity of primal desire and its repression. This event occurs before the subject is capable of articulate thought and, as such, establishes itself in a form that is other than articulate thought. Hence, the processes that issue from the unconscious must also be understood as functioning independently of such thought. In the chapter titled "The Connivances of Desire with the Figural," Lyotard conceives of the unconscious as a "matrix," writing:

> the matrix-figure... is no more visible than it is legible. It does not belong to plastic space any more than it does to textual space. It is difference itself, and as such, does not allow the minimal amount of structural polarity which its verbalization would require, or the minimal amount of construction without which its plastic expression as image or form cannot be obtained.[15]

Something like a mimetic machine, the matrix acts as a force that attracts the contents of the psyche and impresses or imprints itself on them, transforming them, almost in a physical way, into something related to its own image. For Lyotard then the figural, at least when it comes to the unconscious, is what is almost physical. It is an implied physicality that characterizes the figural operations of the unconscious. What differentiates these figural operations from the figurative ones of language is that the transformations of the figural are not undertaken with the aim of producing meaning, but rather to destroy it and disguise it. In the dream, for example, the energetics of unconscious desire combine with figurality to destroy the relation between signification and meaning that structures the discursive dream-thoughts. Figurality comes into play in the relation between the dream-thoughts and the dream-work:

> It is advisable, if one wants truly to grasp Freud's intention, to take seriously the opposition he establishes between the dream-thoughts and

dream-work (*Gedanke and Arbeit*), and the transformative action (*Umformen*) of the dream. The *discourse* which resides at the heart of the dream is the object of this work, its raw material.[16]

More definitely than Freud himself does, Lyotard establishes the discursive and figural dimensions of both the latent and manifest content of the dream and the way one content is *refigured* as the other. The dream-thoughts are more or less discursive, whereas the dream-work is figural. The discursive dream-thoughts comprise the raw material that the dream-work operates on to produce the manifest content of the dream.[17] The dream-work, on the other hand, is a kind of labor; it works over the text of the dream-thoughts in a quasi-physical way. The dream-thoughts are transformed not by recourse to their meaning but because the unique operations of dream-work—condensation, displacement, considerations of representability and secondary revision—seize on the organizational structure or the figurative dimension of discourse and subject it to quasi-physical processes.

The chapter of *Discours, figure* titled "Le travail du rêve ne pense pas" ("The Dream-Work Does Not Think") elaborates each of the primary processes to demonstrate the operation of figurality. It is worth reiterating the figural dimension of these processes here to heed their quasi-physical makeup. Condensation compresses the space of discourse that otherwise ensures its readability—the space of both the signifier-signified relation and the sign-referent relation. Displacement reinforces some zones of the text so that they are preserved despite the compressive force of condensation. Concerning considerations of representability, Lyotard refers to the conversion of the linguistic text into a pictographic script, yet he also writes of a visibility that, no longer visual, haunts the configuration of the dream. Secondary revision simultaneously ensures that the text violated by the other three operations nevertheless appears to make sense. Freud writes of the manner in which secondary revision supplements the limited representational capacity of the pictographic dream images with the additions of logic and causality imparted by the analysand; whereas Lyotard describes the manner in which the revision flattens out the upheavals of the other operations to ensure a semblance of sense, thereby appealing to a plastic operation on the material substance of the dream. Although secondary revision endows the dream with the semblance of intelligibility, in relation to the dream-thoughts this intelligibility is meaningless.

The import of Freud's invention and formulation of the operations of the dream-work is not to be underestimated. As Lyotard more than sufficiently demonstrates, these operations provide a means of understanding how processes that are neither linguistic nor rhetorical impact meaning and nonmeaning. Such operations, far from simply partaking in an abstract transgression of sense, can be examined and analyzed to account for the relation between sense and nonsense. Their facility is nowhere more evident than in the extent to which they form the basis of the psychoanalytic method.

As operations that form the dream, however, the primary processes exist only as inferences. As we noted, Lyotard's emphasis on the physicality of figurality in his reading of Freud is a quasi-physicality. The dream-work does not transform any actual physical thoughts. At the same time, Freud's idea of visuality in "Considerations of Representability" is an implied visuality. We see, in fact, no visible evidence of a pictographic script. Lyotard's repeated reference to aesthetic examples to back up his arguments about the figurality of the dream-work is, in this regard, noteworthy. In so doing, he demonstrates that the primary processes have a reality in the world of culture that is palpable.

Lyotard also furnishes us with an explanation of the extension of the primary process to nonlinguistic signifying material and indeed nonsignifying plasticity is just what he demonstrates in "The Connivances of Desire with the Figural." In this chapter, he explicates the manner in which the unintelligent force of desire constitutes an energetics that dismantles the machinery of not only discourse, but the image and form as well. When the *image-figure* comes into contact with the unconscious, the set of rules that regulate the perceived object is infringed.[18] Now produced "within a space of difference,' the percept, the outline of a figure that defines an object, for instance, is deconstructed; the revealing trace is transgressed.[19] When the *form-figure* comes into contact with the unconscious, a Dionysian energy destroys the unity of the whole.[20] Lyotard gives the example of Jackson Pollock's "passion painting" which succeeds in rendering such "Bacchic delirium."[21] Whereas the unconscious destroys the trace of the object in the *image-figure*, in the *form-figure* the unconscious inhibits form, permitting no recognizable figure as such.

The *matrix-figure* is the most figural figure. According to David Carroll it involves the "transgression of the figure itself" to make "possible another notion of the figural."[22] Lyotard can only define the *matrix-figure* in terms of negatives: neither visible nor legible, it is not seen at all. It does not belong either to textual or plastic space, and it disallows both "the minimal amount of structural polarity which its verbalization would require" and "the minimal amount of construction" necessary for "plastic expression as image or form." It cannot be intelligently apprehended.[23] The *matrix-figure* is not so much a figure that comes into contact with the unconscious as what comprises the unconscious as such. The *matrix-figure* attracts the preconscious material that desire works over to produce the phantasm (of the dream, joke, symptom, and so forth).[24]

THE PLEASURE PRINCIPLE

Lyotard could not have fully developed his notion of figurality without attending to the differences between the operation of the primary and secondary processes, and correspondingly between the flow of psychical energy under the sway of the pleasure principle and the reality principle. Freud himself refers to the importance of these processes to the formation of the joke when he says, toward the end of his discussion of the primary and secondary processes and their relation to repression, that the comic is nothing other than the operations of the primary process that have managed to force their way through to consciousness, thereby providing us with a clear statement of his own recognition of the connection between his work on the dream and his work on the joke.[25] The difference between the primary and secondary processes is between two modes of functioning of the psychical apparatus, two accounts of the flow of energy in the psyche, two mechanical conditions. The difference also respectively correlates topographically with the unconscious and preconscious-conscious systems of the psyche, and the pleasure principle and the reality principle.[26]

For Freud, the psyche in general is regulated by the tendency toward the pleasure principle, a tendency that turns out to be as much an avoidance of unpleasure as anything with positive value.[27] Unpleasure arises as a result of an increase in the quantity of excitation in the psyche, whereas pleasure results from the diminution or discharge of such energy. As a result, the pleasure principle is itself underpinned by the principle of constancy or Fechner's principle of the "tendency toward stability."[28]

The unconscious part of the psyche, however, is regulated by the most primitive state of the pleasure principle. The unconscious comprises repressed ideas and unfulfilled wishes from infancy, which are necessarily inaccessible to consciousness because they give rise to pain rather than pleasure. The continued unfulfillment of these wishes means that they attract large amounts of psychical energy. To counteract this attraction of energy to repressed desire, the unconscious maintains a high degree of mobility of cathectic energy that attaches to the content or ideas of the psyche. In the primary process cathectic energy is free flowing, serving both to "avoid an accumulation of excitations" and to move such excitation by means of discharge.[29] This free flow of cathectic energy is made possible precisely because of the operations of condensation and displacement. An unconscious wish engages a current of energy that starts out as unpleasure and aims at pleasure. The mobility of cathectic energy aims at "a hallucinatory cathecting of the memory of satisfaction" so that the wish is satisfied as quickly as possible.[30] The wish, in other words, is satisfied through fantasy. Condensation and displacement both allow for the hallucination of the satisfaction of desire and make psychical energy very mobile.

But because the unconscious operates in accordance with the most primitive aspect of the pleasure principle, the organism is left "in reality" in an unsatisfied state; the operation of the primary process is without a practical means of addressing the problem of unsatisfied desire. Therefore a second system, the secondary process, comes into operation later on in the development of the subject as a refinement of the primitive and problematic way the primary process operates. The aim of the secondary process is to prevent "the mnemic cathexis" from "proceed[ing] as far as perception,"[31] to prevent, in other words, the hallucinatory cathecting of the memory of satisfaction and to divert the flow of energy so that satisfaction can be arrived at which is both real and tolerable to consciousness. The secondary process is a rational system, organized by a heuristic method of trial and error. It requires both a multitude of memories that can be called up, reviewed, and acted on in accordance with intentional desire and quiescent energy that can be used in small amounts for the activity of sending out and withdrawing feelers. The aim of this system, Freud states, is therefore also to inhibit the free discharge of psychical energy and to transform free energy into quiescent energy.[32]

Whereas the primary process is characterized by the free-flowing cathectic energy of the unconscious system occurring in accordance with the most primitive state of the pleasure principle and aiming at the most immediate satisfaction of a wish, in the secondary process the flow of energy occurs in much smaller intensities, and a certain amount of quiescent energy is available for binding. The pleasure principle is still operative in the secondary process, but it has been modified to the extent that it takes into account the development of the psyche and the existence of the external world. Strictly speaking, it is now called the *reality principle*. The aim of the secondary process is to divert "the excitation arising from the need along a roundabout path which ultimately, by means of voluntary movement, altered that external world in such a way that it became possible to arrive at a *real* perception of the object of satisfaction."[33]

Now Lyotard in fact demonstrates that the hallucinatory fulfillment of a wish in the unconscious, mechanized by the primary process and governed by the pleasure principle, reverses the direction of a purposive action undertaken in accordance with normal thought processes under the operation of the secondary process and governed by the reality principle:

> Action starts from excitation, goes through memory-traces, verbal traces, the motor zones, produces a transformation of reality and finally provides satisfaction as an outward discharge. In the fulfillment of desire, excitation passes through the different layers of the apparatus in the reverse direction and cathects perceptual memories with such an intensity that it induces an hallucination.[34]

CINEMATIC COMEDY

The oft-commented on tension between comedy and narrative that emerges in the 1920s in the comedies of Chaplin, Keaton, and others can, according to a Lyotardian reading of Freud, be further interpreted as a tension between the pleasure principle and the reality principle, and between the operations of the primary and secondary processes. In as much as the pleasure principle prescribes the economic condition of the unconscious under which energy is characteristically unhampered and flows freely from one repressed content to another, it can be used to account for any number of gags orchestrated through the operations of condensation and displacement to bring about the hallucinatory satisfaction of desire. The reality principle, on the other hand, might be called on to explain the operation of narrative. Here energy would be increasingly bound, rather than free, and, being oriented toward the achievement of goals, flow in a controlled manner. Cathexis, or the attachment of energy to an idea, would be undertaken in a stable fashion.

Condensation and displacement are brought into play in cinematic comedy by combining the visual qualities of the cinematic image with the physical performance of the comic actor. From Chaplin's Tramp consuming a pair of boots for Christmas roast in *The Gold Rush*, to Keaton's use of a bomb for a cigarette lighter in *Cops* and a live lobster to cut wire in *The Navigator*, to the reframing that transforms the ominous gallows into a mere signpost at a railway station in Lloyd's *Safety Last!*, the directors of silent cinematic comedy variously used condensation for its comic potential. Where dream condensation compresses two or more images into one, cinematic comedy combines condensation with displacement to pull the image apart. Displacement also figures as the method by which Keaton extends short films into longer narratives. Used most dramatically in his trajectory gags, displacement allows him to inscribe a relentlessly linear form into the most rudimentary scenarios. Displacement, in other words, is the operation underpinning the recursion function that we examined previously. All Keaton's character ever has to do is hold tight and wait until the whirligig on which he is caught delivers him up to the point where resolution can finally take place. Chaplin's Tramp also emblematizes the operation of displacement in so far as he is made destitute by the conditions of modern capitalism and is destined to wander aimlessly through its myriad industrial, social, and cultural formations.

Significantly, condensation and displacement are not used as techniques at the beginning of cinematic comedy and are only found in abundance toward the end of the silent era. As is well documented, film historians generally consider the silent cinematic comedy of the early part of the twentieth century to have undergone a dramatic change between the Keystone era of the 1910s and the beginnings of the comedian comedy of the 1920s, associated with performers such as Chaplin, Lloyd, and Keaton. But they do so without adequately comprehending what is at stake in the nature of comedy or what such comedy implies about cinematic visuality. In the work of these performers, the sight gag signals a transition from a cinema in which the comic predominated to one in which the joke—or something like it—played an increasingly significant role. Understood from a Lyotardian perspective on the joke, the sight gag signals the emergence of figurality in cinema. Indeed, the figurality that characterizes these comedies prompts one to question how cinema might have developed had not the advent of the "talkie" directed its evolution toward an aesthetic of verisimilitude. Increasingly, emphasis came to be placed on the realism of the image on the one hand, and the virtuosity of cinematic technique on the other, while the apparatus became so involved with its own technical possibilities that it reoriented the exploration of the visuality that had been one of the motivating forces in its invention along completely different lines. Chaplin, for one, saw this reorientation as a limitation, declaring around the time he made *City Lights* that talkies were "spoiling the oldest art in the world, the art of pantomime.... They were ruining the great beauty of silence.... They are defeating the meaning of the screen."[35]

CITY LIGHTS

That Cavell rationalizes the specific nature of Chaplin's comedy in terms consonant with the Freudian distinction between the pleasure principle and the reality principle is no accident. He writes, for example, of the Tramp's imaginative solutions to the problems reality posed and his pursuit of happiness in the face of a miserly and infelicitous reality, thereby invoking an important interplay between pleasure and reality.[36] Chaplin, the director, choreographer, performer, and so forth, thus seems to stage for the audience some of the possible vicissitudes of these two principles of mental functioning.[37] Cavell also observes that this imagination embodied in the Tramp's visual capacity, in his character's treatment of an object as "something it is not in fact," is a Wittgensteinian "seeing as."[38] The Tramp's visualization of a pair of boots as a Christmas dinner in *The Gold Rush* exemplifies this "seeing as." Slavoj Žižek, by contrast, suggests in passing in *Enjoy Your Symptom: Jacques Lacan in Hollywood and Out*, that throughout *The Circus* Chaplin puts forward a "wild theory of the origins of comedy from the *blindness* of its audience."[39] He explains:

> the Tramp, on the run from the police, finds himself on a rope at the top of the circus tent; he starts to gesticulate wildly, trying to keep his

balance, while the audience laughs and applauds, mistaking his desperate struggle for survival for a comedian's virtuosity...[40]

Putting Cavell's and Žižek's statements together, one could (erroneously) conclude that the extended vision of the comedian—Chaplin's ability to "see as"—is tied to the audience's diminished vision and the joy obtained from seeing less than the truth. What Žižek calls blindness here is referred to in the terminology of film analysis as the restriction of point of view. Even in Žižek's view, restriction is not simply a limitation but makes possible an "other" interpretation of the image, instituting, in other words, a kind of "seeing as." More important to the operation of the comic in this scene, however, is the fact that the film audience sees the doubling of the conditions in which the act emerges and the restricted point of view of the diegetic audience. The film audience, far from blind, occupies a position of visual omnipotence. And we must note that the Tramp is not the one who in this instance is blessed with special vision, but Chaplin, the extrafictional comedian who performs his Tramp persona, whereas the latter remains ignorant of the circus audience's perception of his performance. In Freudian terms, the scene is doubly comic (in so far as the comic emerges from a comparison between "the is" and "the ought"): one sees the Tramp as a degraded clown and one sees the audience as blind to the real conditions of his performance. But the difference between Charlie and the Tramp also extends the domain of the comic. Charlie's performance of the Tramp exemplifies the primary condensation on which all comedian comedy is based.[41]

Although we commonly use the term *comic vision*, exactly what comic vision is, where it is located within the history and theory of visuality, and what specifically makes it comic is something less often reflected on. We should recall here that psychoanalysis also theorizes the role of the image in the unconscious processes while nevertheless relying on a certain blindness. Freud's discussion of the pleasure principle and the reality principle has profound implications for an understanding of the operation of vision. The pleasure principle implies the imagined image of visual hallucination. It freely permits "the hallucinatory cathexis of the memory of satisfaction," whereas the reality principle's entire function is geared toward averting hallucination.[42] And it is also worth recalling here that just as the primary processes are quasi-physical operations or operations distinguished by their treatment of discourse as a quasi-physical object, the visual regression of the dream-thoughts into pictorial images is in fact a quasi-visuality, there being no eye that sees the dream. As such, the hallucination that comes into play in visual comedy in the doubling of the image is an implied hallucination. Visual condensation in cinema works by the performer or the director implying that the image is something other than what it appears to be. What makes it funny is the fact that it is not coded as an hallucination and it comes on us unexpectedly.

Set in the Roaring Twenties, the story of *City Lights* contrasts the superficiality of the upper-middle class and the noble altruism of the urban poor. The plot is divided into two series, structured around the Tramp's encounters with a poor, blind flower girl and an inebriated millionaire. When the blind girl mistakes the Tramp for a gentleman, the Tramp goes along with it and becomes her suitor and benefactor, providing for her as best he can. Likewise, after saving the rich drunk man from committing suicide, he allows the latter to befriend him and treat him to whatever aspects of the good life he deems appropriate—parties, loads of alcohol, and nights on the town. These two series can also be understood to institute a semantic and formal counterpoint. Symbolically, the contrast between rich and poor reverberates in further oppositions between night and day, present and future tense, the amoral and the morally upstanding, narcissism and altruism, carelessness and responsibility, corruption and purity. At a formal level, each series is expressed by a contrasting mode of enunciation. The drunken millionaire series is comedy; the blind girl series is melodrama, although it includes some slapstick. But they can also be understood through a psychoanalytic frame of reference. The melodrama series is governed by the reality principle and the secondary process; the comic sequences that interrupt the melodramatic narrative (through gags) seem geared by pleasure, and their mechanism must be understood in accordance with the primary process.

Consider, for example, the scene where the Tramp first meets the girl. The Tramp is initially chuffed at being mistaken for a gentleman, then touched when he realizes the girl is blind. The scene is delivered slowly and methodically. We have time to reflect that although the girl's blindness leads her to mistake him for a gentleman, this is because Chaplin's imitation of a gentleman is faultless. (In this sense, blindness allows her to perceive qualities in the Tramp that would otherwise be overlooked.) The pathos of the scene is emphasized by the plaintive, beseeching musical score, that combines the flute with the strings of violins and cello and that are, in turn, echoed in the single melancholy note from the harp. This melodramatic tone continues when the blind girl returns home to her grandmother, in the sparseness and simplicity of their living conditions and in the girl's resentment at the lot she has drawn. The victimization of one character or another is emphasized in subsequent scenes of the girl sick in bed, the arrival of the eviction notice, the penultimate scene of the Tramp utterly denigrated by the paperboys, and the final scene of the girl being "illuminated" to the Tramp's identity. Fortunately the cloying sentimentality of such sequences never extends for long and the scenes detailing the Tramp's encounters with the drunk millionaire do much to lighten the film's social message. The escapades of the

Tramp and the millionaire, on the other hand, are completely lacking in sentimentality. They include more slapstick, more condensation and displacement gags, and more comic performances by Chaplin. The music in these sequences is lighter and racier than it is in the melodrama sequences, and it is also much more closely tied to the rhythms of action than is conventional in melodrama generally.

While Chaplin constitutes the common link between the melodrama series with the girl and the comic series with the drunk, he is also a conduit for the transfer of money from one series to another. A third subseries develops around the world of work as he seeks gainful employment, however, his lack of success in this series is ultimately compensated for in the millionaire series, where he obtains enough cash to pay for both the girl's rent and a trip to Vienna, of all places, for an operation to cure her blindness. The end of the film shows the girl with her vision restored, seeing the Tramp for the first time.

Vision and visuality are significant in this film because Chaplin aligns them with the deployment of such figures as blindness, illumination, and actual hallucination. In addition, they assist in the orchestration of the film's comic dimension, in the deployment, that is, of condensation and displacement. In this respect, their function is bound up with implied hallucination. We will see that tropic vision is a kind of visuality that serves the film's themes and narrative development, whereas comic vision operates quite differently. Considered in relation to comic visuality, Chaplin's inclination toward tropic visuality in fact evidences an ambivalence (perhaps an unconscious one) toward the figurality of the comic.

Chaplin's use of vision as a trope is apparent in the way both of his friendships are constituted through blindness and in the development of the film's scenario from blindness to illumination. Both the Tramp's friends suffer from a lack of vision—the blind girl mistakes him for a gentleman, the blind drunk appears incapable of any discernment whatsoever. The Tramp too turns a blind eye to the consequences his assistance to the girl will have on their relationship.

Another aspect of tropic vision is evident in the film's contemplation of the notion of hallucination. Both the blind girl and the blind drunk envisage the Tramp to be something he is not and, more importantly, to be someone who accords with their desire of what they want him to be. In this sense, blindness facilitates hallucination, facilitates, that is, an imagined image, unverifiable because it is unmediated by the sensory organ of the physical eye. Possibly because of Chaplin's Marxist orientation, the narrative of the film explicitly rejects hallucination and, at the very end, replaces it with illumination (as a Marxist might want to illuminate what is at stake in the false consciousness of the proletariat). Illumination first involves the blind girl's restoration of vision so that she can come to see the Tramp as he is, not as the gentleman she had assumed he was. False vision is here repudiated in favor of true vision, of the visualization of truth and vision as truth. The blind girl's words, "Now I see," signal not just a moment of sensory illumination but of intellectual revelation. It was because she was blind that she could confuse the Tramp with a gentleman, and this in turn made him conform to her desire and act as if he were indeed a gentleman. One hallucination thus engenders another. With her vision restored, she experiences hindsight and in the penultimate shot of the film, during which we see her see, we surmise the entire narrative of the film being replayed, her eyes this time being the lens through which it passes. The link between vision and teleology entailed by hindsight is surely one of the cinema's most powerful epistemological mechanisms. The issue of concern regarding such an inscription of visuality in the film, and pertinent to this particular film as well as Chaplin's oeuvre as a whole, is whether the film's final gesture toward illumination and thus clear and unequivocal vision repudiates not only hallucination but also the visual confusion explicit in his visual comedy.

If tropic vision emerges from the film's narrative, the comic is played out in accordance with Freud's distinction between the comic and the joke. Cinematic techniques such as editing, shot scale, cutting rhythm, camera angle, and so on, undoubtedly enhance Chaplin's intention to ridicule, his deployment of caricature and his degradation of the ideal. Consider, for instance, the context of the Tramp's first appearance in *City Lights*. Two rituals of modernity are intercut: one is the city's unveiling of a new monument, the other a vagrant awakening to a new day. The City Hall streetscape of the first shot duplicates the nighttime shot of the film's opening; except now it is daytime, and the strange monument barely discernible at the image's vanishing point is shrouded by a tarpaulin, and a swelling crowd has replaced the cars and pedestrians. In the first part of the sequence, shot scale becomes progressively closer (an extreme long shot cuts to a less extreme long shot to a medium shot to a medium closeup) to shift the film audience's position from distant theatrical onlooker to cinematic viewer intimately engaged in the amusing details of the travesty to come. The low-angle medium shot of a dignitary gesticulating flamboyantly enhances the caricature by drawing our attention to his protruding belly. Comic degradation is achieved by rendering his speech as cadenced noise, more gestural than significatory, the "blah, blah, blah" of official self-congratulation. The sequence continues to illustrate the pomposity and tedium of civil ceremony: a matronly "Mishes Mashen" (Mrs. Mason perhaps) takes the microphone; the film cuts to an oblique-angled shot showing both the rotund man and "Mishes Mashen" bearing upward and slightly backward, signifying at once their moral rectitude and the shallow (simply formal) premise on which it is based. The strings of the musical score that had been rubbing away at us give way to triumphant brass, and like a parachute in reverse, the tarpaulin shrouding the monument to peace and prosperity is lifted. Beneath, peace is symbolized by a male statue languidly reclining while brandishing his sword, prosperity by a figure standing empty-handed, and behind and between the two presides a seated matriarch. The film cuts to a slightly closer shot to reveal that the flesh-and-blood figure asleep across the stone lap of the female statue is the Tramp.

Rudely awakened from his slumber, the Tramp has a little scratch, first of his head, and then his leg, which he lifts vertically into the air like a dog. A shot from the reverse angle conveys the response of the appalled audience and dignitaries, and from this point until the end of the sequence, the editing follows a shot/reverse-shot pattern. Chaplin thereby institutes a rhythm of cutting between the officials flanked by indignant crowds demanding ever more vehemently that the Tramp quit the scene, and Charlie, dazed but slowly wakening, acknowledging the situation, taking a breather, starting to remove himself, becoming entangled in the ensemble, freeing himself, clambering across it, deciding he will not be hurried, tying his shoelaces and finally climbing one last time over the statues before discreetly backing away over the fence. The rhythm of the montage allows the drama to escalate in the short sharp shots depicting the crowd's angry jeers and to strain in the longer shots (in terms of both time and scale) of Chaplin milking the situation, serially entangling himself in the ensemble until its comic potential is exhausted.

Even so, this aesthetic of comic degradation is a long way from the seeing that signals the eruption of the figural. Throughout the sequence the Tramp interferes further with the already questionable signification of the tableau, and inadvertently fills the scene with sexual innuendo, exhibiting what William Paul has called a preoccupation with the lower body stratum.[43] The Tramp, for example, as Paul notes, impales himself on the sword of the reclining statue through a hole in the rear of his trousers, poses in such a way as to inadvertently thumb his nose to the crowd, and deploys gestures implying that he has stepped in dog shit. The comic doubling that occurs here results from the visual dimension of Charlie's performance. This could be called condensation in as much as the visual quality of the gags provides for at least two readings of a single image.

Condensation and displacement (together with slapstick) occur throughout the film, predominantly in the sequences detailing the escapades of the Tramp and the drunk. The nightclub sequence is one of several in the film where Chaplin uses condensation to incorporate the riotously performative, rough-and-tumble aspects of pantomime into cinema. The millionaire treats the Tramp to a night on the town to repay him for his unwavering determination to save him from the lure of suicide. The two men arrive at a nightclub already well-sozzled, drunkenness justifying to some extent the gags that comprise the sequence as well as the overall comic performance. Intoxication destroys the men's sensory-motor coordination (the Tramp's more than the millionaire's), and the space that harbors them and the objects in it become phantasmatic. In an extreme long shot the dance floor becomes a skating rink for which the Tramp is ill-equipped. Arms and legs flailing, he turns into a ragbag of chaotic limbs and only manages to scramble to his table with the support of his friend and the waiter. A two-shot of the Tramp and his friend trying to smoke cigars shows the Tramp, having lost the sense of the position of his body in space, confusing his own cigar with his friend's, so that every time he goes to light his cigar it is the millionaire's that is in his mouth.

Condensation and displacement gags in this sequence include Charlie eating a streamer as though it were spaghetti and grabbing a woman and recklessly twirling her around the dance floor because he has misinterpreted the gesture of her outstretched arms as an invitation to dance. Figurally speaking, the space in which the dinner guests are seated is transformed into a stage, while the acts performed on it seamlessly run into each other. Comic slapstick thus replaces diegetic realism (and melodrama for that matter). The action of the sequence, on more than one occasion, degenerates into a kind of circus clown routine. When the Tramp finds himself without hat and cane at the beginning of the sequence—the waitress has relieved him of them—he promptly snatches those of another man, who just as promptly snatches them back. A while later, the Tramp's attempt to douse the smoldering gown of a woman with spray from a soda fountain gives way to a fisticuffs routine reminiscent of Punch and Judy. The tension increases when a further altercation ensues between the millionaire and the man at the next table over who is entitled to which chair, which doubles as a tit for tat routine. Camera scale—the long shot—gives the scene a considerably theatrical flavor. As one man takes the chair for himself, the other falls on his behind. From the film audience's point of view, the Tramp and the millionaire turn the nightclub scene into a comedia dell'arte performance. And in this sense the entire scene can be understood as condensation.

The extent to which comic condensation also develops the film's meaning depends on whether it is tendentious or innocent. The condensed image of the Tramp cradled in the arms of the female statue, spread across the body of a would-be Madonna, is tendentious to the extent that it resonates in the ensuing narrative. The Tramp, like Christ, is both society's sacrificial lamb and savior. The dignitaries' outrage at the Tramp's disfigurement of the ensemble puts the point rather bluntly that peace and prosperity are not so much the ideals for the whole society as the bounty of the middle class. On viewing the film a second time, the sexual innuendo of the unveiling ceremony resonates with the film's narrative concerns about the rich shafting the poor and conveys Chaplin's response to the increasing hostility of the middle class to the bawdy elements of his earlier films.

Just as a the comedy sequences have a serious undertone, the melodrama sequences are similarly interspersed with comic moments. A comedy of errors, for example, opens the third sequence of the film. The blind girl assumes the Tramp is rich because he alights from a nearby car, whereas he has in fact improvised a short cut to cross a busy street by sneaking through the back-seat compartment of a stationary vehicle. And the sequence is closed by pure slapstick: the Tramp remains to watch the blind girl without her knowing it, and the girl, assuming the Tramp long gone, throws a bucket of water in his face. While the film has alternating melodramatic and comedic sequences, this does not mean that the operations undertaken in accordance with the pleasure principle and the reality principle, or between the primary and secondary processes, are completely distinguishable. In the comedic sequences at least, the two principles operate at the same time. But, as is typical with Chaplin's feature films, as the film progresses the pleasure principle gives way to the reality principle, comedy to melodrama, play to moral comment.

Thus the comic performances that run throughout the film are nearly always tendentious, telling a second story about the Tramp's marginal social status. Despite the comicality of Charlie gallivanting about town, the sequences of his escapades with the millionaire also have a serious underside: for instance, the millionaire repeatedly attempts suicide, and the Tramp is subjected to the millionaire's unsolicited advances, humiliated at the nightclub, and beaten up during the boxing match.

In spite of Cavell's characterization of Chaplin's comedy as providing imaginary solutions to real problems, it is significant that until the boxing match, the Tramp's uses of condensation and displacement are inadvertent. He does not, for example, intentionally transform the streamer into a strand of spaghetti at the nightclub, and it is a mistake that he attempts to apportion a man's head onto a plate because his party hat resembles the dessert on offer. Indeed, until the boxing match, the condensations and displacements that the Tramp performs are not strategies of the character but accidents resulting from his marginal place in society. While the Tramp is goal-oriented in the melodramatic sequences, that he is otherwise passive is remarkable. In contrast to Keaton, who frequently uses condensation and displacement as strategies of adaptation to the problems the world presents him, the Tramp appropriates the operations of the primary process, as Cavell rightly suggests, only because the extreme circumstances of reality mean no other options are available to him.

This eruption of figurality under the pressure of the extremity of reality is precisely what we see in the boxing sequence. Without doubt the film's comic tour de force, the sequence is nevertheless narratively motivated by the Tramp's determination to earn the money needed for the blind girl's rent. Desperate, the Tramp agrees to fight in a rigged boxing match. When his coconspirator has to leave town in a hurry, the manager recruits another, more formidable opponent for him. The Tramp calls on all available resources to diminish the likelihood of losing the fight: he borrows the good luck charms of another fighter, flutters his eyelashes, tries to seduce his opponent into taking it easy (this, while the camera gaily swings back and forth between them) and, finally, failing in his efforts, resorts, in the ring, to using the referee as a shield to protect himself. The Tramp, in other words, transforms himself into a coquette and the fight into a dance (and undertakes in the process a feminization of masculine performance ritual). Here the intolerable reality that Cavell says motivates Chaplin's comedy forces the Tramp to let the operations of the primary process take over and adopt the kind of strategies toward objects that are much more readily deployed by Keaton's persona.

Even while the performative dimension of the boxing match exceeds its diegetic significance, Chaplin ensures that the Tramp's transformations simultaneously operate as comic degradations and as impotent means of dealing with reality. This point is brought home in the middle of the boxing sequence when the kind of implied hallucination that gives rise to the comic confusion and performative transformation we see in sight gags is replaced with hallucination proper.

Indeed, the boxing sequence can be thought of as a series of rising crescendos of implied hallucinations in the form of visual condensations, the comedy here escalating until the devastating actual hallucination brings us back to the reality of the diegesis. During the interval between rounds, Charlie, beaten half to death, hallucinates that one of the ring assistants is the blind girl and that she soothes him and inspires him to continue. This hallucination, this visual doubling, is significantly found in the form of the film and is not funny. It serves to expose the fact that Charlie's real goal is a preposterous wish. The Tramp's strategies, in other words, in no way prevent the consequences of reality from becoming operative in that he is sorely beaten in the fight and remains penniless for his efforts.[44]

The insertion of a cinematic representation of hallucination is a perfectly conventional means of establishing psychological motivation. It also fits well with the narrative exposition of tropic vision, being carefully and significantly placed in the development of the blindness-hallucination-illumination series. But it also suggests that the appropriation of the hallucinatory operation of the primary process is far from condoned by the director.

What is striking about *City Lights* as a film that uses comic vision is Chaplin's position in relation to it. Certainly, his take on the figurative and the figural in cinema is complex. Arguing this through recourse to his intentions would be impossible but his presentation of hallucination at the climax of the film's comicality and the tropic vision that gives the film its form suggests, in spite of everything, a preference for the figurative over the figural. At the end of the film, Chaplin's desire, apparently, is to no longer have to "see as," but rather to envisage a world that requires neither hallucination nor visual confusion as devices to indicate the problems with reality. In this respect we find a lack of conviction on Chaplin's part as to the promise of the figurality of comic vision. Indeed, by engendering comedy in situations of pure pathos, he appears to want to restrict himself to the humorous disguise of social critique. Chaplin's investment in the comic in this film, his achievements notwithstanding, implies that the efficacy of the primary process is, while entertaining, of limited effectivity. In the case of *City Lights*, the deployment of the comic is predominantly tendentious, ensuring that figural visuality assists making meaning as much as destroying it, whereas Chaplin's replacement of hallucination by clear and unequivocal vision suggests a repudiation rather than a celebration of the unconscious processes of condensation and displacement. At the same time, his cinematic technique has discursive and figurative functions. In the first instance, it serves visual intelligibility. In the second, Chaplin's distinctive cinematic style (particularly his establishment of rhythm through a complex choreography of music, film editing, and the actions and pulsations of his body) can be understood as the comic forepleasure that Freud would say establishes a mood in the audience that will look favorably on the figural eruptions of the unconscious. Without the virtuoso performance, Chaplin's "jokes" would be overly didactic and barely tolerable.

Lyotard's understanding of the operation of the primary process as a figural force or energetics is relevant to philosophical aesthetics not simply to the extent to which it provides for a theorization of modernist artistic practice but as a means of understanding the imbrication of restricted and general economy that operates in cinematic comedy. In art the quasi-physical character of these psychical processes becomes physical. We have seen that Chaplin's Tramp literally performs condensation and displacement. But the visual medium in which the processes are presented gives way at times to something that has been variously designated as blindness, implied hallucination, or "seeing as." We should acknowledge here too that figural vision often works on the basis of visual resemblance so that only a limited blindness comes into play in cinematic comedy. Indeed, the figural vision I have identified here as operating in the sight gag accords only to a limited extent with Woolf's idea of the radically obscene and Kafka's appeal to a "more-visual of vision." The comic formed through the operation of the primary processes is undoubtedly the least compromised of the compromise formations (compromised by the unconscious that is). As Freud notes, the condition of intelligibility is more binding in the joke than it is in the dream. This condition also appears to be more binding in commercial cinema than in, say, the avant-garde films of the surrealists. Lyotard's reworking of the Freudian schema nevertheless shows us that even commercial cinema does not always "hold to the visual" and it calls for a much more thorough analysis of the nature of visuality in the history of cinematic comedy. While the figural has an undeniable presence in the cinematic comedy of the silent period, the brief contrasts drawn here between the work of Chaplin and Keaton suggest that it will be deployed in varying ways by different comic performers. It presents, nevertheless, the possibility of developing a paradigm for further analyses of such comedy.

CHAPTER 9

Preposterous Figurality

Comic Cinema and Bad Metaphor

In the course of trying to set out what comic sovereignty might be, Bataille effectively refuses to entertain the idea that poetry, in the last instance, can be understood as an operation of sovereignty. Poetry for Hegel is the highest form of art; according to Bataille, however, it is rather almost entirely "poetry in decline" or "fallen poetry" (as Derrida calls it) because it relies on metaphors extracted from the "servile domain" of determinate discourse.[1] To conclude this discussion of the comic, I want to return more explicitly to its relation to the poetic. Specifically, I want to consider what cinematic metaphor is, what role the visual plays in the construction of cinematic metaphor, and what differences can be surmised between metaphor and comic figurality in cinema. By articulating the conceptual basis of the difference between metaphor and the comic, or indeed by ascertaining a lack of difference, this analysis will give further nuance to the implications of Freud's theorization of the role played by the primary process in the operation of the comic and Lyotard's insistence that the dream-work "does not think." The relationship between the poetic and the comic will thus be considered through the tension between sense and nonsense, and in the first instance it will be thought that will provide a point of focus. In addition to drawing on by Freud's and Lyotard's arguments that have proved crucial to my study so far, I will consider Deleuze's discussion of metaphor in cinema, Barthes's conception of the film gag as something capable of releasing metaphor from its demonstrative function, and Derrida's deconstruction of the philosophical conceptualization of metaphor. With regard to cinematic comedy, we will, on the one hand, see how the Marx Brothers' gags extend the function of metaphor to the point that it relinquishes its service to meaning. On the other hand, we also see the way the analysis of the relationship between images in cinematic comedy produces what would best be described as bad metaphor. By analyzing the operation of such figures in Keaton's film *The Navigator*, it will become clear that slapstick works to hide thought.

CINEMATIC METAPHOR

In his second book on film, *Cinema 2: The Time-Image*, Deleuze defines verbal metaphor as the practice of "giving a 'subject' the verb or action of another subject."[2] He theorizes the construction of cinematic metaphor as that which is created by dissolving the movement of the image and connecting the image with the whole that it expresses. He gives the following example from Eisenstein's film *Strike* (1925):

> The boss's big spy is first shown the wrong way round, head downwards, his massive legs rising like two tubes which end in a puddle at the top of the screen; then we see the two factory chimneys which seem embedded in a cloud. This is a metaphor with double inversion, since the spy is shown first, and shown upside-down. The puddle and the cloud, the legs and the chimneys have the same harmonics: it is metaphor through montage.[3]

The dissolution of movement in metaphor, through the montage of images, suggests a fusion of images. This occurs, Deleuze insists, not as a result of technical superimposition but because the two images have the same harmonics.[4] Harmonics here might be understood as the visual resemblance that we saw to be at the heart of cinematic condensation. When expressed through montage, cinematic metaphor describes a relation between images. Yet Deleuze says it can also be found in the single image without montage. The cesarean section in Keaton's film *The Navigator* provides an example of the latter. The Keaton character, Rollo Treadway, emerges from the depths of the ocean with half of it in his diver's suit, necessitating that he perform surgery on himself to release the water/amniotic fluid. He does this by slicing through the belly of his suit with a knife in a manner almost as dramatic as the razor dissecting the eye in Luis Buñuel's film *Un chien andalou* (made in 1929, four years after Keaton's film). Deleuze gives the following description of the sequence in *The Navigator*:

> The hero in the life-jacket, strangled, dying, drowning in his life-jacket, is going to be awkwardly saved by the girl. She takes him between her legs to make sure of a grip and finally manages to open the jacket by cutting it, whereupon a flood of water escapes from it. Never has an

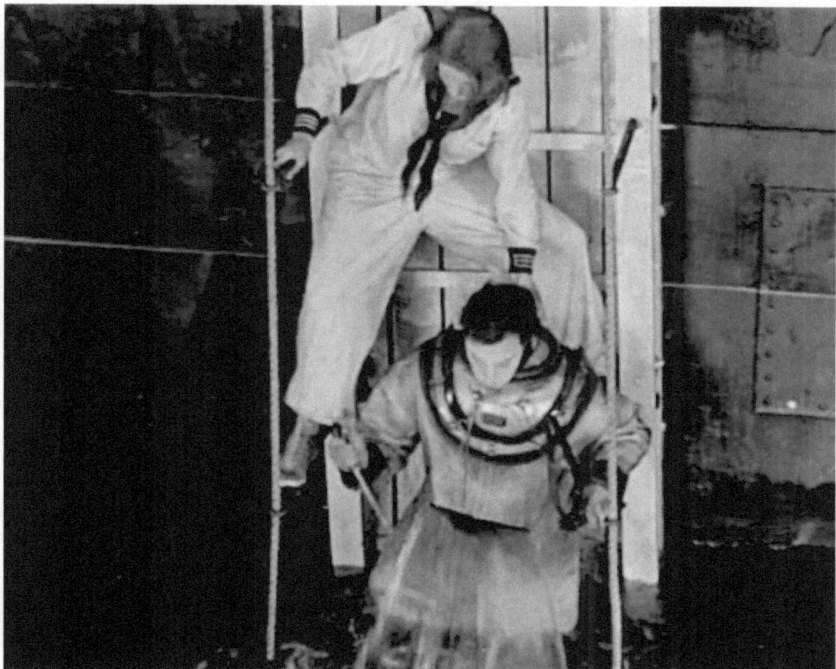

Figure 18. *The Navigator* (1924).

image rendered so well the violent metaphor of giving birth, by caesarean section and explosion of the amniotic sac.[5]

I'm not especially concerned here with Deleuze's misattribution of the surgical task, although his memory makes for a better gag in the fuller symmetry it gives the gender reversal. Deleuze's discussion of cinematic metaphor has two points of interest. The first is that metaphor is one of the means by which thought is introduced into the image. Thought emerges from the relation between images or from a single image and the whole. Encompassing both bodies and movement, the whole is much greater than a set of cinematic images because it implies both change and duration. A change to the whole is not simply a translation of space or a rearrangement of parts, but something much more fundamental—a transformation of relations. The whole is in fact comprised of relations, but relation is, significantly, "not a property of objects":[6]

> Relations do not belong to objects, but to the whole, on condition that this is not confused with a closed set of objects. By movement in space,

the objects of a set change their respective positions. But, through relations, the whole is transformed or changes qualitatively. We can say of duration itself or of time, that it is the whole of relations.[7]

Although Deleuze's account of metaphor conceptualizes the operation of thought in the cinematic image by virtue of the connections between images or between the image and the whole that it expresses, his description of the metaphor of the cesarean section nevertheless ignores the sequence's inherent comicality. He leaves open the question of how cinematic metaphor relates to the equivocity of the small form of the action-image that he discusses in relation to Chaplin's filmmaking: in other words, the question between what he describes earlier as *metaphor* and what the first cinema book theorizes as an instance of *the comic*. Is there, in fact, an equivalence between the image of Keaton being born through cesarean section and another of Chaplin, seen from behind, apparently convulsing with sobs because his wife has left him (where in actuality he is shaking a cocktail to celebrate her departure), or yet another of Keaton filling the mortar of a cannon with gun powder as if he were pinching salt from a salt cellar? Each of these gags similarly rely on the harmonics of the image or of images, whether established through a montage of images or by a second image figurally operating in the first.[8] Deleuze's respective comments on metaphor and cinematic comedy suggest that both equivocity and metaphor involve either a splitting of the image to make two interpretations possible, or a doubling of the image where the literal photographic image of the action is supplemented by a second, figural image. In both cases, the visual qualities of the cinematic image provide the basis for harmonics. If in the cinema books Deleuze shows no interest in distinguishing between the comic and poetic deployment of images, we can nevertheless see that in spite of his suggestion that Chaplin's images are comic and his inference that Keaton's are metaphorical, in both cases we see a very wide gap separating the two images.

THE COMIC AND THE POETIC

The question of the significance of the operation of thought in the poetic and the comic similarly emerges in Lyotard's disagreement with Lacan and Jakobson over their claims that the primary processes have equivalent functions in language. Jakobson claims that condensation and displacement come under the metalinguistic category of contiguity, but Lacan's view has become almost an orthodoxy in language and literature departments the world over: condensation is taken to be synonymous with metaphor and displacement with metonymy.[9] Yet in the case of Lacan, whether jokes and gags are considered subcategories of rhetorical figures, whether the relation between sense (meaning) and nonsense that we had thought specific to the joke in fact derives from the figurative aspects of these devices, or, the inverse, is not altogether clear. Perhaps rhetorical figures rather derive from quasi-physical operations such as condensation and displacement?

Lyotard, for his part, levels a broad criticism at both Jakobson and Lacan, suggesting that the divergence between their ascription of synonymous operations to rhetoric and the primary process "results from applying to one field of expression categories borrowed from another, an undertaking which is motivated by the desire to find in the dream-work the operations of speech."[10] Lyotard's wish is to prove precisely the opposite. That is, that linguistic signs and rhetorical figures are fundamentally different from the operations of the primary process. By equating the dream-work with mechanisms of signification as they are conceived by structural linguistics, both Lacan and Jakobson, he argues, miss the point—the de(con)structive impetus—of the operations of the dream-work. The function of linguistic signs in ordinary signification is based on their intelligibility and meaning, whereas in the dream such signs are subject to a kind of quasi-physical manhandling that destroys the intelligible relation between signifier and signified and skews meaning. Composed of both intelligible signs and rhetorical figures, literary discourse (at least before the advent of psychoanalysis and deconstruction) has meaning because it is attributable to an agent or author who is responsible for ensuring that all the aspects of the work communicate with one another. Coming from the unconscious, on the other hand, the dream results from the conflictual relation between desire and repression. And whereas the rhetorical operations of the figure in literary discourse are open to conventional hermeneutic interpretation, in the field of the dream the meaning of the dream-thoughts can be arrived at only by *undoing* the scrambling of signification that has taken place. In the former, it is a question of finding the meaning of the text. In the latter, it is a matter of restoring its sense.

By Lyotard's reckoning, the operations of the primary process therefore are not reducible to rhetorical figures. Condensation and metaphor, for example, must rather be understood as different kinds of figuration. Whereas metaphor involves the determination of meaning, condensation involves its destruction. For Lyotard, this comes about because the compressive force of condensation treats words as if they were things (and the thing is not synonymous with the signified, although for Lyotard the signified can be treated by the primary process as a thing). The primary process mixes up the components of signification, the sign, the signified, the signifier, and the thing, so that their sense is obliterated. Ironically, Lyotard argues for an irreducibility (a nonmetaphoricity) between the operations of the fields of linguistic discourse and the unconscious.

However apt Lyotard's criticisms of Jakobson and Lacan are with regard to the operations of condensation and displacement in the dream and the figures of language, we have seen already that the configuration of sense and nonsense, and the impact of the primary process on meaning, varies between the dream and the joke. This difference will doubtless also impact the conceptualization of the relation between metaphor and the gag.

The dream, for instance, makes sense in two ways. The first is when secondary revision, the spin doctor of the psyche, operates as the counterforce to the unconscious' exertion of a kind of magnetic pressure on the contents of the preconscious. Secondary revision takes hold of the nonsensical dream and restores to it a façade that appears to make sense. This meaning, however, is completely at odds with the meaning of the "original" dream-thoughts. The second way the dream makes sense comes from its interpretation. The nonsense or revised sense of the manifest content of the dream has its sense restored by the analyst because he or she undoes mechanisms of condensation, displacement, pictographic regression, and secondary revision. In the joke (and in some instances in the gag), the operations of the primary process must be understood in their capacity to permit the *double play* of sense and nonsense. The joke makes sense in two ways, depending on whether it is an innocent joke or a tendentious one. As Freud notes, the joke is a "double-dealing rascal," two-faced, a Janus head. In the innocent joke, a preconscious thought is articulated through irrational processes. The innocence of the innocent joke in this respect can be thought of as the innocence of content and unconscious *desire* manifests itself in the transformation of the innocent joke's *form*. In the tendentious joke, the *content* of the preconscious thought itself is transformed by condensation and displacement to express an unconscious desire. And this desire expresses itself in a conceptual manner. Even so, the meaning of the joke or gag here is produced not as a result of any intentional act but because of the repetition compulsion, that is, "the power of the repressed."[11] This does not mean that compromise formations (such as the joke or gag) are meaningless, but that no consciousness underwrites their meaning. In the cases of both innocent and tendentious jokes, sense is simultaneously made and destroyed. Where Bataille emphasizes the sacrifice of meaning in the sovereign operation of the comic, and Lyotard insists on the destructive nature of the operations of the dream-work, Freud's treatment of the comic delineates multiple and varying relations between sense and nonsense.

THE GAG AND METAPHOR

Barthes is the first theorist of cinema to insist on a "deconstructive" relationship between metaphor and the cinematic gag. Buried among a collection of his most aphoristic writings, we find a brief but tantalizing allusion to a few sequences in the Marx Brothers' film *A Night at the Opera* (1935) and a claim that the comic performs a kind of logical subversion of the text while laughter frees metaphor from the constraint of meaning. Barthes writes:

> What a textual treasury [sic].... If some critical demonstration requires an allegory in which the wild mechanics of the text-on-a-spree explodes, the film will provide it for me: the steamer cabin, the torn contract, the final chaos of opera decors—each of these episodes (among others) is the emblem of the logical subversions performed by the Text; and if these emblems are perfect, it is ultimately because they are comic, laughter being what, by a last reversal, releases demonstration from its demonstrative attribute. What liberates metaphor, symbol, emblem from poetic *mania*, what manifests its power of subversion, is the *preposterous*, that "bewilderment" which Fourier was so good at getting into his examples, to the scorn of any rhetorical respectability (*Sade, Fourier, Loyola*). The logical future of metaphor would therefore be the gag.[12]

While Barthes's summation of the gag and his argument for it as the logical future of metaphor is without doubt very suggestive, the precise steps that inscribe the movement from metaphor to the gag are less than clear. At the very least, Barthes's mobilization of such claims for the gag warrants a further analysis of the difference between metaphor and the gag, a delineation of precisely how laughter "releases demonstration from its demonstrative attribute," and how metaphor is liberated from making sense (meaning). It also begs the question of whether the gag sublates metaphor or constitutes something altogether different.

By examining the Marx Brothers' gags that Barthes cites, we can expand what he has in mind with regard to the preposterous deployment of demonstration, metaphor, symbol, and emblem, and the contribution of the primary processes to the comicality of the sequences. (Mellencamp has previously discussed both Barthes's characterization of the Marx Brothers' gags in relation to condensation and displacement *and* metaphor and metonymy, although she has avoided addressing the issue of how the gag releases metaphor from its demonstrative function and hence whether the operations of the primary process can really be reconciled with rhetorical figures.[13])

In the "torn contract" scene from *A Night at the Opera*, Groucho searches around back stage at the theater looking for a man who has been described to him as "the greatest tenor in the world." When Groucho announces his quest to Chico, Chico understands "the tenor" in question as his own client, Ricardo. This "confusion" can, in Freudian terms, be understood as a kind of condensation. Groucho immediately wants to sign up Ricardo for the New York Opera Company and after a brief discussion of matters monetary, he hands Chico a contract for his perusal and signature. In terms of narrative exposition, the farce that follows gives Chico and Ricardo a reason to go to New York. It also reveals certain aspects of Groucho's shyster character and Chico's illiteracy:

DRIFTWOOD : Now here are the contracts. Put his name at the top and you sign at the bottom. There's no need of you reading that because these are duplicates. Yeah, they's a duplicates...
FIORELLO: (*quietly and without either fully understanding or wanting to admit it*): Duplicates.
DRIFTWOOD: I say they're duplicates.
FIORELLO: Why sure they's a duplicates
DRIFTWOOD: Don't you know what duplicates are?
FIORELLO: Sure, those five kids up in Canada.
DRIFTWOOD: Well, I wouldn't know about that. I haven't been to Canada in years. Well go ahead and read it.
FIORELLO: What does it say?
DRIFTWOOD: Well, go on and read it.
FIORELLO: You read it.
DRIFTWOOD: All right, I'll read it to ya. Can you hear?
FIORELLO: I haven't heard anything yet. Did you say anything?
DRIFTWOOD: Well, I haven't said anything worth hearing.
FIORELLO: Well that's why I didn't hear anything.
DRIFTWOOD: Well that's why I didn't say anything.
FIORELLO: Can you read?
DRIFTWOOD: (*struggling to read the fine print*): I can read, but I can't see it. I don't seem to have it in focus here. If my arms were a little longer I could read it. You haven't got a baboon in your pocket have ya? Here, here, here we are, now I've got it. Now pay particular attention to this first clause because it's most important. It says the uh, "the party of the first part shall be known in this contract as the party of the first part." How do you like that? That's pretty neat, eh?
FIORELLO: No, it's no good.
DRIFTWOOD: What's the matter with it?
FIORELLO: I don't know. Let's hear it again.
DRIFTWOOD: It says the, uh, "The party of the first part shall be known in this contract as the party of the first part."
FIORELLO (*pausing*) It sounds a little better this time.
DRIFTWOOD: Well it grows on ya. Would you like to hear it once more?
FIORELLO: Uh, just the first part.
DRIFTWOOD: What do you mean? The party of the first part?

FIORELLO: No! The first part of the party of the first part.
DRIFTWOOD: All right. It says the, uh, "The first part of the party of the first part shall be known in this contract as the first part of the party of the first part shall be known in this contract"—look why should we quarrel about a thing like this. We'll take it right out, eh?
FIORELLO Yeah, it's a too long anyhow. (*They both tear off the tops of their contracts.*) Now, what do we got left?
DRIFTWOOD: Well I've got about a foot and a half. Now its says, "The party of the second part shall be known in this contract as the party of the second part."
FIORELLO: Well I don't know about that...
DRIFTWOOD: Now what's the matter?
FIORELLO: I don't like the second party either.
DRIFTWOOD: Well, you should've come to the first party. We didn't get home 'til around four in the morning.... I was blind for three days!
FIORELLO: Hey look, why can't a the first part of the second party be the second part of the first party? Then you gotta something.
DRIFTWOOD: Well, look, uh, rather than go through all of that again, what do you say?
FIORELLO: Fine. (*They rip out a portion of the contract.*)
DRIFTWOOD: Now, uh, now I've got something you're bound to like. You'll be crazy about it.
FIORELLO: No, I don't like it.
DRIFTWOOD: You don't like what?
FIORELLO: Whatever it is, I don't like it.
DRIFTWOOD: Well, don't let's break up an old friendship over a thing like that. Ready?...
FIORELLO: OK! (*Another part is torn off.*) Now the next part I don't think you're gonna like.
DRIFTWOOD: Well your word's good enough for me. (*They rip out another part.*) Now then, is my word good enough for you?
FIORELLO: I should say not.
DRIFTWOOD: Well that takes out two more clauses. (*They rip out two more parts.*) Now, "The party of the eighth part..."
FIORELLO: No, that'sa no good. (*more ripping.*) No.
DRIFTWOOD: "The party of the ninth part..."
FIORELLO: No, that'sa no good too. (*they rip the contracts again until there's practically nothing left.*) Hey, how is it that my contract is skinnier than yours?
DRIFTWOOD: Well, I don't know, you must have been out on a tear last night. But anyhow we're all set now aren't we?

FIORELLO: Oh, sure.
DRIFTWOOD: (*Offering his pen to sign the contract*): Now just, uh, you just you put your name down there and then the deal is legal.
FIORELLO: I forgot to tell you I can't write.
DRIFTWOOD: Well, that's all right, there's no ink in the pen anyhow. But listen, it's a contract isn't it?
FIORELLO: Oh sure.
DRIFTWOOD: We got a contract...
FIORELLO: You bet.
DRIFTWOOD: No matter how small it is...
FIORELLO: Hey wait, wait, what does this say here? This thing here.
DRIFTWOOD: Oh, that? Oh, that's the usual clause. That's in every contract. That just says uh, it says uh, "If any of the parties participating in this contract is shown not to be in their right mind, the agreement is automatically nullified."
FIORELLO: Well I don't know...
DRIFTWOOD: It's alright, that's in every contract. That's, that's what they call a "sanity clause."
FIORELLO: Ha ha ha ha ha! You can't fool me! There ain't no Sanity Clause!

The dialogue of the sequence is crucial both to the scene's overall comic effect and, to some extent, to the illustration of how condensation and displacement release metaphor from its demonstrative function. The metaphorical function of the sequence involves the exploitation of the illiterate, naïve, and gullible Fiorello (Chico) by the hoodwinker Driftwood (Groucho). As the occasion for the demonstration of contractual arrangement, the sequence bears on the nature of negotiation and exchange. Chico's verbal illiteracy is acknowledged and his broken English further demonstrates his lack of verbal acumen. But his linguistic incapacity also becomes the means for him to turn the tables on Groucho at strategic moments in the negotiating process. Furthermore, in the dialogue the nonsense of condensation and displacement (duplicates/quintuplets, party/party, sanity clause/Santa Claus) is only relative to the more thoroughgoing nonsense of Chico's complete sacrifice of sense to the maintenance of his bargaining position and Groucho's willingness to go to any length to humor him. The sequence thus becomes a parody of a haggling ritual between business associates. The posturing and the preening in turn give way to more preposterous absurdities: one party cannot read, the contract lacks pertinence to the deal being negotiated, and the one thing not ripped from the contract is the implicitly nullified sanity clause. Indeed, could either of these men be said to be of sound mind?

The extension of metaphorical demonstration into preposterous spectacle is also brought about visually. Throughout the sequence the framing predominantly shows Groucho and Chico standing side by side, both facing the camera as though performing a duet. The camera, however, occasionally cuts to a single shot of one of them. Mostly it cuts to Groucho and the effect is to make his communication with the audience more immediate than Chico's. Indeed, Chico's exclusion from view at these points, coupled with Groucho's wide-eyed incredulous responses to his comic naïvete, make him the butt of the jokes. This mode of direct address also serves to inscribe the audience as a presence within the film, positioning them, as Mellencamp has suggested, as the third person of the joke relationship, the one whose laughter confers the status of the joke upon the enunciation.[14] The episode, so framed, is more operatic or theatrical than cinematic.

Barthes cites the steamer cabin sequence as another case in point. Here the demonstration of the uncomfortable smallness of Groucho's room quickly gives way to the emblematization of condensation and displacement operating together. The scene uses vaudevillian style comic performance to displace plausible realism. Interestingly, the point is not that physical space is being compressed as much as its contents are multiplied many times over. Groucho has arrived at his cabin on board the steamship to find it somewhat cozier than expected, and fittingly delivers the first of a series of verbal jokes complaining about the size of the room, suggesting to the steward that he might as well put the cabin in his trunk as put the trunk in his cabin. The trunk fills almost the entire floor space of the cabin. When Groucho opens it, who should emerge but Chico, Ricardo, and Harpo, and they only agree to leave the cabin if they are first given something to eat. Groucho rings for the steward, and the conversation between them sets the tenor for the pandemonium that follows. Groucho not only asks for everything under the sun, but includes all variations on every genre of sustenance. Moreover, his ordering is interspersed with a chorus from Chico and Harpo—Chico intermittently insists on having two hard-boiled eggs, Harpo follows with a honk.

Inside the cabin, the expectation of the four men awaiting the arrival of food is thwarted many times over by a constant stream of unknown personages into the room. The first knock sees the entry of two maids who have come to make up the bed. Groucho admits them into the, needless to say, already overcrowded room while Ricardo lifts the sleeping Harpo so that the women can perform their tasks. Harpo is unconscious in more than one sense, somnambulism providing him with a cover to sleepily grope the women. One woman stands on top of the bed; Ricardo is squashed behind the trunk; the second maid, Harpo, Chico, and Groucho fill the bottom of the frame, lined up like sardines in a can. A second rap on the door signals the arrival of the electrician who has come to turn off the heat. Next enters the manicurist, who is promptly given Harpo's foot to groom. As each person struggles within the cabin's rapidly decreasing space, the frame becomes saturated with increasingly compromised gestures. Still, the compression continues. A huge engineer's assistant enters, then a stranger looking for her Aunt Minnie, then the cleaner to mop up, and finally four servants bearing the platters of food.

If the quality in need of metaphorical demonstration is the smallness of the room, smallness is conveyed as soon as the trunk is inserted. To transform the metaphor into a gag, the image, like Groucho's "verbosity," is milked for all its possible significations, all of its mutative potential. Our interest in the smallness of the room is quickly lost to the unrelenting demonstration of the point, to the variety of means the brothers summon to make it again and again, to the spectacle of signification itself rather than its meaning, and, one might even say, to the spectacle of condensation. This episode has no development of meaning; its purpose is to exhibit rather than to tell. And what it exhibits is the gag's capacity to proliferate. Condensation and displacement are the means by which metaphor, taken to the level of the comic, is "liberated" from meaning. They open restricted economy to the pandemonium of general economy.

ARISTOTELIAN METAPHOR

To better ascertain how the comic liberates signification from restricted meaning, we need a more rigorous formulation of the conceptual basis for metaphor. Derrida affords us some satisfaction in his theorization of both the demonstrative function of metaphor and its limits in his essay, "White Mythology: Metaphor in the Text of Philosophy."[15] The locus of his enquiry is for the most part concentrated on the operation of metaphor in philosophical conceptualization. He justifies his focus on the Aristotelian definition of metaphor on the basis that it is a definition that has barely altered since its inception, and its logic encompasses subsequent formulations and refinements:

> Metaphor (*metaphora*) consists in giving (*epiphora*) the thing a name (*onomatos*) that belongs to something else (*allotriou*), the transference being either from genus to species (*apo tou genous epi eidos*), or from species to genus (*apo tou eidous epi to genos*), or from species to species (*apo tou eidous epi eidos*), or on the grounds of analogy (*e kata to analogon*). ("WM," 231)

Aristotelian metaphor involves the substitution of one term for another on the basis that the things that the two terms designate share a common property. It is the practice of giving a thing a name that properly belongs to something else. Derrida proposes that the necessary condition for such metaphor, for the "extractions and exchanges" that underwrite its existence, "is that the essence of a concrete subject be capable of several properties, and then that a particular permutation between essence and what is proper to (and inseparable from) it be possible, within the medium of a quasi-synonymy" ("WM," 249). It also implies the structure of analogy (indeed, Derrida suggests that analogy is Aristotelian metaphor par excellence): where the property A is to B as the property C is to D. D can thus replace B because it is authorized by the equivalence between A and C.

What metaphor demonstrates then is a "theoretical" likeness between things. In the first three kinds of metaphor, where substitution or eclipse is involved, the demonstration entails indicating an absent property or thing. In the case of analogy, the likeness is demonstrated with all the terms being present.

Worth mentioning, if only parenthetically, is that by mapping Lyotard's reading of the Lacanian algorithm onto the Aristotelian formula for analogy we can see that Lacan's model of metaphor is indeed a reconceptualization of the Aristotelian structure of analogy along semiotic lines. The Lacanian definition of metaphor is expressed in the following algorithm:

$$f\left(\frac{S'}{S}\right) S \cong S(+)s$$

Lyotard reads the algorithm according to the following key: S = signifier; s = signified; S' = metaphor itself—the term which eclipses s; $f\left(\frac{S'}{S}\right)$ = the metaphoric function (the eclipsing of one signifier by another—hence S is underneath or buried by S'); $S (+) s$ = the emergence of signification; the bar (—) "separates the signifier and the signified, it is the mark of 'nonsense.' Crossed (+) by the metaphor, it re-establishes contact between signifier and signified and thus establishes meaning."[16]

The classical (Aristotelian) model can be substituted for Lacan's where $S = B$, $s =$ either A or C, $S' = D$. Although Lacan claims that his model is consistent with Saussurean semiotics, Lyotard argues that what underwrites the stability of the signified has nothing to do with the linguistic realm, but instead comes from the sensible world (of the referent). In other words, the relationship it implies between the signifier, signified, and the sign differs from the one specified by Saussurean linguistics. In the latter, the arbitrary and transparent relationship between the signifier and the signified makes language *intelligible*, whereas the Lacanian definition implies that the relation constituted between the signifier and the signified is one of *meaning*. The Saussurean theory of signification is, according to Lyotard, a theory of the intelligibility of language, whereas the Lacanian theory of metaphor, while claiming to be structuralist, inscribes a relation between language and the sensible world to produce meaning. Rather than the formula proving the existence of the signified, the substitution is authorized by the preexistent meaning of the terms in question, and in this respect, metaphor is demonstrative.

The Aristotelian conception of metaphor, Derrida shows, is embroiled in a particular set of relationships between language, thought, meaning, and truth, so the importance of the demonstrative function of metaphor lies not simply in its capacity to create meaning, but in its situation within a conceptual scaffolding, a powerful ontology that institutes:

> a certain systematic indissociability of the value of metaphor and the metaphysical chain holding together the values of discourse, voice, noun, signification, meaning, imitative representation, resemblance; or, in order to reduce what these translations import or deport, the values of logos, *phone, semantike, semainein, onoma, mimesis, homoiosis.* ("WM," 237)

The consequences of the Aristotelian schema are such that philosophy conceives meaning to be independent of language, emanating, however indirectly, from nature revealing itself mimetically through language. Meaning is understood to preexist the language through which it is simply transported. Which is to say that the emphasis of the Aristotelian theory of metaphor is that metaphor is meaningful because meaning exists in the natural world (*physis*). Metaphor demonstrates this meaning either indirectly, by substituting one term for another, or directly, by showing that two terms share a common property as in the case of analogy. Because of this independence from the (linguistic) form that articulates it, philosophical thought thinks it is justified in claiming itself to be true.

In delimiting "the general functioning and effective limits of this chain," Derrida discloses how the schema does not simply describe indisputable and value-free conditions but privileges a certain conception of metaphor at the expense of others ("WM," 230). The one it privileges is no less than the demonstrative metaphor that rests unobtrusively within the schema, contained by it, and functioning to support it. This is good metaphor. It is metaphor in which the properties of the things being compared can both be named and judged to belong to them properly. Good metaphors are generally considered to be substantives (nouns and verbs, sometimes adjectives and adverbs, but definitely not conjunctions and elements that can claim no existence in the natural world). Such metaphors demonstrate the property of the thing they replace and are therefore approved and supported by a metaphysics whose imperative is the constitution of truth.

Nevertheless Derrida also shows that not all metaphors demonstrate properties that, although temporarily elided in language, in fact exist in the real world. Bad metaphors by contrast are catechreses, words that do not participate in the unity of being because they have no substantive basis. Derrida argues, for example, that the metaphysical conception of good, authentic, legitimate metaphor, metaphor that is kept good by being restricted to naming through analogy the authentic properties of the thing, is called into question as soon as metaphor loses its point of reference in the natural world, and it is acknowledged, on the one hand, that metaphors exist that have no properties (as in the example of the wineless cup of Ares), and, on the other hand, metaphors that name nonexistent properties (such as the sun that sows).

Bad metaphor is also permitted a more extensive play than good metaphor. The adventure of meaning that bad metaphor embarks on comes about because language can produce thought and meaning internally through its own form. As such, Derrida proposes a metaphoricity that endlessly displaces meaning and gives rise to a general condition of overdeterminability, a condition where all words begin to mean more than they designate and run the risk of sending meaning off on a course independent from nature. This conceptual possibility, he argues, is implicit in the Aristotelian definition, but repressed or disavowed because it undermines his theory of truth, the proper and the whole system of concepts on which the philosopheme of metaphor is based:

> It risks disrupting the semantic plenitude [the identity of meaning and being] to which it should belong. Marking the moment of the turn or the detour [*du tour ou du détour*] during which meaning might seem to venture forth alone, unloosed from the very thing it aims at however, from the truth which attunes it to its referent, metaphor also opens the wandering of the semantic. ("WM," 241)

The metaphor of metaphor, the metaphor that doubles its metaphysical counterpart, has the tendency to lead off to unknown places. Indeed, it has the capacity to embark on just those kinds of adventure that we expect from the primary process.

Although Derrida does not explicitly enter into the debate about the analogy between rhetorical figures and Freud's mechanisms of the dreamwork, he nevertheless makes an explicit reference to Freud's *Interpretation of Dreams* at the beginning of the section, "The Flowers of Rhetoric: The Heliotrope," citing Freud's comments that "[dreams] show a particular preference for combining contraries into a unity or for representing them as one and the same thing," that dream formation has a preference for relations of "similarity (*Ähnlichkeit*), consonance (*Übereinstimmung*) or approximation (*Berührung*)," and that "Aristotle remarked in this connection that the best interpreter of dreams was the man who could best grasp similarities" ("WM," 245–46). Yet the concept of overdetermination that Derrida uses to question the parameters of the field within which metaphor traditionally has been considered to operate entails precisely the condensation and displacement that Freud specifies as the operations of the primary process:

> The metaphorization of metaphor, its bottomless overdeterminability, seems to be inscribed in the structure of metaphor, but as its negativity. As soon as one admits that all the terms in an analogical relation already are caught up, one by one, in a metaphorical relation, everything begins to function no longer as a sun, but as a star, the punctual source of truth or properness remaining invisible or nocturnal. ("WM," 243–44)

Derrida thus deconstructs the historical opposition between good and bad metaphor to show not the limitation of the latter by the former, but the prevalence of the latter—of bad metaphor—and of its capacity as a concept to contaminate all usage of language, both linguistic and rhetorical.

So the divergence between the structuralist homogenization of poetic devices and unconscious operations and Lyotard's insistence on their irreducibility on the grounds that the purpose of poetic metaphor is to make meaning and that of the primary process is to destroy it ("the dream-work does not think") is to some extent displaced by both Deleuze's and Derrida's more rigorous conceptual expositions of metaphor. Deleuze's and Derrida's attention to the precise nature of language's generation of thought, and indeed their departure from classical metaphysical assumptions about the subordination of language to representational meaning, is borne out in Deleuze's emphasis on relationality and his insistence that relations are not properties of the thing but come from the whole and Derrida's deconstruction of the tendency to subordinate bad metaphor to good metaphor. The rigorous conceptual grounding of metaphor also goes some way toward displacing Bataille's arguments against the possibility of the sovereignty of the poetic. This is because for both Deleuze and Derrida meaning is not something that discourse represents, and thought is not some intangible, elusive thing whose only guarantee is its mimetic relation to nature. Rather, discourse generates thought. Overdeterminability shows that the thought that language generates is not contained by it, that thought unloosed from its representational function has the capacity to go off on its own adventure.

Whereas contemporary writers Paul Patton and François Zourabichvili have examined the correspondences between Deleuze's and Derrida's articulations of metaphoricity to demonstrate their reconceptualization of philosophical metaphor along antirepresentational lines and to emphasize philosophy's generation of concepts through language,[17] I want to pursue the consequences of this poststructuralist conception of thought along slightly different lines. In particular, I want to consider the consequences of Derrida's restitution of bad metaphor for the "classical" cinema with which this book has been concerned. I want to think through the way the comic operates in accordance with the conditions of "bad metaphor" and how it derives from the visual conditions of cinema a special capacity to generate bad metaphors. In line with the Derridean conception of metaphor, these instances of the comic emerge from the overdetermination of the image, from the visual image's ability to generate meaning independently of the world it represents. They emerge, in other words, from the cinema's own figural conditions. We've seen abundant evidence of this already—in comic literalizations emerging from the relation between words and images, in the condensation of visual gags and the displacement that forms the basis of narrative structure. In the discussion that follows, I also want to consider how slapstick—another figural dimension of cinema—operates to hide them.

CINEMATIC METAPHOR AND COMIC VISUALITY

If the operation of metaphor in language works by mobilizing the properties of two things and swapping between linguistic terms on the basis of the similarity of these properties, metaphor in cinema comes into play through visual means. Philosophically speaking, the issue of visual resemblance presents an interesting set of problems. On the one hand, Derrida very convincingly shows the importance of vision in the operation of philosophical catechresis. Philosophy has a propensity to make the light of the sun, as a precondition for vision, a trope for knowledge (evident in terms such as *elucidate, illuminate,* and so forth). Philosophy as such orbits around the figure of the sun. And yet philosophy in general also distrusts the capacity of the senses to apprehend the truth. Certainly it does not hold to the axiom that seeing is believing. Nor does it trust the visual image's capacity to produce knowledge. This is not just emblematized by Descartes in the *Dioptrics*. It dates back to the deceptive appearances visually apprehended by the prisoners in Plato's Cave and his subsequent determination to exclude artists and their simulacra from the Republic. In this regard, it might be just as well that cinema has not claimed for itself the capacity to philosophize in the traditional sense of the term (as part of the Aristotelian ontology that philosophy both produces and situates itself within). In traditional terms, whether *visuality* is a valid property for identifying common likeness between things, whether it upholds the distinction between essences and properties that authorizes the metaphorical production of truth, is altogether questionable.

On the other hand, metaphor in cinema does not substitute *the names* of properties to produce theoretical (conceptual) knowledge of the relations between things. It produces meaning on the basis of visual resemblance. The arbitrary relationship between signifier and signified that supports the philosophical conception of metaphor by providing a supposedly neutral medium

Figure 19. *Sherlock Jr.* (1924).

in which to represent the truth of nature is in cinema replaced by a motivated iconic or indexical one and the metaphors that emerge do not eclipse the things or their properties but retain them. The very disposition toward the poetic that this visuality affords to cinema is, however, more often than not abstained from—in favor of asserting the cinema's predisposal to realism and its capacity to imitate reality—or set aside for the comic.

Cinematic metaphor would be bad metaphor in as much as it is produced by and often denotes nothing more than specious visual resemblance or sensory harmonics. Visuality is first and foremost what disposes cinema to a kind of poetics (although this does not preclude the possibility of aural harmonics or even synaesthesic ones). The unrestrained use of such harmonics, their extension beyond the production of meaning through motif and theme, turns the poetic into the comic. And as far as the comic has a capacity to insinuate itself into every structure of meaning, it redeploys metaphor for its own ends by appropriating the "turns" of bad metaphor, by orchestrating "figurative" exchanges. In such exchanges, we find properties that lack equivalence (either by being less than them in the case of the comic, or other to them in the case of the joke), or images that are drawn to each other only by numerous specious connections between the intermediate terms (the recursion

Figure 20. *The Navigator* (1924). Courtesy of Photofest.

function) or notions that embark on semantic detours or adventures that don't return to the truth (as in the Marx Brother's gags).

Let's return, by way of example, to the maternal figure, or the birth image, encountered in the cesarean section gag in *The Navigator*. Numerous other comical references to the maternal can be located in the film. It is notable that both Rollo and the girl are motherless, and that they both take to sleeping in storage compartments of the ship that resemble huge womblike orifices. The ship, once set adrift, becomes their mother, apprentices them to the tasks of domestic living and affords them the opportunity to learn how to nurture and care for themselves and each other. Another such reference to the maternal, or at least to being born, occurs when, on the second day of their adventure adrift on the ship, the couple, desperately searching for each other, finally give up the chase, and Rollo is sucked down one of the funnels and delivered, this time breech birth, to the girl on the deck below. Once acknowledged, the maternal figure starts to contaminate everything, starts proliferating virtual images, subjecting the mise-en-scène to both figurative meaning and comic ridiculousness. The film starts to be about the absent mother, these lost children.

Certain other images link the absence of the mother to the thematic of navigation. The source of the figure of navigation is both the title of the film and the name of the boat on which Rollo and the girl have been set adrift. When the boat is unmoored, it is not simply that Rollo and the girl cannot navigate the ship—to begin with they cannot perform or control the most rudimentary domestic tasks. Rollo's navigational ineptitude gives provision for numerous gags—he determines to marry on the basis of a passing whim (following the example of African-American newlyweds whom he happens to spy from his bedroom window in what is undoubtedly a racist joke) and demonstrates a remarkable incompetence at interpreting signs, whether it is the prevailing wind, the girl's desire or the ship's compass.

The figurative dimension of some of these gags from *The Navigator* may come to the fore only in the descriptive mode of film analysis. The resemblance between images is produced through an interpretation of the cinematic object by analysis, more often than by laughter. Although many of the images and sequences are humorous, they are not always sight gags in the strictest sense of the term. We do not get them as we do a joke, they are not readily intelligible in the way that visual puns are. One could not prove, for instance, that the mother was there at all. The maternal figure is a very distant attractor for many of the visual quips in the film. Indeed, *the mother, navigation*, and as we will see, *the treadmill* operate almost like rebuses. Absent words, indeed concepts, exert a pressure on the film. These words transformed into visual quips, once acknowledged, seem somewhat cheesy today, as if the correspondence between word and image were too literal. This explains why claims for their existence will make some people uncomfortable. Perhaps these gags are not just bad metaphors, but bad jokes.

Slapstick, however, functions to disguise such symbolic ordering, as if the truth of cinema's aesthetic capabilities, its poetic propensity, were too much to bear. For example, the breech birth gag is not an isolated gag but tops a comic sequence orchestrated both to bring Rollo and the girl together and to delay their meeting as long as possible. The two characters are thus held apart so that the scene can be milked for comic effect and then finally brought together so that the story can continue. The couple chase each other around the balconies of the upper and lower decks. A long shot shows Rollo and the girl running in opposite directions, fore and aft, alternately covering the port and starboard sides of the boat, each following the other, inscribing not two converging points or lines (as is conventional in chase sequences) but a rotating circle, the two of them representing equidistant points. As the protagonists search for one another on the upper and lower decks, the director pulls the camera back to a long establishing shot, creating in the process the figural image of a treadmill, constructed from the ship's deck (the vertical axis of the treadmill is dropped down onto the horizontal plane), and then a moebius strip, a nightmare image of the eternal impossibility of meeting.

Despite the figure giving rise to thought in these images, the rhythm and movement of slapstick dominates. The characters are caught in a loop; the velocity of movement increases; the shots get shorter. Each perpetually runs after the other until the final surprise delivery of Rollo to the girl. The audience's attention is thus absorbed by the slapstick orchestration of time and space. Such absorption renders other aspects of the mise-en-scène, such as the pictorial harmonics of the birth canal and Keaton's breech delivery, however much they overdetermine the images, almost to nonsymbolic banality. Thus the maternal figure deployed in the sight gag is simultaneously inscribed in the cinematic image and disguised by the slapstick. The maternal figure is there in the harmonics of the image, but the slapstick of the sequence draws the audience's attention to the orchestration of events, to the protraction of narrative time and space, and their final fortuitous contraction in the protagonists' meeting. So, if metaphor affords thought to the image, slapstick simultaneously works to hide it. The slapstick orchestration of time and space both hides figurative meaning and presents it in a form where its "truth" might be taken as nonsense. But "in truth" what it does not quite succeed in hiding is the nonsense that lies at the origin of sense.

ை

From its birth, the *magic* of cinema has generally been understood not just as its capacity to "capture" movement but as its ability to defy the laws of the physical universe, whether by reversing time, conjuring things from nothing, resuscitating the dead, or killing the living. In addition we might think about comic montage, about the special capacity of cinema to bring together images that stand on opposite sides of the universe, as part of the this magic. This pa(i)ring of images, this displacement and condensation, involves more than what Lev Kuleshov demonstrated in his "creative geography" experiments in the 1910s that spliced images of people on the streets in Russia with images of the White House to produce a seamless syntagmatic construction. Indeed, we should heed Lyotard's insistence that we not forget that the physicality of condensation implies both compression and a change in the state of things (such as when gas becomes liquid). A new configuration of space is born by compressing the three dimensional visual field into the two dimensions of the frame, then adding movement to the two-dimensional image, then pausing and connecting it with the whole, and thereby setting it in motion once again. This new space engenders images that can never quite be contained and that are capable of regenerating themselves. The fruit of the connection between images, or between the image and the whole, affords cinema a fundamental break with the realism that so many theorists think constitutes its essence. Whether inadvertently or intentionally, the 1920s' comedians were attuned to not so much the medium's capacity for representing reality, but its means of constituting it.

Notes

INTRODUCTION

1. Andrew Sarris, *The American Cinema: Directors and Directions 1929–1968* (New York: Dutton, 1969); Sarris, "Notes on Auteur Theory in 1962" in Gerald Mast et al., eds., *Film Theory and Criticism: Introductory Readings*, 4th ed. (New York: Oxford University Press, 1992).

2. Jean-Patrick Lebel, *Buster Keaton*, trans. P. D. Stovin (London: Zwemmer Limited, 1967).

3. Daniel Moews, *Keaton: The Silent Features Close Up* (Berkeley: University of California Press, 1977).

4. Of course other monographs on Buster Keaton could be mentioned here. For a thorough bibliography of published literature on Keaton, see Joanna E. Rapf and Gary L. Green, *Buster Keaton: A Bio-Bibliography* (Westport: Greenwood Press, 1995).

5. Walter Kerr, *The Silent Clowns* (New York: Knopf, 1975).

6. Although Mast probably gives more attention to Sennett films than most other historians of cinematic comedy, he deals with them in a relatively perfunctory way in one chapter of his book. Mast's justification for this is his declaration that his book is concerned with "the intellectual complexity of comic films," with establishing that "a specific breed of clown...did think" (1), and his assertion that "the most strikingly serious element of Keystone capers is that they do not contain a single serious element." Gerald Mast, *The Comic Mind: Comedy and the Movies*, 2nd ed. (Chicago: University of Chicago Press, 1979), 53.

7. Steve Seidman, *Comedian Comedy: A Tradition in Hollywood Film* (Ann Arbor: University Microfilms International Research Press, 1981).

8. Frank Krutnik, "The Clown-Prints of Comedy," *Screen* 25.4–5 (1984); Peter Kramer, "Derailing the Honeymoon Express: Comicality and Narrative Closure in Buster Keaton's *The Blacksmith*," *The Velvet Light Trap* 23 (1989).

9. Dana Polan, "Being and Nuttiness: Jerry Lewis and the French," *Journal of Popular Film and Television* 12.1 (1984); Michael Selig, "*The Nutty Professor*: A 'Problem' with Film Scholarship," *The Velvet Light Trap* 26 (1990). See also Frank Krutnik, *Inventing Jerry Lewis* (Washington, DC: Smithsonian Institution Press, 2000).

10. Tom Gunning, "The Cinema of Attraction: Early Film, Its Spectator and the Avant-Garde," *Wide Angle* 8.3–4 (1986).

11. Miriam Hansen, *Babel and Babylon: Spectatorship in American Silent Cinema* (Cambridge, MA: Harvard University Press, 1991).

12. Henry Jenkins, *What Made Pistachio Nuts? Early Sound Comedy and the Vaudeville Aesthetic* (New York: Columbia University Press, 1992).

13. Robert Knopf, *The Theater and Cinema of Buster Keaton* (Princeton, NJ: Princeton University Press, 1999).

14. Jerry Palmer, *The Logic of the Absurd: On Film and Television* (London: British Film Institute, 1987).

15. Steve Neale and Frank Krutnik, *Popular Film and Television Comedy* (London: Routledge, 1990).

16. Jim Cook, ed., *The Television Sitcom: BFI Dossier* 17 (1982).

17. Steve Neale, "Psychoanalysis and Comedy," *Screen* 22.2 (1981); Mick Eaton, "Laughter in the Dark," *Screen* 22.2 (1981).

18. Claire Johnston and Paul Willemen, eds., *Frank Tashlin* (Edinburgh: Edinburgh Film Festival in association with *Screen*, 1973).

19. Patricia Mellencamp, "Jokes and Their Relation to the Marx Brothers," in Stephen Heath and Patricia Mellencamp, eds., *Cinema and Language* (Los Angeles: American Film Institute, 1982).

20. Samuel Weber, "The Divaricator: Remarks on Freud's *Witz*," *Glyph: Johns Hopkins Textual Studies* 1 (1977); Weber, *The Legend of Freud* (Minneapolis: University of Minnesota Press, 1982); Weber, "Laughter in the Meanwhile," *MLN* 102.4 (1987).

1. THE PHILOSOPHY OF LAUGHTER: BATAILLE, HEGEL, AND DERRIDA

1. For a discussion of the relation between play and meaning in the joke see Weber, *The Legend of Freud*.

2. Henri Bergson, *Laughter: An Essay on the Meaning of the Comic*, trans. Cloudesley Brereton and Fred Rothwell (1911; Copenhagen: Green Integer, 1999), 178–9.

3. Georges Bataille, *The College of Sociology (1937–39)*, ed. Dennis Hollier, trans. Betsy Wing (Minneapolis: University of Minnesota Press, 1988); Bataille, *Inner Experience*, trans. Leslie Anne Boldt (Albany: State University of New York Press, 1988); Bataille, *Guilty*, trans. Bruce Boon (Venice, CA: Lapis Press, 1988).

4. See Jacques Derrida's comments on this in "The Pit and the Pyramid: Introduction to Hegel's Semiology," in *Margins of Philosophy*, trans. Alan Bass (Chicago: University of Chicago Press, 1982), 91, n. 19, as well as Hegel, *Aesthetics*, vol. II, trans. T. M. Knox (Oxford, England: Oxford University Press, 1975), 1036; Bataille, *Inner Experience*, 147; Derrida, "From Restricted to General Economy: A Hegelianism without Reserve," in *Writing and Difference*, trans. Alan Bass (Chicago: University of Chicago Press, 1978), 262.

5. For an elaboration of the philosophical, literary, and anthropological influences on Bataille's thought and in turn the influence of his work on postmodernist thinkers, particularly Jean Baudrillard, see Julian Pefanis, *Heterology and the Post-Modern: Bataille, Baudrillard and Lyotard* (Durham: Duke University Press, 1991).

6. Michel Foucault, *L'ordre du discours* (Paris: Gallimard, 1971), 74 , quoted by Vincent Descombes, *Modern French Philosophy*, trans. L. Scott-Fox and J. M. Harding (Cambridge, England: Cambridge University Press, 1980), 12.

7. Derrida, "From Restricted to General Economy," 272.

8. G. W. F. Hegel, *Phenomenology of Spirit*, trans. A. V. Miller (Oxford, England: Oxford University Press, 1977).

9. Georges Bataille, "Un-knowing: Laughter and Tears," *October* 36 (1986): 93.

10. For a discussion of the elaboration of community and contagion throughout Bataille's work see Paul Hegarty, *Georges Bataille: Core Cultural Theorist* (London: Sage, 2000).

11. Bataille, "Un-knowing: Laughter and Tears," 90.

12. Ibid.

13. See Nick Land, *The Thirst for Annihilation: Georges Bataille and Virulent Nihilism* (London: Routledge, 1992), 105–20, and Joseph Libertson, *Proximity: Levinas, Blanchot, Bataille and Communication* (The Hague, Netherlands: Martinus Nijhoff, 1982), 2.

14. Kant, *Critique of Pure Reason*, 2nd ed., trans. Norman Kemp Smith (Basingstoke, England: Macmillan, 1929), 307; Diana Coole, *Negativity and Politics: Dionysus and Dialectics from Kant to Poststructuralism* (London: Routledge, 2000), 29.

15. Nick Land quotes the following passage from Kant:

> The supreme concept with which it is customary to begin a transcendental philosophy is the division into the possible and the impossible. But since all division presupposes a concept to be divided, a still higher one is required, that this is the concept of an object in general, taken problematically, without its having been decided whether it is something or nothing.

The Thirst for Annihilation, 105; Kant, *Collected Works*, vol. III, 305–6.

16. Land, *The Thirst for Annihilation*, 114.

17. Ibid., 116.

18. Libertson, *Proximity*, 1. Hereafter cited in text as *P*.

19. Stanley Rosen comments that Kojève's "interpretation of Hegel is arbitrary and philologically unsound, despite the fact (somehow unexplained by his orthodox academic critics) that it remains the best in the sense of the most philosophical single book ever written about Hegel...." ("Kojève's Paris: A Memoir," *parallax* 4 [1997], 9), and Derrida writes in an endnote to "From Restricted to General Economy," "...for Bataille there was no fundamental rupture between Kojève's reading of Hegel, to which he openly subscribed almost totally, and the true instruction of Marxism" (334), both illustrating the general perception of the incorrectness of Kojève's and Bataille's interpretations of Hegel.

20. Bataille's repudiation of anti-intellectualism and the specificity of his approach to it is indicated in his response to Hemingway:

> ...I think that this anti-intellectualism accounts for that which is basically very limited and entirely anachronistic in the affirmation of the master's morality pursued throughout his work.
>
> ...I believe, in any case, that if the seduction of Hemingway, which is linked to ignorance, can be attained, it will be on one condition only: that we go to the extreme limit of knowledge. It is only beyond knowledge, and perhaps in that un-knowing which I have presented, that we can win the right to ignorance. "Un-knowing: Laughter and Tears," 101–2.

21. Ibid., 102.

22. "Un-Knowing and Its Consequences," *October* 36 (1986): 81.

23. "Un-Knowing: Laughter and Tears," 93.

24. Ibid., 95.

25. Bataille, *Inner Experience*, 108.

26. Bataille, "Hegel, Death and Sacrifice," trans. Jonathan Strauss, *Yale French Studies* 78 (1990),: 11.

27. Ibid., 12.

28. Ibid.

29. Ibid., 13.

30. In "Attraction and Repulsion I: Tropisms, Sexuality, Laughter and Tears," Bataille writes, "[i]f in a communicative reaction of exuberance and general joy a third term interferes, one partaking of the nature of death, it is to the extent that the very dark, repulsive nucleus, around which all turbulence revolves, has created the principle of life out of the category of death, springing out of falling." *The College of Sociology*, 111.

31. Hegarty, *Georges Bataille*, 91.

32. Bataille, "Hegel, Death and Sacrifice," 13.

33. Derrida, "From Restricted to General Economy," 255. Hereafter cited in text as "FRGE."

34. Hegel, *Phenomenology of Spirit*, 115; Derrida, "From Restricted to General Economy," 255.

35. Hegel, ibid., 114–5.

36. Derrida writes for example that the *Aufhebung* "signifies the *busying* of a discourse losing its breath as it reappropriates all negativity for itself."

37. Derrida, 256, Bataille, "*Conférences sur le non-savoir*," *Tel Quel*, 10 (1962).

38. Bataille, "Un-knowing: Laughter and Tears," 89.

39. Michael Richardson, ed., *Georges Bataille: Essential Writings* (London: Sage, 1998), 188.

40. *L'expérience intérieure* (Paris: Gallimard, 1943), 237. Quoted by Derrida, "From Restricted to General Economy," 274.

41. Joseph C. Flay, "Hegel, Derrida and Bataille's Laughter" and Judith Butler, "Commentary on Joseph Flay's 'Hegel, Derrida and Bataille's Laughter,'" in William Desmond, ed., *Hegel and His Critics: Philosophy in the Aftermath of Hegel* (Albany: State University of New York Press, 1989).

42. Butler, "Commentary," in *Hegel and His Critics*, 175.

43. Flay, "Hegel, Derrida and Bataille's Laughter," in Desmond, ed., *Hegel and His Critics*, 166.

44. *Reconfigurations: Critical Theory and General Economy* (Gainesville: University Press of Florida, 1993), 20.

2. RESTRICTED AND GENERAL ECONOMY: NARRATIVE, GAG, AND SLAPSTICK IN *ONE WEEK*

1. Neale and Krutnik, *Popular Film*, 109–1.

2. Roland Barthes, "Introduction to the Structural Analysis of Narratives," in *Image-Music-Text*, trans. Stephen Heath (Glasgow, Scotland: Fontana/Collins, 1977), 79.

3. Robert Stam, Robert Burgoyne, and Sandy Flitterman-Lewis, *New Vocabularies in Film Semiotics: Structuralism, Post-Structuralism and Beyond* (London: Routledge, 1992), 70; Gerald Prince, *A History of Narratology* (Lincoln: University of Nebraska Press, 1987), 60.

4. Hayden White, *The Content of Form: Narrative Discourse and Historical Representation* (Baltimore: Johns Hopkins University Press, 1987), 1.

5. Robert Burgoyne summarizes and analyzes the detail and vicissitudes of these influences in the chapter on film narratology in *New Vocabularies in Film Semiotics*.

6. Raymond Bellour, "To Alternate/To Narrate," trans. Inge Pruks, *Australian Journal of Screen Theory* 15–16 (1983): 35.

7. Janet Bergstrom, "Alternation, Segmentation, Hypnosis: Interview with Raymond Bellour," trans. Susan Suleiman, *Camera Obscura* 3–4 (1979): 84, my emphasis.

8. Jean-François Lyotard, "Acinema," *Wide Angle* 2.3 (1978): 53–4.

9. Barthes, "The Third Meaning: Research Notes on Some Eisenstein Stills," in *Image-Music-Text*, 52–68. Hereafter cited in text as "TTM."

10. Bordwell, *Narration in the Fiction Film* (Madison: University of Wisconsin Press, 1985), 50. Hereafter cited in text as *NFF*.

11. In addition to Bordwell, see Edward Branigan, *Narrative Comprehension and Fiction Film* (London: Routledge, 1992).

12. Neale and Krutnik, *Popular Film*, 27.

13. Northrop Frye, *Anatomy of Criticism: Four Essays* (Princeton, NJ: Princeton University Press, 1957).

14. Neale and Krutnik, *Popular Film*, 31. They are citing Bordwell's comments in *The Classical Hollywood Cinema: Film Style and Mode of Production to 1960*, cowritten with Janet Staiger and Kristin Thompson (London: Routledge and Kegan Paul, 1985).

15. Neale and Krutnik, *Popular Film*, 31–2, my emphasis. Hereafter cited in text as *PFTC*.

16. Donald Crafton, "Pie and Chase: Gag, Spectacle and Narrative in Slapstick Comedy" in Kristine Brunovska Karnick and Henry Jenkins, eds., *Classical Hollywood Comedy* (New York: Routledge, 1995), 107. Hereafter cited in text as "PAC."

17. Neale and Krutnik, *Popular Film*, 119. David Robinson argues that André Deed was "the first true movie clown" where "the personality of the comic actor was central to the humour." Both Deed and his rival Max Linder worked at the Pathé Studio in Paris. *The Great Funnies: A History of Film Comedy* (London: Studio Vista Limited, 1969), 11–2.

18. Neale and Krutnik cite both Lloyd and Keaton as claiming to have moved beyond the slapstick tradition, *Popular Film*, 120.

19. Don B. Wilmeth, *The Language of American Popular Entertainment: A Glossary of Argot, Slang, and Terminology* (Westport, CT: Greenwood Press, 1981), 245.

20. Larry Langman, *Encyclopedia of American Film Comedy* (New York: Garland, 1987), 548. The *OED*'s definition of the term confirms the first definition and a range of citations of its usage support this meaning. What is interesting in these citations, which are too numerous to include here, is that *slapstick* was always associated with low comedy and is used to express a pejorative judgment about low comedy from the outset.

21. Freud, *Jokes and Their Relation to the Unconscious*, trans. and ed. James Strachey, Penguin Freud Library, vol. 6 (1905; Harmondsworth: Penguin, 1976), 293. Hereafted cited in text as JTRU.

22. Robinson, *The Great Funnies*, 43.

23. Ibid., 41–2.

24. Durgnat, *The Crazy Mirror: Hollywood Comedy and the American Image* (London: Faber and Faber, 1969), 70; Bergson, *Laughter*, 39.

25. Ibid., 69.

26. Doug Riblet, "The Keystone Film Company and the Historiography of Early Slapstick," in Kristine Brunovska Karnick and Henry Jenkins, eds., *Classical Hollywood Comedy*, 176.

27. Ibid., 172.

28. Ibid., 175–6, my emphasis.

29. Riblet writes:

These second half action sequences often involved crosscutting between up to four or five lines of action. Along with the fast-paced editing, the construction of these rapid-fire climactic sequences also generally featured rapid and/or violent movement in each shot, a withholding of intertitles which might interrupt the rhythm, and occasional slight undercranking. Even in sequences not involving crosscutting, Keystone films often employed quick cutting between adjacent spaces to follow knockabout action or interplay between characters. (ibid., 179)

30. James Agee, "Comedy's Greatest Era," in *Agee on Film: Reviews and Comments* (New York: Peter Owen, 1949), 3.

31. *Oxford English Dictionary*, 3rd ed., s.v. "farce."

32. White, *The Content of Form*, 5.

33. Ibid., 16.

3. THE MACHINE OF COMEDY: GUNNING, DELEUZE, AND BUSTER KEATON

1. Gilles Deleuze, *Cinema 1: The Movement-Image*, trans. Hugh Tomlinson and Barbara Habberjam (Minneapolis: University of Minnesota Press, 1986).

2. Gilles Deleuze, *Cinéma 1: L'image-mouvement* (Paris: Les Éditions de Minuit, 1983).

3. Deleuze, *Cinema 1*, 176–7. Hereafter cited in text as *C1*.

4. *Oxford English Dictionary*, 3rd ed., s.v. "recursive."

5. Deleuze, *Cinema 2: The Time-Image*, trans. Hugh Tomlinson and Robert Galeta (London: Athlone, 1989).

6. Deleuze, *Cinema 2*, 26.

7. Buster Keaton with Charles Samuels, *My Wonderful World of Slapstick* (New York: Da Capo Press., 1982), 173-4.

8. From the time Keaton parted company with Arbuckle in 1920 until he started to make features, he made nineteen two-reeler films. Most of these were cowritten and codirected with Eddie Cline. Two films (*The Goat* [1921] and *The Blacksmith* [1922]) were collaborations with Malcolm St. Clair, and

the last, *The Love Nest* (1923), Keaton directed alone. In the features Keaton shares the credits for directing with Cline, Jack Blystone, Clyde Bruckman, and Donald Crisp. Critics and commentators have generally acknowledged that the directorial responsibility for Keaton's films was largely his, despite other directors being listed in the credits. Even Keaton's gag writer and sometime codirector Bruckman said that Keaton "was his own best gagman" and that his crew members were "overpaid from the strict creative point of view. Most of the direction was his" (Rudi Blesh, *Keaton*, New York: Macmillan, 1966, 149; 150).

9. Keaton, *My Wonderful World*, 173–4.

10. Ibid., 176.

11. Bordwell et al., *The Classical Hollywood Cinema.*

12. Bordwell, "Happily ever after, Part Two," *The Velvet Light Trap* 19 (1982): 2; Neale and Krutnik, *Popular Film*, 30.

13. Tom Gunning, "Crazy Machines in the Garden of Forking Paths: Mischief Gags and the Origins of American Film Comedy" in Karnick and Jenkins, eds., *Classical Hollywood Comedy.* Gunning derives this concept from Neil Harris's study of P. T. Barnum's entrepreneurial success, *Humbug: The Art of P. T. Barnum* (Boston: Little, Brown, 1973). Harris details the exploits of Barnum, the wily, nineteenth-century pragmatist who would do almost anything to make a buck, including dramatizing the reality effects of his shows and flagrantly manipulating the truth to deceive his audiences. He achieved fame and fortune by blurring the distinction between the circus and museum, orchestrating such one-act attractions as the 161-year-old slave Joice Heth who he advertised as having nursed George Washington. Harris develops the idea of an operational aesthetic to account for the attraction of the U.S. public to such hoaxes. Barnum's special contribution to Jacksonian America was to present conundrums and illusions to the public which responded with a requisite amount of skeptical fascination. His aesthetic sought to focus his audience's attention on the "structures and operations" of his exhibits and hoaxes alike, all of which were "empirically testable, and enabled—or at least invited—audiences and participants to learn how they worked'" (Harris, *Humbug*, 57). The operational aesthetic then was "an approach to experience that equated beauty with information and technique, accepting guile because it was more complicated than candor" (Harris, *Humbug*, 57). Significantly, Harris conceives this aesthetic more broadly than is suggested by Gunning's application of the concept to the cinema, where it is taken as simply part of an endemic fascination with the machine and its illusory capabilities.

14. Gunning, "The Cinema of Attraction."

15. Gunning, "Crazy Machines," 88.

16. Ibid. The Lumière Brothers' film *La charcuterie mécanique* (*The Mechanical Butcher*, 1895) can be understood as an allegory for the cinematic process itself, a point taken up many years later by Jean Eustache and Jean-Michel Barjol in their 1970 film *Le Cochon*.

17. Gunning, "Crazy Machines," 90.

18. Ibid., 96.

19. Ibid., 100.

20. See Noël Carroll, "An In-Depth Analysis of Buster Keaton's *The General*," (PhD diss., New York University; Ann Arbor, MI: Xerox University Microfilms, 1976).

21. Gunning, "Crazy Machines," 95.

22. Gunning holds the view that cinema could only really produce *dramatic* narratives through the development of character psychology and the exploration of character motivation. For him, *comedic* narratives emerged only at that point that gags could be "intricately worked into comic personas." Gunning, "Crazy Machines," 97.

23. Gunning, "Response to 'Pie and Chase,'" in Karnick and Jenkins, eds., *Classical Hollywood Comedy*, 121.

24. Ibid.

25. Lebel, *Buster Keaton*, 124–7.

26. Ibid., 122–3.

27. Ibid., 124.

28. Inwood, *A Hegel Dictionary* (Oxford: Blackwell, 1992), 82.

29. Ibid., 83.

30. Ibid., 82.

31. *Mechanism* is a device, means, machine, or instrument. Inwood proposes that Hegel understands it in terms of an "arrangement and interaction of objects on mechanical principles." (181). Mechanism for Hegel is neither organic nor behavioral to the extent that "[t]he category of mechanism applies primarily to inorganic nature. But mechanism essentially consists not in the relations of *physical or material bodies*, but in *external* RELATIONS of *persistent, independent* objects" (181). Chemismus or chemism refers to the arrangement and interaction of things in accordance with chemical principles. Inwood notes Hegel's differentiation between chemism and mechanism: "[a]n object in a mechanistic system might in principle exist,... even if it

were detached from the system and thus unrelated to other objects. But chemical substances or stuffs are intrinsically related by their OPPOSITION to and affinity for each other" (182).

32. Ibid., 182–3.

33. Indeed, in so far as cinematic melodrama has been theorized as exploring the problematic constitution of masculinity, the intrusion of the epic form (which conversely deploys an unproblematic representation of masculinity) explicitly addresses the representation of masculinity in melodrama. By creating an oxymoron—epic masculinity versus melodramatic masculinity—Keaton's films make fun of both constructions. See Geoffrey Nowell-Smith, "Minnelli and Melodrama," in Christine Gledhill, ed., *Home Is Where the Heart Is: Studies in Melodrama and the Woman's Film* (London: BFI Publishing, 1987), 70–4.

34. In addition to Lebel, many theorists of Keaton's comedy make the mistake of presuming that the Keaton character surpasses himself because of the challenges he confronts. (See, for example, Carroll, "An In-Depth Analysis," and Moews, *Keaton*).

35. Seidman, *Comedian Comedy*; Kramer, "Derailing the Honeymoon Express."

36. "*L'originalité profonde de Buster Keaton, c'est d'avoir rempli la grande forme d'un contenu burlesque qu'elle semblait récuser, d'avoir réconcilié contre toute vraisemblance le burlesque et la grande forme*" (Deleuze, *Cinéma 1*, 237). Unfortunately in the wording of the English translation Deleuze's reference to what is specifically comic is lost. The English translators, for instance, write that Keaton merely "gives" the large form a burlesque content and the multiple senses of the term *toute vraisemblance* are not evident in the English "against all odds." The idiom is usually translated as "in all likelihood" or "in all probability" but the term *vraisemblance* also carries with it the meanings verisimilitude, likelihood, plausibility and probability. The latter two words are especially significant because their opposites, *implausibility* and *improbability*, are often used to specify the nature of comedy. See, for instance, Palmer, *The Logic of the Absurd*, and Neale and Krutnik, *Popular Film*. The connotation of verisimilitude is also important given that Deleuze claims that the action-image constitutes the cinema of realism and that while the large form of the action-image is usually reserved for the great realist genres of the epic, the documentary and the Western, the small form of the action-image is properly comedic. He proposes at the same time that it does not necessarily give rise to comedy and can be used for dramatic effects as much as comic effects.

37. George Wead has noted that the narrative is adapted from a real story in the American Civil War. In 1862 a Union spy stole a passenger train at Big Shanty in Georgia. His plan was to travel to Chattanooga and along the way destroy the telegraph wires and track. The plan failed because the spy was pursued by the train's engineer and a road-shop foreman. The spy and his accomplices were captured and hanged ("The Great Locomotive Chase," *American Film* 2.9 [1977]).

38. Moews, *Keaton*, 221–2.

39. Bergson, *Laughter*.

4. FOOL'S GOLD: METAMORPHOSES IN *SHERLOCK JR.*

1. Carroll, "An In-Depth Analysis," 9.

2. Ibid., 6.

3. Carroll argues that in *The General* "[t]he types of automatism and inattention that Johnnie evinces can be readily stigmatized as a sort of stupidity. Rigidity of thought, the incapacity to re-evaluate the situation and to modify behavior accordingly clearly is a form of dimwittedness." (ibid., 58). For Carroll, the flip-side of automatism is insight: in the character's supreme adroitness "it becomes apparent that automatism alone does not represent a full picture of Keaton's portrayal of adaptability" (ibid., 71).

4. Seidman, *Comedian Comedy*, 3.

5. James Naremore, *Acting in the Cinema* (Berkeley: University of California Press, 1988).

6. Ibid., 78.

7. Ibid., 128.

8. *Fatal Strategies*, trans. Philip Beitchman and W. G. J. Niesluchowski (New York: Semiotext(e), 1990), 113–4.

9. Carroll is not the only theorist to proffer such a reading. Along the same lines, Moews suggests that Keaton's nocturnal sojourn constitutes the transformational interval between the two aspects of the character. This reading is also presented by Peter F. Parshall: "A consistent trait of Keaton's feature films was that the central character changed from ineffectual dolt to resourceful hero." "Buster Keaton and the Space of Farce: *Steamboat Bill, Jr.*, versus *The Cameraman*," *Journal of Film and Video* 46.5 (1994): 30; and Moews, *Keaton*, 3. Kevin W. Sweeney, alternatively, argues that Moews account is inadequate: "he is incorrect to understand the film as being mainly

structured by 'a law of reversal.' Keaton has more structural options available than basis/reversal and competence/incompetence." ("The Dream of Disruption: Melodrama and Gag Structure in Keaton's *Sherlock Junior*," *Wide Angle* 13.1 [1991]: 107).

10. Baudrillard, *Fatal Strategies*, 120.

11. Ibid., 121.

12. Ibid.

13. Baudrillard himself cites the comic performance of Harpo Marx who, called on to utter the password "swordfish," presents an actual swordfish (*Fatal Strategies*, 121). See also Freud, *Jokes*; and Mellencamp, "Jokes and Their Relation to the Marx Brothers."

14. Keaton, *My Wonderful World*, 261–2.

15. Redundancy is readily associated with Bergson's interpretation of the comic as the element of the mechanical encrusted upon the living. *Laughter*.

16. Jean Baudrillard, *The Evil Demon of Images*, trans. Paul Foss and Paul Patton (Sydney: Power Institute Publications, 1987), 44.

17. See Carroll, "Notes on the Sight-Gag," in Andrew Horton, ed., *Comedy/Cinema/Theory*, (Berkeley: University of California Press, 1991).

18. In a psychoanalytic context this is exactly the process that Lyotard describes when desire comes into contact with the figure. See "The Connivances of Desire with the Figural," in Roger McKeon, ed., *Driftworks* (New York: Semiotext(e), 1984).

19. Seidman, *Comedian Comedy*, 7.

20. Derrida, "From Restricted to General Economy," 264.

21. Ibid., 265.

22. Ibid., 256.

23. Ibid.

24. Krutnik, "The Clown-Prints of Comedy."

25. Seidman, *Comedian Comedy*, 5–6.

26. Keaton is not distinctive here. The same could be said, and indeed has been said, of Chaplin.

27. Lebel writes of Keaton's cinema in terms of perfect geometry but there is also a temporal factor that demands consideration. *Buster Keaton*.

28. Kramer, "Derailing the Honeymoon Express," 113.

29. Geoff King, *Film Comedy* (London: Wallflower Press, 2002), 40.

30. Ibid., 42.

31. The exploration of the extremity of improbability is something cinema inherited from the circus and vaudeville under the aegis of the stunt.

5. JOKES AND THEIR RELATION TO...

1. In "Un-knowing: Laughter and Tears," Bataille writes:

> We can, with fair precision, observe and define the various themes of the laughable; it in no way eludes the clarity of knowledge or of methodological investigation. Moreover, once we have seen the cause of laughter in its various aspects, we can reproduce its effects at will. We possess veritable recipes, we can in various ways provoke laughter, in exactly the same way as all the other effects known to us. We can, in short, produce objects of laughter. Or one might say, and indeed it has been said, that knowing means knowing how. (89).

2. See Weber, "The Divaricator," *The Legend of Freud*, and "Laughing in the Meanwhile"; Jeffrey Mehlman, "How to Read Freud on Jokes: The Critic as *Schadchen*," *New Literary History* 6.2 (1975); Jean-Luc Nancy, "*Menstruum universale* (Literary Dissolution)," *Sub-stance* 21 (1978).

3. Mellencamp, "Jokes and Their Relation to the Marx Brothers"; Neale, "Psychoanalysis and Comedy"; Eaton, "Laughter in the Dark."

4. See George McFadden, *Discovering the Comic* (Princeton, NJ: Princeton University Press, 1982).

5. Weber, *The Legend of Freud*.

6. "De Poetica," trans. Ingram Bywater, chap. 5, in *The Complete Works of Aristotle*, vol. XI, (Oxford, England: Clarendon, 1946), 1449a.

7. Marcel Gutwirth, *Laughing Matter: An Essay on the Comic* (Ithaca, NY: Cornell University Press, 1993), 30.

8. Ibid., 31. Gutwirth writes, "[a] first consequence of this functional bias, which directed comic theory toward an assessment of how well laughter serves social ends, was to set the framework in which comedy as a genre was analyzed and described well into the late eighteenth century" (30). He locates Pierre Corneille, Dr. Johnson, Jean de Santeul, John Dryden, Wilhelm von Schlegel, Denis Diderot, George Meredith, and Bergson among others within this tradition.

9. Ibid., 25.

10. Bergson, *Laughter*, 19-20. Indeed, George Meredith, in "An Essay on Comedy" conceives that too much elasticity is as much a problem as too much tension and thus considers the dilemma of the hypergelasts, those excessive laughers "who are so loosely put together that a wink will shake them." In Wylie Sypher, ed., *Comedy* (Garden City, NY: Doubleday, 1956), 4.

11. Bergson, *Laughter*, 19. Hereafter cited in text as L.

12. Quote from Victor Hugo, *Marion Delorme*.

13. Bergson has a second conception of *wit*, a narrow one, which is by contrast pertinent to his theory of laughter. It is restricted to the witty exchanges between interlocutors in theatrical comedy. Wit is here distinguished from the comic of words only as far as it uses figures of speech (103). In the end, both wit in the narrow sense of the word and the comic of words remain obedient to the laws of the comic (132).

14. Although one could argue that Bergson does not explicitly theorize the comic in terms of degradation—indeed, he argues that exaggeration is a form of the comic opposite to degradation—one could also argue that it is implicit in his general definition of *the comic*.

15. Freud, *Jokes*, 239. Hereafter cited in text as *JTRU*.

16. Weber, "Laughing in the Meanwhile," 700-4.

17. We might ask whether comparison and degradation are not also the techniques of the joke in as much as Freud makes a comparison between form and content in his explication of the joke technique—the form or expression might be seen as a degraded rendition of the thought or content. Freud does, after all, argue that precisely the difference between form and content contributes to the joke's distinctiveness. On the one hand, this brings us back to the fact that the joke nevertheless still belongs to the comic, which means that its comparative aspect does not have to be extinguished to support its identity. On the other hand, it calls our attention to Freud's repeated insistence that technique alone is insufficient to explain the joke's laughter compelling effect.

18. Ferdinand de Saussure, *Course in General Linguistics*, ed. Charles Bally, Albert Sechehaye, and Albert Reidlinger, and trans. Roy Harris (La Salle, IL: Open Court, 1983).

19. So named after one of the most famous jokes in Freud's book:

"A. borrowed a copper kettle from B. and after he had returned it was sued by B. because the kettle now had a big hole in it which made it unusable. His defence was: "First, I never borrowed a kettle from B. at all; secondly, the kettle had a hole in it already when I got it from him; and thirdly, I gave him back the kettle undamaged." (100)

20. Freud paraphrased.

21. Weber, *The Legend of Freud*, 89; Freud, *Jokes*, 92.

22. Weber, *The Legend of Freud*, 89.

23. Weber, "Laughing in the Meanwhile," 701.

24. Lyotard, "The Dream-Work Does Not Think," in *The Lyotard Reader*, ed. Andrew Benjamin (Oxford, England: Blackwell, 1989), 41.

25. J. Laplanche and J. B. Pontalis, *The Language of Psychoanalysis* (London: Karnac Books, 1988), 474.

26. Ibid., 339.

27. Lyotard, "The Dream-Work."

28. Laplanche and Pontalis, *The Language of Psychoanalysis*, 325.

29. Ibid., 171.

30. Ibid., 339.

31. See Weber's "Laughing in the Meanwhile" for a detailed analysis of cathexis and decathexis in the joke process. Freud conceived the relation of pleasure and unpleasure and their role in the maintenance of the equilibrium of the psyche along the lines of thermodynamics. The human being is like a complex combustion engine that must necessarily relieve itself of surplus energy to maintain a state of equilibrium.

32. Ibid., 699.

33. Freud makes an analogy here to language: "But actually I do not carry the imitation through, any more than I still spell words out if I learnt to read by spelling."(*Jokes*, 251).

34. Freud, *Jokes*, 300, original emphasis. We should note that within this definition Freud is also incorporating the production of comic affect in jokes, because he goes on to suggest that jokes differ from the comic in so far as in the joke "the difference between two simultaneous methods of viewing things, which operate with a different expenditure" occurs in the third person in the joke process and that one of these views develops through the unconscious and the other from the preconscious to the conscious (ibid). We should note that in discussing both the joke and the comic as the application of two ideational methods to one act of ideation, Freud is doing so to distinguish both of them from humor.

35. Neale reads Freud's conception of the comic as constituted by identification, empathy, and oscillation and suggests that this foregrounds the instability of the subject who finds something comic. Yet Freud argues against precisely this notion of oscillation, contending that apprehension of the comic involves a comparison of cathectic expenditures and not an oscillation between them. Neale, "Psychoanalysis and Comedy," 35–6.

6. THE COMIC: DEGRADATION AND REFINEMENT IN 1920s' CINEMATIC SLAPSTICK

1. In the *Critique of Judgment*, Kant's discussion of laughter forms the basis of his "Comment" that concludes the first division, "Analytic of Aesthetic Judgment," of the "Critique of Aesthetic Judgment." The "Comment" comes immediately after the section on the "Comparison of Aesthetic Value in the Various Fine Arts"—where, significantly, he has just finished arguing that poetry is the highest ranking of the various fine arts (196)—so that the theory of laughter occupies not simply a marginal space, but a limiting space in relation to the fine arts. The play of thought or wit as the cause of laughter is set apart from the fine arts (such as poetry, the visual arts, and music) because it involves a gratification, a "furtherance of bodily well-being," health. Whereas aesthetic experience involves "*what we like when we merely judge it* [fine art]" (201), laughter pertains to the good health of the subject. It is gratifying in the same manner that food is, and what it satisfies is some sort of bodily need. Immanuel Kant, *Critique of Judgment*, trans. Werner S. Pluhar (Indianapolis: Hackett Publishing, 1987).

2. Aristotle, "De Poetica," chap. 5, 1449a.

3. Bergson, *Laughter*, 31.

4. In a footnote, Freud also cites the English term *degradation*, quoting Alexander Bain, "The occasion of the Ludicrous is the Degradation of some person or interest, possessing dignity, in circumstances that excite no other strong emotion." (Freud, *Jokes*, 261). Bain, *The Emotions and the Will*, 2nd ed. (London: Longmans, Green, 1865, 248). Gutwirth says that Bain's view "neatly suits the Victorian scheme of things, in which dignity mightily prevails," (*Laughing Matter*, 25).

5. Freud, *Jokes*, 260–1. Hereafter cited in text as *JTRU*.

6. Freud lists the following in his paradigm of comic possibilities:

[The comic] is found in people—in their movements, forms, actions and traits of character, originally in all probability only in their physical characteristics but later in their mental ones as well or, as the case may be, in the expression of those characteristics. By means of a very common sort of personification, animals become comic too, and inanimate objects. At the same time, the comic is capable of being detached from people, in so far as we recognize the conditions under which a person seems comic. In this way the comic of situation comes about, and this recognition affords the possibility of making a person comic at one's will by putting him in situations in which his actions are subject to these comic conditions. The discovery that one has it in one's power to make someone else comic opens the way to an undreamt-of yield of comic pleasure and is the origin of a highly developed technique. One can make *oneself* comic, too, as easily as other people. The methods that serve to make people comic are: putting them in a comic situation, mimicry, disguise, unmasking, caricature, parody, travesty, and so on. (248–9)

7. The movement of Groucho Marx springs to mind here. The overall effect of him lowering his torso toward the ground and his huge lunging strides is to diminish his size and his stature.

8. Freud's theorization of the comic has presented certain difficulties for theorists of cinematic comedy. Neale and Krutnik suggest Freud's conceptualization of the comic only has a limited pertinence to the study of cinematic comedy because the rule of the comic is deduced from instances that are found rather than made. In their book *Popular Film and Television Comedy*, they insist that Freud's concept of the comic is not synonymous with theirs. The situations of the comic that occur in everyday life, while undoubtedly operating in a semiotic sense, are not acts of enunciation as are comic incidents in cinematic comedy. They thus contend that the comic that operates in cinematic comedy has a structure of address closer to Freud's conception of the joke (62–8). Referring to Palmer's book, *The Logic of the Absurd*, they propose that the comic in cinema gives rise to a double interpretation or reading, one of which is incompatible with its syntagmatic context, a semantic anomaly, whereas the other is paradigmatically compatible. For Neale and Krutnik, the comic that occurs in comedy has a witty dimension that is not present in Freud's conception of the comic. Although Neale and Krutnik make no mention of the fact that Freud includes numerous examples of the enunciation of the comic within his delimitation of the concept (that is, mimicry, caricature, parody, travesty, and unmasking), one can nevertheless argue that the reduction of the comic to a notion of degradation significantly overlooks the formal and semantic richness to which such operations must surely, at least on some occasions, give rise. Neale and Krutnik have a point—Freud's theorization of the comic in the narrow sense opposed to the joke does not give provision for wit.

9. Gutwirth, *Laughing Matter*, 2.

10. Plato, *Philebus and Epinomis*, trans. A. E. Taylor (London: Nelson, 1956), 167–9.

11. Bergson, *Laughter*, 23.

12. Neale and Krutnik, *Popular Film*, 72.

13. Gerald Mast, *The Comic Mind*, 43.

14. Riblet, "The Keystone Film Company," 168–89.

15. Mast, *The Comic Mind*, 43.

16. Jay Leyda, "California Slapstick: A Definition," in Eileen Bowser, *The Slapstick Symposium*, (Brussels, Belgium: Federation Internationale des Archives du Film, 1988), 1–3.

17. Neale and Krutnik, *Popular Film*, 110.

18. Charles J. Maland, *Chaplin and American Culture: The Evolution of a Star Image* (Princeton, NJ: Princeton University Press, 1989), 17.

19. Kerr, *The Silent Clowns*, 63.

20. Riblet, "The Keystone Film Company," 175.

21. Benayoun, *The Look of Buster Keaton*, ed. and trans. Randall Conrad (New York: St. Martin's Press, 1983), 17.

22. Lebel, *Buster Keaton*, 30.

23. Ibid.

24. Ibid., 31.

25. See Benayoun, *The Look of Buster Keaton*, 17.

26. Lebel, *Buster Keaton*, 19.

27. Ibid., 16.

28. Riblet, "The Keystone Film Company," 175–6.

29. Mast, *The Comic Mind*, 49.

30. Ibid., 50.

31. This last point is invariably the reason for his rejection by the girl of the film. His lesson usually involves the attainment of recognition; but Keaton himself either remains oblivious to the real necessity behind his actions or only seeks recognition as a means to an end, that is, because the girl has demanded it.

32. Deleuze, after Benayoun, calls it his periscopic vision (*Cinema 1*, 173).

33. Kerr, *The Silent Clowns*, 70.

34. Riblet, "The Keystone Film Company," 182.

35. Ibid.

36. Seidman, *Comedian Comedy*, 19.

37. Neale and Krutnik, *Popular Film*, 111.

38. Donald W. McCaffrey, *Four Great Comedians: Chaplin, Lloyd, Keaton, Langdon* (London: Zwemmer, 1968), 67.

39. Ibid., 56.

40. Richard Dyer MacCann, *The Silent Comedians* (Metuchen, NJ: Scarecrow Press, 1993), 196.

41. McCaffrey, *Four Great Comedians*, 53.

42. Belton, *Cinema Stylists* (Metuchen, NJ: Scarecrow Press, 1983), 313–4.

43. Ibid., 314–6.

44. Mast, *The Comic Mind*, 152.

45. Seidman, *Comedian Comedy*, 2.

46. This is the term Gilles Deleuze uses to describe Lloyd's slapstick (*Cinema 2*, 64).

47. Mast, *The Comic Mind*, 152–3.

48. Although rare and colloquial, in French *façade* is sometimes used interchangeably with *visage* (face): *se refaire la façade* can mean to redo one's face or to have a face lift, whereas *il va te démolir la façade* means he's going to smash your face in (*Collins Robert French Dictionary*, 5th ed. [Glasgow: HarperCollins, 2003]).

49. Fischer cited in Freud, *Jokes*, 40, original parenthesis.

50. Ernst Kris, *Psychoanalytic Explorations in Art* (New York: Schocken Books, 1952), 174.

51. Ibid.

52. Ibid., 175.

53. Ibid., 176. In this respect, Kris, like Neale and Krutnik, wants to extend the Freudian definition of the comic as essentially degradation.

54. In the seventeenth century, neoclassicist Ben Jonson distinguished between the crude and scurrilous Old Comedy of Aristophanes and the more refined New Comedy of Menander and his Roman imitators by advocating the latter's moral worth. This distinction has played itself out many times over in the history of the theory and criticism of comedy, and is doubtless an

attempt to rescue at least some instances of comedy from the systematic devaluation that the genre so often meets with. D. J. Palmer, ed., *Comedy: Developments in Criticism* (London: Macmillan, 1984). See D. J. Palmer "Introduction," 8–22, and Ben Jonson, "Wise and Foolish Laughter," 37–8.

55. Rudolf Arnheim, *To the Rescue of Art: Twenty-Six Essays* (Berkeley: University of California Press, 1992), 101.

56. Deleuze, *Cinema 2*, 64.

57. Ibid.

58. André Martin, "Le Mécano de la Pantomime," *Cahiers du Cinéma* 86 (1958), cited by Lebel, *Buster Keaton*, 47.

59. Lebel, *Buster Keaton*, 46–7.

60. Lebel for one argues against a Bergsonian reading of Keaton's comedy:

> [I]t would be wrong to liken him to a robot, even were one to liken him to the most highly perfected mechanical robot possible. The precision, rigor, perfection and achievement of his gestures and trajectories are not determined by some greater power exterior to him, but, on the contrary, are the fruits of an auto-dynamism and an unparalleled intensity. (ibid., 44)

61. Noël Carroll, "Buster Keaton, *The General*, and Visible Intelligibility," in *Close Viewings: An Anthology of New Film Criticism*, ed. Peter Lehman (Tallahassee: Florida State University Press, 1990). See also "Keaton: Film Acting as Action," in *Making Visible the Invisible: An Anthology of Original Essays on Film Acting* ed. Carole Zucker, (Metuchen, NJ: Scarecrow Press, 1990).

7. FROM WORDS TO IMAGES (GAGGING)

1. *Oxford English Dictionary*, 3rd ed., s.v. "gag."

2. Neale and Krutnik, *Popular Film*, 51.

3. Carroll, "Notes on the Sight Gag."

4. Weber, "The Divaricator." This was not a bad thing in itself, although, as I will indicate in my discussion of Eaton's essay "Laughter in the Dark," it led to some rather skewed conclusions.

5. Eaton, "Laughter in the Dark," 24. This tension was taken as a significant point of focus by Weber.

6. We saw in chapter 6 that the jest precedes the joke both in its emergence on the scene at an early stage of the subject's psychical development and in complexity.

7. Freud, "Beyond the Pleasure Principle" (1920), in *On Metapsychology: The Theory of Psychoanalysis*, trans. James Strachey, Penguin Freud Library, vol. 11, (London: Penguin Books, 1984).

8. Eaton, "Laughter in the Dark," 25.

9. Ibid.

10. "[W]hilst comedy can be directed *against* anything, it cannot be analytical *of* anything." (Eaton, "Laughter in the Dark," 25). Even though Eaton appears to follow the argument articulated in "The Divaricator," he makes a distinct break from it. He contends that Freud implicitly revokes his preliminary claim that play comprises the essential characteristic of the joke and proposes instead that it is the kind of meaning that comes from the good joke. Although Weber does, indeed, note that *meaning* distinguishes the good joke from the bad joke, and gives the joke its authenticity by likewise distinguishing it from the jest, he, nevertheless, argues that the "bad joke" comprises the essence of the joke:

> if the joke consists of two elements, a negative and a positive one, and if the negative one involves the use of meaning to allay the critique of reason, while the positive factor inheres in nothing but verbal play itself, then the empty, meaningless word-play of the jest or "bad" joke comprises the essence of the *Witz*, engaging the pleasure of play in its purest form. On the other hand, it is precisely the necessity of an *impure* form of play and of pleasure—the *Aufhebunglust* involved in the relaxation and relief from inhibitions—that makes the joke proper and good. ("The Divaricator," 17)

11. Mehlman, "How to Read Freud on Jokes."

12. Neale, "Psychoanalysis and Comedy," 38.

13. Ibid.

14. Ibid., 34.

15. Ibid.

16. Ibid., 38.

17. Ibid., 34.

18. For Neale one possibility of a transgressive cinema remains, which would be realized if jokes and gags could somehow break out of narration and

discourse, oppose the Law and reorder the Symbolic. To transgress the Law, according to Neale:

> that rhythm of transgression and familiarization outlined by Mick Eaton would have, itself, to be transgressed. And for that to occur modes of discourse and signification other than those characteristic of mainstream novelistic narration would have to be employed for the context of the jokes and gags themselves. For the Law is not simply a matter of the ideological content of discourse, but of the orders of the articulation of meaning and sense themselves. The mode of discursive inscription and narration of jokes and gags would have to take different forms, which themselves oppose the orders of discourse and language characteristic of the Law, if these jokes and gags are to achieve a re-ordering of the Symbolic that is in any way radically effective. (40–1)

19. Mellencamp, "Jokes and Their Relation to the Marx Brothers."

20. Ibid., 74.

21. Ibid., 66.

22. While Mellencamp does not come straight out and say this, she nevertheless hints at it in her inclusion of a quote from Luce Irigaray, which theorizes the look as the privilege of men who use it to distance, objectify, and master, and which, through being privileged over the other senses, ensures the domination of the male sex because of its overt visibility (doubtless manifested in the penis). Mellencamp explicitly binds this privilege to the resultant objectified, distanced, and mastered female body (64).

23. Ibid.

24. Mary Ann Doane, "The Film's Time and the Spectator's Space," in *Cinema and Language*, cited by Mellencamp, ibid., my emphasis.

25. Mellencamp, "Jokes and Their Relation to the Marx Brothers," 64.

26. Jacques Lacan, "The Agency of the Letter in the Unconscious or reason since Freud," *Écrits: A Selection*, trans. Alan Sheridan (New York: Norton, 1977).

27. Freud, *Jokes*, 219.

28. Ibid.

29. Indeed, in his book on the joke and his discussion of the comic, Freud deems ideational mimetics to be a form of expression readily seen in children, common people, and "members of certain races." (Freud, *Jokes*, 252).

30. Carroll, "Notes on the Sight Gag," 27.

31. Ibid.

32. See chap. 5 for a discussion of this joke.

33. Carroll's definition is also unable to account for the articulated gags that I discussed in chapter 3 which are temporal rather than instantaneous ("Notes on the Sight Gag").

34. Ibid., 26.

35. Ibid., 25–42.

36. Ibid., 37.

37. Ibid.

38. Ibid., 37–8.

39. Stanley Cavell, *Themes Out of School: Effects and Causes* (Chicago: University of Chicago Press, 1984), 174.

40. Ibid., 175.

41. Neale and Krutnik, *Popular Film*, 109–31.

42. Carroll, "Notes on the Sight Gag," 25–6.

43. Freud, *The Interpretation of Dreams*, trans. James Strachey, Penguin Freud Library, vol. 4 (1900; Harmondsworth: Penguin, 1976), 422–3.

44. Ibid., 422.

45. Ibid., 424–5.

46. Ibid., 455.

47. Ibid., 460.

48. Ibid., 455.

49. Mellencamp, "Jokes and Their Relation to the Marx Brothers," 65.

50. Ibid., 66.

51. Ibid.

52. Freud, *Dreams*, 460.

53. Freud, "The Unconscious" (1915), in *On Metapsychology*, 207.

54. Freud, *Dreams*, 381–82.

55. Ibid., 382.

56. Garrett Stewart, "Keaton through the Looking Glass," *The Georgia Review* 33.2 (1979): 355.

57. Sylvain du Pasquier, "Buster Keaton's Gags," trans. Norman Silverstein, *Journal of Modern Literature* 3.2 (1973): 276.

8. FIGURAL VISION: FREUD, LYOTARD, AND *CITY LIGHTS*

1. Heath, "Cinema and Psychoanalysis: Parallel Histories," in ed. Janet Bergstrom, *Endless Night: Cinema and Psychoanalysis, Parallel Histories* (Berkeley: University of California Press, 1999), 29.

2. Ibid., 30.

3. Ibid.

4. Ibid., 31.

5. Ibid.

6. Ibid.

7. Jean-François Lyotard, *Discours, figure* (Paris: Éditions Klinksieck, 1985). See in particular David Carroll, *Paraesthetics: Foucault, Lyotard, Derrida* (New York: Methuen, 1987); Geoffrey Bennington, *Lyotard: Writing the Event* (Manchester: Manchester University Press, 1988); Bill Readings, *Introducing Lyotard: Art and Politics* (London: Routledge, 1991).

8. See Bennington, *Lyotard: Writing the Event*; and Readings, *Introducing Lyotard*.

9. Mary Lydon, "Veduta on *Discours, figure*," *Yale French Studies* 99 (2001): 24.

10. Lyotard, "The Dream-Work," 33.

11. Lyotard, "Connivances."

12. Lyotard, "The Dream-Work," 19.

13. Ibid.

14. Lacan, "The Agency of the Letter."

15. Lyotard, "Connivances," 64–5.

16. Lyotard, "The Dream-Work," 20–1, my emphasis.

17. While Lyotard calls these thoughts discursive, it does not follow that they are intelligible. The dream-thoughts cannot be intelligible discourse because the unconscious is not an intelligent thinking agency.

18. Lyotard, "Connivances," 63.

19. Ibid.

20. Ibid., 64.

21. Ibid. He describes such painting as "a plastic screen entirely covered with chromatic flows, no stroke, not even a 'trace,' no effects of echo or

rhythm coming from the repetition or reentry of forms, values, or colors on the surface of the painting, thus no recognizable figure," (ibid).

22. Carroll, *Paraesthetics*, 38.

23. Lyotard, "Connivances," 65.

24. Ibid., 57.

25. Freud, *Dreams*, 766.

26. Laplanche and Pontalis, *The Language of Psychoanalysis*, 325–32, 379–82.

27. Freud, "Beyond the Pleasure Principle" (1920), in *On Metapsychology*, 278.

28. Ibid., 277.

29. Freud, *Dreams*, 757.

30. Ibid., 758.

31. Ibid., 758.

32. Ibid., 759.

33. Ibid., 758, my emphasis.

34. Lyotard, "Connivances," 60.

35. Chaplin cited in Maland, *Chaplin and American Culture*, 113.

36. Cavell, *Themes Out of School*, 176.

37. See William Paul's essay for a third conceptualization of vision in the film concerning the relation between vision and power, in "Charles Chaplin and the Annals of Anality," in ed. Horton, *Comedy/Cinema/Theory*.

38. Cavell, *Themes Out of School*, 176.

39. Žižek, *Enjoy Your Symptom: Jacques Lacan in Hollywood and Out* (London: Routledge, 1992), 4, my emphasis.

40. Ibid.

41. We have already seen that the genre of comedian comedy is identified precisely because of the comic doubling of character by performer (Seidman, *Comedian Comedy*).

42. In *The Interpretation of Dreams*, Freud proposes that the aim of the reality principle is to work against hallucination—to "prevent the mnemic cathexis" from "proceeding as far as perception" (758), to prevent, in other words, the hallucinatory cathecting of the memory of satisfaction and to divert the flow of energy so that satisfaction can be arrived at which is both real and tolerable to consciousness.

43. Paul, "The Annals of Anality," 111.

44. Comedy does not completely disappear after the boxing match—there is another sequence with the drunk millionaire—but a lack of consistency is to be expected in comedy.

9. PREPOSTEROUS FIGURALITY: COMIC CINEMA AND BAD METAPHOR

1. Bataille, *Inner Experience*, 147; Derrida, "From Restricted to General Economy," 262. Bataille does, however, associate the risk of sovereignty with modernism.

2. Deleuze, *Cinema 2*, 160.

3. Ibid., 160.

4. Ibid., 160.

5. Ibid., 160–1.

6. Deleuze, *Cinema 1*, 10.

7. Ibid.

8. Deleuze argues that Chaplin had an unsurpassed ability to create a laughter-emotion circuit by finding an action or gesture that corresponded to two situations that were far apart (ibid., 171). Although Deleuze seems to imply here that the comic is found in only one of the situations, the other creating an intense emotional cathexis, he also notes—to put it in Freudian terms—that the circuit doubles back on itself, intensifying both the cathexis of emotion and the discharge of cathexis in laughter. As such, the comic emerges not just from one part of the contrast but additionally from the contrast between the two—precisely like the play between form and meaning in Freud's conception of the joke.

9. Lyotard, "The Dream-Work."

10. Ibid., 33.

11. "Beyond the Pleasure Principle," 290–4. Although Freud does not explicitly theorize the eruption of jokes as resulting from the repetition compulsion, it seems a fair enough inference to make given his focus on the joke's relation to the unconscious.

12. Roland Barthes, *Roland Barthes*, trans. Richard Howard (New York: Hill and Wang, 1977), 80–1.

13. Mellencamp, "Jokes and Their Relation to the Marx Brothers," 72–3.

14. Ibid., 70–1.

15. Derrida, "White Mythology: Metaphor in the Text of Philosophy," in *Margins of Philosophy*. The term *white mythology* itself comes from the work of Anatole France who, within the parodic theatricality of a dialogue between two characters—Aristos and Polyphilos—sets out to show how metaphysics is nothing but a series of abstractions that have erased their physical (hence, literal) origin. Philosophy uses words with a sensory origin as metaphors. Yet the figurality of these metaphors is subsequently forgotten to produce abstract concepts. Thus Polyphilos attempts to convince Aristos that:

> any expression of an abstract idea can only be an analogy. By an odd fate, the very metaphysicians who think to escape the world of appearances are constrained to live perpetually in allegory. A sorry lot of poets, they dim the colors of the ancient fables, and are themselves but gatherers of fables. They produce white mythology. (213)

In the essay, Derrida cites Freud's *Studies in Hysteria, Jokes and Their Relation to the Unconscious, Beyond the Pleasure Principle, Introductory Lectures on Psycho-Analysis* and *The Question of Analysis* among the texts of others (Renan, Nietzsche, Bergson, and Lenin) as necessary tools to the interpretation of the significance of the claim that metaphysics is but a white (anaemic) mythology that "has erased within itself the fabulous scene that has produced it" (213). Hereafter cited in text as "WM."

16. Lyotard, "The Dream-Work," 36. See also, Lacan, "The Agency of the Letter," 149, 164.

17. Paul Patton, "Mobile Concepts, Metaphor and the Problem of Referentiality in Deleuze and Guattari," in ed. Maria Margaroni and Effie Yiannopoulou, *Metaphoricity and the Politics of Mobility* (Amsterdam: Rodopi, 2006); François Zourabichvili, "Are Philosophical Concepts Metaphors? Deleuze's Problematic of Literality," trans. Paul Patton (Paper presented at the International Association for Philosophy and Literature Conference, Syracuse, NY, 2004).

Bibliography

Agee, James. *Agee on Film: Reviews and Comments.* New York: Peter Owen, 1949.

Aristotle. "De Poetica." In *The Complete Works of Aristotle*, Translated by Ingram Bywater, vol. XI. Oxford, England: Clarendon Press, 1946.

Arnheim, Rudolf. *To the Rescue of Art: Twenty-Six Essays.* Berkeley: University of California Press, 1992.

Bain, Alexander. *The Emotions and the Will.* 2nd ed. London: Longmans, Green, 1865.

Barthes, Roland. *Image-Music-Text.* Translated by Stephen Heath. Glasgow, Scotland: Fontana/Collins, 1977.

———. *Roland Barthes.* Translated by Richard Howard. New York: Hill and Wang, 1977.

Bataille, Georges. *The College of Sociology (1937–39).* Edited by Dennis Hollier. Translated by Betsy Wing. Minneapolis: University of Minnesota Press, 1988.

———. "Conférences sur le non-savoir." *Tel Quel* 10 (1962): 3–20.

———. *L'expérience intérieure.* Paris: Gallimard, 1943.

———. *Guilty.* Translated by Bruce Boon. Venice, CA: Lapis Press, 1988.

———. "Hegel, Death and Sacrifice." Translated by Jonathan Strauss. *Yale French Studies* 78 (1990): 9–28.

———. *Inner Experience.* Translated by Leslie Anne Boldt. Albany: State University of New York Press, 1988.

———. "Un-Knowing and Its Consequences," *October* 36 (1986). 80–5.

———. "Un-knowing: Laughter and Tears." *October* 36 (1986). 89–102.

Baudrillard, Jean. *The Evil Demon of Images*. Sydney: Translated Paul Foss and Paul Patton. Power Institute Publications, 1987.

———. *Fatal Strategies*. Translated by Philip Beitchman and W. G. J. Niesluchowski. New York: Semiotext(e), 1990.

Bellour, Raymond. "To Alternate/To Narrate." Translated by Inge Pruks. *Australian Journal of Screen Theory* 15–16 (1983): 35–43.

Belton, John. *Cinema Stylists*. Metuchen, NJ: The Scarecrow Press, 1983.

Benayoun, Robert. *The Look of Buster Keaton*. Edited and translated by Randall Conrad. New York: St. Martin's Press, 1983.

Bennington, Geoffrey. *Lyotard: Writing the Event*. Manchester, England: Manchester University Press, 1988.

Bergson, Henri. *Laughter: An Essay on the Meaning of the Comic*. Translated by Cloudesley Brereton and Fred Rothwell. 1911. Reprint, Copenhagen: Green Integer, 1999.

Bergstrom, Janet. "Alternation, Segmentation, Hypnosis: Interview with Raymond Bellour." Translated by Susan Suleiman. *Camera Obscura* 3–4 (1979): 71–103.

———, ed. *Endless Night: Cinema and Psychoanalysis, Parallel Histories*. Berkeley: University of California Press, 1999.

Blesh, Rudi. *Keaton*. New York: Macmillan, 1966.

Bordwell, David. "Happily Ever After, Part Two." *The Velvet Light Trap* 19 (1982): 2–7.

———. *Narration in the Fiction Film*. Madison: University of Wisconsin Press, 1985.

Bordwell, David, Janet Staiger, and Kristin Thompson. *The Classical Hollywood Cinema: Film Style and Mode of Production to 1960*. London: Routledge and Kegan Paul, 1985.

Bowser, Eileen, ed. *The Slapstick Symposium*. Brussels, Belgium: Federation Internationale des Archives du Film, 1988.

Branigan, Edward. *Narrative Comprehension and Fiction Film*. London: Routledge, 1992.

Butler, Judith. "Commentary on Joseph Flay's 'Hegel, Derrida and Bataille's Laughter.'" In *Hegel and His Critics*, edited by William Desmond.

Carroll, David. *Paraesthetics: Foucault, Lyotard, Derrida*. New York: Methuen, 1987.

Carroll, Noël. "Buster Keaton, *The General*, and Visible Intelligibility." In *Close Viewings: An Anthology of New Film Criticism*, edited by Peter Lehman.

———. "An In-Depth Analysis of Buster Keaton's *The General*." PhD diss., New York University. Ann Arbor, MI: Xerox University Microfilms, 1976.

———. "Keaton: Film Acting as Action." In *Making Visible the Invisible: An Anthology of Original Essays on Film Acting*. Edited by Carole Zucker.

———. "Notes on the Sight-Gag." In *Comedy/Cinema/Theory*. Edited by Andrew Horton.

Cavell, Stanley. *Themes Out of School: Effects and Causes*. Chicago: University of Chicago Press, 1984.

Cook, Jim, ed. *The Television Sitcom: BFI Dossier* 17 (1982).

Coole, Diana. *Negativity and Politics: Dionysus and Dialectics from Kant to Poststructuralism*. London: Routledge, 2000.

Crafton, Donald. "Pie and Chase: Gag, Spectacle and Narrative in Slapstick Comedy." In *Classical Hollywood Comedy*, edited by Kristine Brunovska Karnick and Henry Jenkins.

Deleuze, Gilles. *Cinéma 1: L'image-mouvement*. Paris: Les Éditions de Minuit, 1983.

———. *Cinema 1: The Movement-Image*. Translated by Hugh Tomlinson and Barbara Habberjam. Minneapolis: University of Minnesota Press, 1986.

———. *Cinema 2: The Time-Image*. Translated by Hugh Tomlinson and Robert Galeta. London: Athlone, 1989.

Derrida, Jacques. "From Restricted to General Economy: A Hegelianism without Reserve." In *Writing and Difference*, translated by Alan Bass. Chicago: University of Chicago Press, 1978.

———. *Margins of Philosophy*. Translated by Alan Bass. Chicago: University of Chicago Press, 1982.

Descombes, Vincent. *Modern French Philosophy*. Translated by L. Scott-Fox and J. M. Harding. Cambridge, England: Cambridge University Press, 1980.

Desmond, William, ed. *Hegel and His Critics: Philosophy in the Aftermath of Hegel*. Albany: State University of New York Press, 1989.

Doane, Mary Ann. "The Film's Time and the Spectator's Space." In *Cinema and Language*, edited by Stephen Heath and Patricia Mellencamp.

Durgnat, Raymond. *The Crazy Mirror: Hollywood Comedy and the American Image*. London: Faber and Faber, 1969.

Eaton, Mick. "Laughter in the Dark." *Screen* 22.2 (1981): 21–5.

Flay, Joseph. "Hegel, Derrida and Bataille's Laughter." In *Hegel and His Critics*, edited by William Desmond.

Foucault, Michel. *L'ordre du discourse*. Paris: Gallimard, 1971.

Freud, Sigmund. "Beyond the Pleasure Principle" (1920). In *On Metapsychology*, edited and translated by James Strachey.

———. *The Interpretation of Dreams*. Edited and translated by James Strachey. Penguin Freud Library, vol. 4. 1900. Reprint, Harmondsworth: Penguin, 1976.

———. *Jokes and Their Relation to the Unconscious*. Edited and translated by James Strachey. Penguin Freud Library, vol. 6. 1905. Reprint, Harmondsworth: Penguin, 1976.

———. "The Unconscious" (1915). In *On Metapsychology: The Theory of Psychoanalysis*, Edited and translated by James Strachey, Penguin Freud Library, vol. 11. London: Penguin Books, 1984.

Frye, Northrop. *Anatomy of Criticism: Four Essays*. Princeton, NJ: Princeton University Press, 1957.

Gledhill, Christine, ed. *Home Is Where the Heart Is: Studies in Melodrama and the Woman's Film*. London: BFI Publishing, 1987.

Gunning, Tom. "The Cinema of Attraction: Early Film, Its Spectator and the Avant-Garde." *Wide Angle* 8.3–4 (1986): 63–70.

———. "Crazy Machines in the Garden of Forking Paths: Mischief Gags and the Origins of American Film Comedy." In *Classical Hollywood Comedy*, edited by Kristine Brunovska Karnick and Henry Jenkins.

———. "Response to 'Pie and Chase.'" In *Classical Hollywood Comedy*, edited by Kristine Brunovska Karnick and Henry Jenkins.

Gutwirth, Marcel. *Laughing Matter: An Essay on the Comic*. Ithaca, NY: Cornell University Press, 1993.

Hansen, Miriam. *Babel and Babylon: Spectatorship in American Silent Cinema*. Cambridge, MA: Harvard University Press, 1991.

Harris, Neil. *Humbug: The Art of P. T. Barnum*. Boston: Little, Brown, 1973.

Heath, Stephen. "Cinema and Psychoanalysis: Parallel Histories." In *Endless Night: Cinema and Psychoanalysis, Parallel Histories*, edited by Janet Bergstrom.

Heath, Stephen, and Patricia Mellencamp, eds. *Cinema and Language*. Los Angeles: American Film Institute, 1982.

Hegarty, Paul. *Georges Bataille: Core Cultural Theorist*. London: Sage, 2000.

Hegel, G. W. F. *Aesthetics*. Translated by T. M. Knox. Vol. II. Oxford, England: Oxford University Press, 1975.

———. *Phenomenology of Spirit*. Translated by A. V. Miller. Oxford, England: Oxford University Press, 1977.

Horton, Andrew, ed. *Comedy/Cinema/Theory*. Berkeley: University of California Press, 1991.

Inwood, Michael. *A Hegel Dictionary*. Oxford, England: Blackwell, 1992.

Jenkins, Henry. *What Made Pistachio Nuts? Early Sound Comedy and the Vaudeville Aesthetic*. New York: Columbia University Press, 1992.

Johnston, Claire, and Paul Willemen, eds. *Frank Tashlin*. Edinburgh, Scotland: Edinburgh Film Festival in association with *Screen*, 1973.

Jonson, Ben. "Wise and Foolish Laughter." In *Comedy: Developments in Criticism*, edited by D. J. Palmero.

Kant, Immanuel. *Critique of Judgment*. Translated by Werner S. Pluhar. Indianapolis, IN: Hackett, 1987.

———. *Critique of Pure Reason*. Translated by Norman Kemp Smith. 2nd ed. Basingstoke, England: Macmillan, 1929.

Karnick, Kristine Brunovska, and Henry Jenkins, eds. *Classical Hollywood Comedy*. New York: Routledge, 1995.

Keaton, Buster, with Charles Samuels. *My Wonderful World of Slapstick*. New York: Da Capo Press, 1982.

Kerr, Walter. *The Silent Clowns*. New York: Knopf, 1975.

King, Geoff. *Film Comedy*. London: Wallflower Press, 2002.

Knopf, Robert. *The Theater and Cinema of Buster Keaton*. Princeton, NJ: Princeton University Press, 1999.

Kramer, Peter. "Derailing the Honeymoon Express: Comicality and Narrative Closure in Buster Keaton's *The Blacksmith*." *The Velvet Light Trap* 23 (1989): 101–16.

Kris, Ernst. *Psychoanalytic Explorations in Art*. New York: Schocken Books, 1952.

Krutnik, Frank. "The Clown-Prints of Comedy." *Screen* 25.4–5 (1984): 50–9.

———. *Inventing Jerry Lewis*. Washington, DC: Smithsonian Institution Press, 2000.

Lacan, Jacques. "The Agency of the letter in the Unconscious or Reason since Freud." In *Écrits: A Selection*, translated by Alan Sheridan. New York: Norton, 1977.

Land, Nick. *The Thirst for Annihilation: Georges Bataille and Virulent Nihilism*. London: Routledge, 1992.

Langman, Larry. *Encyclopedia of American Film Comedy*. New York: Garland, 1987.

Laplanche, J., and J. B. Pontalis. *The Language of Psychoanalysis*. London: Karnac Books, 1988.

Lebel, Jean-Patrick. *Buster Keaton*. Translated by P. D. Stovin. London: Zwemmer, 1967.

Lehman, Peter, ed. *Close Viewings: An Anthology of New Film Criticism*. Tallahassee: Florida State University Press, 1990.

Leyda, Jay. "California Slapstick: A Definition." In Bowser, ed. *The Slapstick Symposium*, edited by Eileen Bowser.

Libertson, Joseph. *Proximity: Levinas, Blanchot, Bataille and Communication*. The Hague, Netherlands: Martinus Nijhoff, 1982.

Lydon, Mary. "Veduta on *Discours, figure*." *Yale French Studies* 99 (2001): 10–26.

Lyotard, Jean-François. "Acinema." *Wide Angle* 2.3 (1978): 53–4.

———. "The Connivances of Desire with the Figural." In *Driftworks*, edited by Roger McKeon. New York: Semiotext(e), 1984.

———. *Discours, figure*. Paris: Éditions Klinksieck, 1985.

———. "The Dream-Work Does Not Think." In *The Lyotard Reader*, edited by Andrew Benjamin. Oxford: Basil Blackwell, 1989.

MacCann, Richard Dyer. *The Silent Comedians*. Metuchen, NJ: Scarecrow Press, 1993.

Maland, Charles J. *Chaplin and American Culture: The Evolution of a Star Image*. Princeton, NJ: Princeton University Press, 1989.

Martin, André. "Le Mécano de la Pantomime." *Cahiers du Cinéma* 86 (1958): 18–30.

Mast, Gerald. *The Comic Mind: Comedy and the Movies*. 2nd ed. Chicago: University of Chicago Press, 1979.

McCaffrey, Donald W. *Four Great Comedians: Chaplin, Lloyd, Keaton, Langdon*. London: A Zwemmer, 1968.

McFadden, George. *Discovering the Comic*. Princeton, NJ: Princeton University Press, 1982.

Mehlman, Jeffrey. "How to Read Freud on Jokes: The Critic as *Schadchen*." *New Literary History* 6.2 (1975): 439–61.

Mellencamp, Patricia. "Jokes and Their Relation to the Marx Brothers." In *Cinema and Language*, edited by Stephen Heath and Patricia Mellencamp.

Meredith, George. "An Essay on Comedy." In *Comedy*, edited by Wylie Sypher. Garden City, NY: Doubleday, 1956.

Moews, Daniel. *Keaton: The Silent Features Close Up*. Berkeley: University of California Press, 1977.

Nancy, Jean-Luc. "*Menstruum universale* (Literary Dissolution)." *Sub-stance* 21 (1978): 21–35.

Naremore, James. *Acting in the Cinema*. Berkeley: University of California Press, 1988.

Neale, Steve. "Psychoanalysis and Comedy." *Screen* 22.2 (1981): 29–43.

Neale, Steve, and Frank Krutnik. *Popular Film and Television Comedy*. London: Routledge, 1990.

Nowell-Smith, Geoffrey. "Minnelli and Melodrama." In *Home Is Where the Heart Is: Studies in Melodrama and the Woman's Film*, edited by Christine Gledhill.

Palmer, D. J., ed. *Comedy: Developments in Criticism*. London: Macmillan, 1984.

Palmer, Jerry. *The Logic of the Absurd: On Film and Television*. London: British Film Institute, 1987.

Parshall, Peter F. "Buster Keaton and the Space of Farce: *Steamboat Bill, Jr.* versus *The Cameraman*." *Journal of Film and Video* 46.5 (1994): 29–46.

Pasquier, Sylvain du. "Buster Keaton's Gags." Translated by Norman Silverstein. *Journal of Modern Literature* 3.2 (1973): 269–91.

Patton, Paul. "Mobile Concepts, Metaphor and the Problem of Referentiality in Deleuze and Guattari." In *Metaphoricity and the Politics of Mobility*, edited by Maria Margaroni and Effie Yiannopoulou. Amsterdam, Netherlands: Rodopi, 2006.

Paul, William. "Charles Chaplin and the Annals of Anality." In *Comedy/Cinema/Theory*, edited by Andrew Horton.

Pefanis, Julian. *Heterology and the Post-Modern: Bataille, Baudrillard and Lyotard*. Durham: Duke University Press, 1991.

Plato. *Philebus and Epinomis*. Translated by A. E. Taylor. London: Nelson, 1956.

Plotnitsky, Arkady. *Reconfigurations: Critical Theory and General Economy*. Gainesville: University Press of Florida, 1993.

Polan, Dana. "Being and Nuttiness: Jerry Lewis and the French." *Journal of Popular Film and Television* 12.1 (1984): 42–6.

Prince, Gerald. *A History of Narratology*. Lincoln: University of Nebraska Press, 1987.

Rapf, Joanna E., and Gary L. Green. *Buster Keaton: A Bio-Bibliography*. Westport, CT: Greenwood Press, 1995.

Readings, Bill. *Introducing Lyotard: Art and Politics*. London: Routledge, 1991.

Riblet, Doug. "The Keystone Film Company and the Historiography of Early Slapstick." In *Classical Hollywood Comedy*, edited by Kristina Brunovska Karnick and Henry Jenkins.

Richardson, Michael, ed. *Georges Bataille: Essential Writings*. London: Sage, 1998.

Robinson, David. *The Great Funnies: A History of Film Comedy*. London: Studio Vista, 1969.

Rosen, Stanley. "Kojève's Paris: A Memoir." *parallax* 4 (1997): 1–2.

Sarris, Andrew. *The American Cinema: Directors and Directions 1929–1968*. New York: Dutton, 1969.

———. "Notes on Auteur Theory in 1962." In *Film Theory and Criticism: Introductory Reading*, edited by Gerald Mast et al. 4th ed. New York: Oxford University Press, 1992.

Saussure, Ferdinand de. *Course in General Linguistics*. Edited by Charles Bally, Albert Sechehaye, and Albert Reidlinger. Translated by Roy Harris. La Salle, IL: Open Court, 1983.

Seidman, Steve. *Comedian Comedy: A Tradition in Hollywood Film*. Ann Arbor, MI: University Microfilms International Research Press, 1981.

Selig, Michael. "*The Nutty Professor*: A 'Problem' with Film Scholarship." *The Velvet Light Trap* 26 (1990): 42–56.

Stam, Robert, Robert Burgoyne, and Sandy Flitterman-Lewis. *New Vocabularies in Film Semiotics: Structuralism, Post-Structuralism and Beyond*. London: Routledge, 1992.

Stewart, Garrett. "Keaton through the Looking Glass." *The Georgia Review* 33.2 (1979): 348–67.

Sweeney, Kevin W. "The Dream of Disruption: Melodrama and Gag Structure in Keaton's *Sherlock Junior*." *Wide Angle* 13.1 (1991): 104–20.

Wead, George. "The Great Locomotive Chase." *American Film* 2.9 (1977): 18–24.

Weber, Samuel. "The Divaricator: Remarks on Freud's *Witz*." *Glyph: Johns Hopkins Textual Studies* 1 (1977): 1–27.

———. *The Legend of Freud*. Minneapolis: University of Minnesota Press, 1982.

———. "Laughter in the Meanwhile." *MLN* 102.4 (1987): 691–706.

White, Hayden. *The Content of Form: Narrative Discourse and Historical Representation*. Baltimore, MD: The Johns Hopkins University Press, 1987.

Wilmeth, Don B. *The Language of American Popular Entertainment: A Glossary of Argot, Slang, and Terminology*. Westport, CT: Greenwood Press, 1981.

Žižek, Slavoj. "Why Does a *Letter* always Arrive at Its Destination?" In *Enjoy Your Symptom: Jacques Lacan in Hollywood and Out*. London: Routledge, 1992.

Zourabichvili, François. "Are Philosophical Concepts Metaphors? Deleuze's Problematic of Literality." Translated by Paul Patton. Paper presented at the International Association of Philosophy and Literature Conference, Syracuse, NY, 2004.

Zucker, Carole, ed. *Making Visible the Invisible: An Anthology of Original Essays on Film Acting*. Metuchen, NJ: Scarecrow Press, 1990.

Index

abstraction, 56, 101, 126, 138, 139, 140
acting, 5, 90, 122, 127, 131–132, 150, 159
Acting in the Cinema, 90
action-image, 61, 75–82, 85, 194, 223n36
aesthetics, 1, 3–5, 11–12, 15–16, 35–39 passim, 60–61, 68–70, 72, 81, 85, 105–108, 125–126, 129–130, 132, 137, 141, 144, 170–172, 175, 179, 184, 210, 221n13, 229n1
affect, 10, 17, 25
Agee, James, 49
aggression, 150
Allen, Woody, 5
alterity, 8, 17, 19, 27–28
American Dream, 134
Apollonian, 172
apperception, 111, 121
Arbuckle, Roscoe, 2, 49, 63, 220n8
Aristophanes, 232n54
Aristotle, 10, 107–108, 114, 125–126, 202–205, 207
Arnheim, Rudolf, 126, 138–140
Arrivée d'un train en gare à La Coitat, 69
art, 15–16, 108, 111, 125, 131, 137–139, 158, 172, 179, 188, 191, 229n1
art history, 1, 11, 137
At the Circus, 93
Atkinson, Rowan, 5
attraction and repulsion, 18, 139

Aufhebung, 24, 27, 29–32, 74, 217n36
auteurism, 3
automatism, 88, 108–109, 126, 224n3
avant-garde film, 37, 189

backwardation, 17, 21, 25–26, 28
Bain, Alexander, 229n4
Bakhtin, Mikhail, 2
Ball, Lucille, 5
Balloonatic, The, 63, 70, 80
Barjol, Jean-Michel, 222n16
Barnum, P. T., 221n13
Barthes, Roland, 9, 12, 36–39, 191, 196–197, 201
Bataille, Georges, 2, 7–8, 10, 15–32, 35, 39, 97–98, 105–106, 113, 191, 196, 206, 216nn19–20, 217n30, 226n1
Baudrillard, Jean, 1, 10, 91–94, 99, 215n5
beauty, 16, 26, 130–131, 172, 179, 221n13
Bellour, Raymond, 9, 37
Belton, John, 133
Benayoun, Robert, 130–131, 231n32
Bennington, Geoffrey, 237n7
Bergson, Henri, 2, 11, 16, 48, 85, 88, 93, 107–109, 114, 125–126, 128, 143, 225n15, 227n14
  élan vital, 143
  la mécanisation de la vie, 11, 16, 48, 85, 108, 126

Bergstrom, Janet, 218n7, 237n1
binomial, 76–77, 79
Blacksmith, The, 63, 70, 100, 214, 220n8
Blanchot, Maurice, 19
Blesh, Rudi, 221n8
blindness and the comic, 179–182, 188
Blystone, Jack, 221n8
Boat, The, 63, 70, 72
Bordwell, David, 9, 38–41, 50, 54, 66, 68
Bowser, Eileen, 231n16
Branigan, Edward, 218n11
Buñuel, Luis, 192
Burch, Noël, 38
Burgoyne, Robert, 218n5
burlesque, 81, 129, 140, 147, 223n36
Butcher Boy, The, 63
Butler, Judith, 31–32
butt of the joke, 110, 121, 143, 201
Byron, Marion, 77

California slapstick, 129
Cameraman, The, 64, 224n9
caricature, 11, 22, 25–26, 113–114, 126–127, 129, 133, 136–139, 144, 183, 229–230n6
Carrey, Jim, 5
Carroll, David, 175
Carroll, Noël, 87–90, 102, 144, 148, 153–156, 224n3, 230n6
cartoons, 46, 60, 139
cathectic energy, 120, 163, 176–177
cathexis, 47, 118, 120, 163, 176–178, 228n31
causality, 10, 12, 26, 40–43, 45, 48, 53, 60, 63, 67–68, 70, 72, 74, 84, 100, 102–103, 139–140, 156, 158, 166, 174
Cavell, Stanley, 155, 179, 180, 186–187
censorship, 107, 118, 120
Cervantes, Miguel de, 31
chance, 9, 40, 43, 60, 67, 96, 100–102, 143–144, 166
Chaplin, Charles, 1, 3–4, 12, 42, 46, 53, 70, 79–80, 90, 91, 95–96, 100, 125, 129, 132–136, 138–139, 143, 155, 166, 171, 178–189, 194, 225n26, 239n8
character and characterization
  agency and identity, 44
  and extradiegetic status of performer, 4, 79, 89, 134
  and performer, 10, 89, 90–99, 238n41
  and persona, 132–136
  Chaplin's Tramp character, 95, 139, 178
  character-oriented cinema, 132
  in genteel comedy, 133
  inelasticity of, 128
  Keaton's character, 42–43, 54, 61–94 passim, 102, 132, 163–164, 178
    as comic 'type,' 88
    behavioral disposition of, 4, 80–81, 87–88, 92, 99–100, 102–103, 224n3, 224n9
    comic sovereignty of, 92, 96–103
    mode of perception of, 155
  Lloyd's glasses character, 133–136
  psychology, 136–137, 222n22
  other comic characters, 42
chase films, 129
choreography, 3, 56, 100, 131, 143–144, 188
Cinema 1: The Movement-Image, 60–61, 88, 223n36, 231n32, 239n8
Cinema 2: The Time-Image, 61, 192
cinema of attraction, 68–69
circus, 47, 93, 95, 129, 179–180, 185, 221n13, 226n31
Circus, The, 95, 179
City Lights, 12, 100, 169, 171, 179, 181, 183, 187–188
classical Hollywood realism, 4, 5
Cline, Eddie, 220–221n8
code, 36–37, 111, 171
coincidence, 40–41, 44, 63, 67, 72, 85, 101
College, 64, 78, 84, 157,
comedia dell'arte, 185
comedian comedy, *see* comedy
comedy
  anarchistic comedy, 7, 48, 89, 129

comedy, *Cont'd*
   and meaning, 151
   and philosophy, 3, 13, 17–18
   and psychoanalysis, 6
   comedian comedy, 4–5, 10, 46, 78–79, 88–89, 91, 95–96, 98, 100–101, 106, 132–134, 155, 178, 180
   genteel comedy, 4, 11, 132–135, 138, 155
   high and low comedy, 4, 219n20
   knockabout comedy, 48–49, 129, 131, 220n29
   New Comedy, 40, 138, 232–233n54
   Old Comedy, 138, 232–233n54
   physical comedy, 47–48, 56, 133, 135, 139, 155–156
   polite comedy, 133
   realist comedy, 7
   risk comedy, 135, 151
   situation comedy, 63
   slapstick comedy, *see* slapstick
   sure-fire comedy, 135
   theatrical comedy, 2, 147, 227n13
   thrill comedy, 135, 166
comic, the
   and aesthetics, 129
   and appearance, 22
   and automatism, 88
   and character, 130
   and comparison, 2, 26, 111, 113–114, 116–117, 122, 125, 127–128, 138, 141, 143, 161, 180, 227n17, 229n35
   and contingency of time and space, 100–102, 166
   and eccentricity, 134
   and editing, 49, 56, 59, 84, 140–141, 143–144, 161, 183–184, 188, 220n29
   and exaggeration, 129, 137–139, 227n14
   and excess, 36
   and graphic qualities, 3, 56, 94, 106, 138
   and incongruity, 65, 154, 156

   and machines and mechanisms, 9, 48, 60–61, 68–70, 72, 79, 81, 83–85, 143, 173, 221n13, 222–223n31
   and movement, 121
   and narrative, 44, 47–48, 75, 84
   and nonsense, 12, 117, 119
   and objects, 87, 92, 99
   and performance, 90–99 passim, 134, 182, 185–186, 201
   and performers, 4, 132, 189
   and persona, 4, 50, 78–79, 132–135, 137, 180, 187
   and props, 47–48, 52, 57, 64, 66, 109, 139, 158–159, 206–207, 210
   and rhythm, 56, 100, 131–132, 183–184, 188, 211, 220n29
   and spectacle, 12
   and types and stereotypes, 89, 108, 134
   and words, 109, 227n13
   and vision, 180, 182, 187–188
   process, 7, 18, 26, 32, 97
   techniques, 11, 105
commercial cinema, 189
communication theory, 110
comparison, *see* the comic and comparison
compromise formations, 106, 118, 188, 196
condensation
   and equivocity, 145
   and metaphor, 173, 194–196, 205–207
   as a technique of the joke, 11, 26, 111-119, 121-123, 145, 152, 161
   as unconscious (primary) process, 2, 152, 157, 174, 176, 194–196, 211
   facilitated by visual regression and pictorial form, 12, 148
   in the dream, 42, 96, 111, 118–119, 152, 157–160, 194–196
   in the gag, 154–156, 165, 197, 200–202, 207, 211
   in the sight gag, 156, 161, 178, 180, 182, 184–186, 188

condensation, *Cont'd*
    of the figurative and the literal, 94
    visual resemblance and harmonics, 192
Coney Island, 51, 63
consciousness, 19–23, 27, 31, 49, 97, 111, 120, 176–177, 196, 238n42
considerations of representability, 148, 153, 158, 166, 169–170, 174
contiguity, 194
Convict 13, 43, 63, 70, 80
Cook, Jim, 214n16
Coole, Diana, 18
Cops, 63, 70, 80, 178
Corneille, Pierre, 226n8
Crafton, Donald, 9, 45–47
Crane, Ward, 94
creative geography, 211
Crisp, Donald, 221n8
critical theory, 6

Daumier, Honoré, 139
Davis, Mildred, 134
Daydreams, 63, 64 fig. 5
death, 2, 8, 17, 22–25, 27–32, 67, 77, 134, 187
deconstruction, 17, 27, 31, 191, 195, 206
Deed, André, 46, 219n17
deformity, 108, 126
degradation
    and comic form, 3, 108, 113, 123, 125–145, 183–184
    and Lebel's understanding of Keaton's comedy, 3
    and mimesis, 11, 108
    and the Aristotelian conception of the comic, 10, 108, 126
    and the superiority theory of humor, 127–128
    as comic technique, 2, 5, 111, 113, 137, 183–184
    ethics of, 96
    in Bergson's study of laughter, 126, 227n4
    in cinematic comedy, 11–12, 125–145, 183–184
    in Freud's study of comic, 11, 108, 111, 113, 117, 123, 125–127, 137, 229n4, 230n8, 232n53
    of philosophy, 7
Deleuze, Gilles, 9, 12, 59–61, 75–76, 79–82, 85, 88, 139, 156, 191–194, 206, 223n36, 239n8
    action-image, 61, 75–82, 85, 194, 223n36
    binomial, 76–77, 79
    large form, 75–83, 85, 223n36
    minoration, 79–85
    small form, 75–76, 79, 80–83, 194, 223n36
    synsign, 76–79, 81
Demolition d'un mur, 69
Derrida, Jacques, 1, 7–8, 12, 15, 17–18, 23–33 passim, 97–98, 191, 202–207, 240n15
Descartes, René, 207
Descombes, Vincent, 17
desire, 91, 115, 120, 152, 160, 171–173, 175–178, 182–183, 188, 195–196, 225n18
Desmond, William, 31
destiny, 40, 95, 101–102
deus ex machina, 67, 100
dialectic, 3, 7–8, 10, 17, 20, 21–32, 37, 39–40, 43, 67, 72–75, 77, 83–84, 88, 92, 97–98, 106, 123, 151
Diderot, Denis, 226n8
diegetic, 4, 23, 29, 37, 52, 79, 89–90, 95–96, 100, 134, 165, 180, 185, 187
différance, 30
Dionysian, 172, 175
Discours, figure, 171, 174
discourse
    and intelligibility, 237n17
    and meaning, 8, 10, 24, 28–29, 105, 160, 204, 206, 217n36
    and metaphor, 93
    and sovereignty, 97, 105
    and the comic, 32, 36, 93, 95, 151, 165, 167, 234–235n18

discourse, *Cont'd*
  and the image, 158, 160, 180
  determinate discourse, 32, 105, 191
  discourse, figure, 12, 170–172, 174–175, 180
  discursive thought, 160
  inadequacy of discourse, 19
  literary discourse, 195
  postmodern and poststructuralist discourse, 1
  theoretical discourse, 36
  verbal discourse, 93, 95, 158, 167
displacement
  and intelligibility, 119
  and trajectory gags, 178
  as a technique of the joke, 11, 26, 111–119, 121–123, 145, 152, 161
  as unconscious (primary) process, 2, 152, 157, 174, 176, 194–196, 211
  facilitated by visual regression and pictorial form, 12, 148
  in the dream, 42, 96, 111, 118–119, 152, 157–60, 194–196
  in the gag, 154–56, 165, 197, 200–202, 207, 211
divine intervention, 75, 85
Doane, Mary Ann, 235n24
Don Quixote, 31
double meaning, 113
dreams
  considerations of representability, 148, 153, 158, 166, 169–170, 174
  dream logic in cinema, 42–43, 63–64, 66, 96, 99, 101–102, 160–167
  dream-content, 118–162
  dream-thoughts, 119, 158, 160, 162, 165, 173–174, 180, 195–196, 237n17
  dream-work, 118–119, 152, 159–160, 169–170, 172–175, 191, 195–196, 205–206
  Freud's study of the dream, 106–107, 115, 148–149, 152–153, 157–160, 162, 165–166, 160–170
  Lyotard on the figurality of the dream, 172–175, 195–196

  means of representation, 157–160
  relation between dreams and jokes, 106–107, 111, 118–119, 144, 152, 176
  secondary revision, 152, 174, 196
Dryden, John, 226n8
Durgnat, Raymond, 48

early cinema, 5, 9, 56, 68–70, 106, 139
Eaton, Mick, 6, 106, 149, 151, 234–235nn10, 18
Eco, Umberto, 130
ecstasy, 17, 20–21, 25
ego, 6, 10, 99, 150
Eisenstein, Sergei, 5, 192
Electric House, The, 63, 71, 72
empathy, 122, 127–128, 152, 229n35
enunciation, 12, 28, 30, 152, 181, 201, 230n8
epic, 83, 87, 223n33
epistemology, 12, 16, 23, 25, 156, 183
equivocity, 80–81, 83, 145, 156, 194
ethics, 85, 95–96
Eustache, Jean, 222n16
Evanthius, 40
experimental cinema, 37

fabula, 38, 41, 43, 50–51, 53
farce, 9, 48, 50, 63, 72, 198
fate, 9, 10, 40–41, 44, 67, 84, 91, 96, 102
feature-length films, 3, 9, 46, 57, 65, 70, 79
Fechner, Gustav, 176
feminism, 6
Fields, W. C., 5
figurality, 12, 170–176, 179, 182, 186, 188, 191
figurative, the, 12, 93–95, 136, 161–162, 170, 173–174, 187–188, 195, 208, 210–211
film history, 155, 178
film industry, 189
film theory, 1, 7, 103, 152, 170
Firgo, 41
Fischer, Kuno, 107, 137

fixation, 87–88
Flay, Joseph C., 31–32
Fliess, Wilhelm, 106
Flitterman-Lewis, Sandy, 218n3
fort-da game, 149, 153, 170
fortuitousness, 40, 56, 85, 101, 211
fortune, 40–41, 67, 136
Foucault, Michel, 17
Freud, Sigmund
    and psychoanalysis, 10
    and psychoanalysis and film theory, 37, 170
    cited by Derrida, 240n15
    importance of work for study of cinematic comedy, 12, 148–156, 161–162, 229n35, 230n8, 234n10
    interpreted by Lacan, 173
    interpreted by Lyotard, 12, 173–174, 177–178, 188, 191
    on caricature, 137–138
    on comic degradation, 229n4, 232n53. *See also* degradation
    on conditions favoring the comic, 10
    on considerations of representability (regression to the visual), 156–160, 162, 165, 169–170
    on distinction between the comic and the joke, 105–123, 183
    on distinction, between the joke and the dream, 118–119, 144, 188, 196
    on ideation and ideational mimetics, 228n33, 228n34, 235n29. *See also* ideation
    on jokes, 6, 11, 105–123, 170, 239n8, 239n11
    on the comic, 7, 105–123, 125–128, 196, 229–230n6
    on the dream-work, 174, 205. *See also* dreams
    on the pleasure principle and the reality principle, 176–177, 180, 238n42
    on the unconscious transformation of words and thoughts, 11
    on thermodynamic conception of the psyche, 228n31
    significance for poststructuralist and postmodernist treatments of the comic, 2
    significance for the study of cinematic comedy, 148
Frozen North, The, 41, 63
Frye, Northrop, 40, 43

gag writing, 93
gags
    articulated gags, 9, 46–47, 49, 51, 54–57, 70, 140, 236n33
    ascending façade gags, 135
    bombarder-mortar-cannon gag, 73, 143
    boomgate gag, 99, 141
    breech birth gag, 210
    chimney gag, 54–56
    chopping wood gag, 83
    clown audition gag, 95
    descending façade gag, 77
    deus ex machina gag, 67–68
    dressing the general gag, 83
    framed gag, 164
    gadget gags, 70–71
    Hank chauffeurs the newly weds gag, 51
    hoser hosed gag, 69
    impossible gags, 65–66
    literalization gags, 148
    lost dollars gag, 96
    machine gags, 9, 84–86
    men at work gag, 66
    perfect misunderstanding gag, 59–60
    projection gags, 164–167
    pulling tooth gag, 70
    ravine gag, 61–62
    riding the handlebars gag, 102–103
    running gags, 45, 101
    sausage machine gag, 69
    shadow gag, 94
    shaking a cocktail gag, 80, 194
    sight gags, 11–12, 148, 153–157, 170, 179, 188, 211
    solution gags, 154
    steamer cabin gag, 197, 201
    straw that broke the camel's back gag, 93

gags, *Cont'd*
  swordfish gag (Keaton), 66
  swordfish gag (Marx Brothers), 225n13
  torn contract gags, 197–201
  trajectory gags, 9, 83–84, 99, 101, 178
  underwater traffic cop gag, 66
Garage, The, 63
general economy, 2, 8–10, 24, 27, 30–47 passim, 57, 85, 88–91, 98, 101, 103, 105–107, 123, 151, 165, 172, 188, 202
General, The, 64, 66–67, 73, 77, 83, 87, 137, 140, 154, 162, 224n3
genre, 4–5, 7, 10, 11, 15, 39–40, 66, 78, 88, 89, 91, 107, 130, 132–135, 201, 223n36, 232–233n54, 238n41
genteel comedy, 4, 11, 132–135, 138, 155
geometrification, 141, 225n27
Gledhill, Christine, 223n33
Go West, 14 fig. 1, 63, 142
Goat, The, 63, 220n8
Godard, Jean-Luc, 100
Gold Rush, The, 90, 178–179
Goldberg, Rube, 60
Green, Gary L., 213n4
Greimas, Algirdas Julien, 37
Griffith, David Wark, 66, 129
Guilty, 16
Gunning, Tom, 5, 9, 59, 68–74, 85, 222n22
Gutwirth, Marcel, 108, 229n4

hallucination, 12, 165, 176–178, 180–183, 187–188, 238n42
Hansen, Miriam, 5
happy ending, 40
Hard Luck, 63
harmonics, 192, 194, 208, 211
Harris, Neil, 221n13
Haunted House, The, 63, 80
Heath, Stephen, 169–170
Hegarty, Paul, 22

Hegel, Georg Wilhelm Friedrich, 7, 8, 10, 15–32, 74–75, 77, 97, 113, 191, 216n19
Heidegger, Martin, 22
Heine, 111, 116
Hemingway, Ernest, 216n20
High Sign, The, 63, 80
Hines, Johnny, 133
Hobbes, Thomas, 128
Hollier, Denis, 16
Horton, Andrew, 225n17
Hugo, Victor, 109
humanism, 88, 91–92
humor, 48
Huston, John, 169
hybridity, 42, 70, 80, 102

id, 10, 150
ideation, 111, 120–122, 125, 127, 228n34, 235n29
identity, 8, 10, 17, 26, 27, 43–44, 54, 56, 79, 81, 88–90, 95, 97–98, 109, 169, 181, 205
imaginary, 6, 170, 186
implausibility, 65, 81, 101, 134, 141
impossibility, 211
impossible gags, 65, 66
improbability, 47, 81, 101, 134, 223n36, 226n31
indeterminacy, 10, 30, 105, 138
index, 80
inelasticity, 108, 126, 128
inhibition, 115, 120
Inner Experience, 16, 26
innocent jokes, 115–117, 196
insight, 22, 32, 87–88, 132, 155, 224n3
intelligibility, 11, 118–119, 121, 144, 171, 174, 188, 195, 203
intentionality, 2, 7, 48, 71, 107, 110, 115, 139, 164, 173, 183
interpretation
  and meaning, 119, 195
  comic interpretation, 99, 154–155, 180
  of the comic, 210

Interpretation of Dreams, The, 173
Intolerance, 66
intuition, 19
Inwood, Michael, 74
Irigaray, Luce, 235n22
irony, 31, 132, 136
irrational, 17, 41, 91, 166, 196
iterability, 32

Jakobson, Roman, 12, 194–196
Janus head, 114–115, 196
Jenkins, Henry, 214, 219
jest, 129, 149, 234n6
Johnson, Samuel, 226n8
Johnston, Claire, 6
jokes
    bad joke, 210, 234n10
    blind man joke, 116
    condensation jokes, 113, 122, 154
    displacement jokes, 112–113, 122
    double structure of, 109, 114–115
    innocent jokes, 116, 117
    Janus head, 114–115, 196
    kettle joke, 227–228n19
    salmon mayonnaise joke, 112
    smutty jokes, 110, 121
    technique of, 122, 227n17
    tendentious jokes, 116, 196
Jonson, Ben, 232–233n54
jouissance, 37, 56

Kafka, Franz, 130, 170, 188
Kant, Immanuel, 17, 18, 19, 216n15, 229n1
Karnick, Kristine Brunovska, 219n16
Keaton, Buster, 1–5, 9, 11–13, 35–36, 41–102 passim, 125–126, 130–145 passim, 148, 155, 157 fig. 16, 162–167, 178–179, 186–187, 189, 192, 194, 211, 219n18, 220–221n8, 223nn34, 223nn36, 224n3, 224–225n9, 225n27, 231n31, 236n60
Kerr, Walter, 4, 129, 132
kettle logic, 113
Keystone films, 35, 46, 48, 125, 129, 132, 144, 213n6, 220n29

King, Geoff, 101
Klee, Paul, 138–139
Knopf, Robert, 5
Kojève, Alexandre, 20
Kramer, Peter, 5, 79, 98, 100
Kris, Ernst, 126, 137–138
Krutnik, Frank, 5, 6, 9, 40–41, 43–47, 68, 98, 101, 128, 133, 147, 155, 219n18, 230n8, 232n53
Kuleshov, Lev, 211

Lacan, Jacques, 12, 152–153, 173, 179, 194–196, 203
Land, Nick, 17–19
Langdon, Harry, 4, 133–134, 136, 139, 155
Langman, Larry, 47
Laplanche, Jean, 119
latent content, 118
Laughing Matter: An Essay on the Comic, 108
laughter
    and gagging, 148, 154, 156
    and morality, 143
    and philosophy, 2, 7, 15, 18, 21, 25, 32, 105–106
    and slapstick, 47, 57, 64, 139
    and the comic, 12–13, 25, 93, 97–99, 101, 108–109
    and the joke, 111, 119, 120–122, 127
    and transgression, 45, 87, 149, 197
    as a social gesture, 128
    as comic pleasure, 120–123, 126
    as discharge of surplus energy, 114, 120–122, 127
    as figure in postmodernist and post-structuralist discourse, 1
    as operation of sovereignty, 10, 87, 97–98
    as opposed to interpretation, 210
    Bataille's, 7–8, 16–28, 30–32, 35, 226n1
    in Bergson, 128, 143–144
    in Kant, 229n1
    in Meredith, 227n10
    intention to laugh and to arouse laughter, 48, 50, 64

laughter, *Cont'd*
   "laughing at" and "laughing with," 95–96
   laughter-emotion circuit in Chaplin's oeuvre, 239n8
Laurel and Hardy, 130–131
law of forbidden montage, 77
Le Cochon, 222n16
Lebel, Jean-Patrick, 3–4, 73–75, 130, 131, 141, 223n34, 225n27, 233n60
Levinas, Emmanuel, 19
Levi-Strauss, Claude, 37
Lewis, Jerry, 5
Leyda, Jay, 129
Libertson, Joseph, 17–19, 21, 27
Linder, Max, 46, 219n17
linguistics, 36, 93, 152–153, 159, 172, 174, 195, 200, 203–204, 206–207
Lipps, Theodor, 107
literalization and the literal, 47, 93–95, 100, 113, 148, 160–165, 167, 194, 210
literary theory, 1, 15, 35, 106, 130, 135, 195
Lloyd, Harold, 1, 3–4, 11, 46, 125, 133–136, 139, 151, 155, 166, 178–179, 219n18
Loewenberg, Jacob, 31
logic, 158, 160–165
Love Nest, The, 63, 70, 142 fig. 15, 220–221n8
luck, 9, 40–41, 67, 134, 187
Lumière brothers, 69, 222n16
Lydon, Mary, 171
Lyotard, Jean-François, 1, 12, 37, 56, 115, 118, 169–177, 188–189, 191, 194–196, 203, 206, 212, 225n18, 237n17, 237–238n21

MacCann, Richard Dyer, 232n40
machines in comedy, 9, 48, 60–61, 68–70, 72, 79, 81, 83–85, 143, 173, 222n16
Mack, Marion, 67
Maland, Charles, 129
Manichaeism, 94

manifest content, 118–119, 158, 160, 174, 196
Martin, André, 141
Martin, Steve, 5
Marx Brothers, 1, 3, 6, 12, 93–94, 100, 151–152, 160–162, 166–167, 191, 197–202, 225n13, 230n7
Marxism, 6, 91, 182, 216n19
masculinity, 3, 77, 223n33
Mast, Gerald, 4, 129, 131, 134–136, 213n6
master-slave dialectic, 8, 23–24, 31–32
mastery, 8, 27, 31–33, 37, 73, 92, 97–99, 102, 152
McCaffrey, Donald, 133
McFadden, George, 226n4
McGuire, Kathryn, 67, 94
McKeon, Roger, 225n18
McLean, Douglas, 133
meaning and nonmeaning, 29–30, 33, 107, 110, 116, 174
means of representation, 157–160
Mehlman, Jeffrey, 106, 150
Mellencamp, Patricia, 6, 106, 151–153, 160–162, 197, 201, 235n22
melodrama, 66, 129, 134, 181, 186, 223n33
Menander, 232n54
Meredith, George, 227n10
metamorphosis, 4, 10, 28, 36, 42, 92, 95–96, 99
metaphor, 12, 23, 29–30, 32, 60, 92–94, 112–114, 160, 173, 191–197, 200, 202–208, 211, 240n15
metaphysics, 17, 26, 29, 204, 240n15
metonymy, 173, 194, 197
metteur-en-scène, 75, 99–103, 106, 143, 164
Metz, Christian, 152
mimesis, 11, 105, 107–109, 114, 138, 173, 206
mimetic degradation, 11, 105, 107–109
mimicry, 11, 113, 126–127, 229–230n6
minoration, 79–85
mirror phase, 153
mischief films, 69, 72

mise-en-abîme, 29
mise-en-scène, 9, 37, 42, 99, 102, 131, 137, 140, 144–145, 160, 164, 167, 210, 211
Modern Times, 143
modernism and modernist art, 126, 130, 139, 188, 239n1
modernity, 77, 126, 183
Moews, Daniel, 3, 84
morality, 95, 216n20
Moving Picture World, 129
Murphy, Eddie, 5
mutual interference gags, 95
My Wife's Relations, 59, 63, 73

Nancy, Jean-Luc, 106
narcissism, 150, 181
Naremore, James, 90–91
narration and narrative
  adventure narratives, 63
  and causality, 60–61, 63, 67–68
  and dialectic, 36–37, 39, 74–75
  and interpretation, 10, 63
  and melodrama, 181–182
  and minoration, 79–84
  and the comic and the joke, 149–151
  and the operational aesthetic, 68–72
  as restricted economy, 9, 36, 41, 151
  as story-telling machine, 59–86
  contrivance and comic destiny, 100–102, 141
  Deleuze on, 61
  demand and impact, 35, 49, 64–65
  dramatic narrative, 74, 222
  exposition and tropic vision, 182–83, 185–87
  farce narrative, 9, 50, 198
  in comedian comedy, 89, 97–98, 100–102
  in Lloyd's comedy, 4, 133–134, 136
  in Keaton's cinema, 3, 35–86
  in Sennett's Keystone comedies, 4, 155-156
  in task films, 70
  in twenties' slapstick, 4, 35–86, 155–156

narrative agency, 63
narrative closure, 41
narrative comedy, 40, 43, 44
narrative economy, 5, 36
narrative structure, 6, 15, 60–61, 65–66, 68, 70, 72–79, 137, 207
parametric narration, 38–39
quest narratives, 63
recursion in Keaton's narratives, 61, 84–86
relation to slapstick, 7–9, 36, 38–39, 40, 45–47
relation to the comic, 9, 35–86, 178
relation to the gag, 7–9, 40, 44–45, 54–57, 59, 69, 72–73, 106, 149
theorization and analysis, 35–39
National Board of Censorship, 129
Navigator, The, 13, 64–68, 68 fig. 7, 81, 100, 137, 140, 162, 178, 192, 193 fig. 18, 209 fig. 20, 210
Neale, Steve, 6, 9, 40–41, 43–47, 68, 106, 128, 133, 147, 150–151, 155, 230n8, 232n53, 234–235n18
negativity and negation, 8, 19, 22–25, 27, 29–33, 38, 45, 108, 123, 156, 158, 206, 217n36
Neighbors, 63, 65 fig. 6
Nelson, T.G.A., 130
New Comedy, *see* comedy
Nietzsche, Friedrich, 2, 18–19, 172
Night at the Opera, A, 197
non-savoir, 16, 18–19, 25
nonsense, 8, 10, 20, 33, 44, 86, 105–106, 116, 119, 122, 154, 162, 172, 191, 195–196, 200, 203, 211
normativity, 56, 108
noumenon, 17–19, 23, 38
Nowell-Smith, Geoffrey, 223n33

objects in comedy, 87, 92, 99
Oedipus complex, 37, 170
Old Comedy, *see* comedy
One Week, 8–9, 35–36, 49, 52 fig. 2, 53, 55 fig. 3, 63, 66, 70–72, 80
operational aesthetic, 9, 68–72, 83–85, 140, 221n13

organic form, 74–75, 77
Our Hospitality, 66, 77
overdetermination, 3, 138, 205–207

Paleface, The, 61, 62 fig. 4
Palmer, D. J., 232–233n54
Palmer, Jerry, 5
pantomime, 179, 184
parody, 11, 46, 47, 66, 77, 113–114, 127, 200, 229-230n6
Parshall, Peter F., 224n9
Pasquier, Sylvain du, 165
Patton, Paul, 206
Paul, William, 184, 238n37
Pefanis, Julian, 215n5
Peirce, Charles Sanders, 76
phenomenology, 172
Phenomenology of Spirit, 7, 18, 20, 21, 23–25, 30–32
Philebus, 128
philosophy, 1–5, 7, 10–15, 16–22, 25, 28–29, 32, 35, 39, 91, 105–106, 108, 125, 143, 188, 191, 202, 204–207
philosophy and comedy, 3, 5
physical comedy, 47–48, 56, 133, 135, 139, 155–156
physicality, 3–4, 12, 47–49, 56, 87–88, 94, 96, 131–133, 135, 139–140, 144, 155–156, 158, 166, 173, 175, 178, 182, 188, 201, 211–212, 229n6
pictoriality, 11, 56, 106, 125–126, 137–138, 148, 153, 157–163, 165, 172, 180, 211
Pierrot le fou, 100
Plato, 128, 207
play, 1, 6, 10, 29, 37, 60, 103, 115–116, 149, 154, 159, 173, 186, 196, 205, 214n1, 229n1, 234n10, 239n8
Playhouse, The, 63, 90 fig. 10
pleasure principle, 10, 12, 118, 176–180, 186
Plotnitsky, Arkady, 17, 32
poetics, 16, 21, 26, 39, 48, 71, 100, 108–109, 140, 144, 158, 172, 191, 194, 197, 206, 208, 210, 229n1
Polan, Dana, 5

Pollock, Jackson, 175
polysemy, 106, 113
Pontalis, J. B., 119, 169
postmodernism, 1, 5, 106
poststructuralism, 1, 5, 106
preconscious, 2, 105, 111, 114, 116–120, 123, 138, 151, 167, 175, 196, 228n34
preconscious-conscious system, 10, 118, 161, 176
primary process, 10, 12, 42, 105, 107, 115, 117–118, 122–123, 126, 138, 152–153, 158, 160–161, 165, 169–170, 173–177, 180–181, 186–188, 191, 194–197, 205–206
Prince, Gerald, 218n3
Propp, Vladimir, 37
props, 48, 61, 64, 144
Proust, Marcel, 19
psychical topography, 117, 161
psychoanalysis, 1, 6, 10, 12, 18, 37–38, 91, 114, 148, 150, 152–153, 165, 169–172, 175, 180–181, 195, 225n18
Psychoanalytic Explorations in Art, 137
puns, 210

Rapf, Joanna E., 213n4
Ray, Charles, 133
Readings, Bill, 237n7
realism, 5, 7, 10, 39, 56, 66, 72, 79, 89, 90, 95–96, 133–134, 162, 179, 185, 201, 208, 212, 223n36
realist and comic acting, 90
reality principle, 10, 12, 118, 120, 176–181, 186, 238n42
reason, 7, 15–18, 24–25, 27, 30, 33, 38, 41, 100, 106, 113, 123, 165, 173, 234n10
rebus, 162, 210
recursion function, 9, 60–62, 79, 83–85, 178, 208
referentiality, 161, 203, 205
regression, 12, 21, 148, 153, 156–157, 161, 165, 167, 169–180, 196
repression, 115, 118, 120, 122, 159, 173, 176, 178, 195–196, 205

restricted economy, 8, 9, 24, 27, 30, 32–33, 35–37, 39, 41, 43–44, 57, 85, 89, 98, 103, 105, 123, 151, 172, 202
rhetoric, 46, 195
Riblet, Doug, 48, 129–132, 220n29
Rice, Arthur, 103
Richardson, Michael, 25
ridiculous, 108
risk of death, 8, 23, 26, 77, 106
Roach, Hal, 133
Roberts, Joe, 42, 70
Robinson, David, 48
Rodin, Auguste, 138–139
romance, 4, 83
Rosen Stanley, 216n19
Russian formalists, 9, 37

sacred, 16–18, 20–22, 85
sacrifice, 8, 17, 22–25, 103, 196, 200
Safety Last!, 132, 134–135, 178
Santeul, Jean de, 226n8
Saphead, The, 133
Sarris, Andrew, 3
Sartre, Jean-Paul, 169
satire, 47
Saussure, Ferdinand de, 113
Scaliger, 40
Scarecrow, The, 63, 70–71, 80
Schenck, Joe, 2
Schlegel, Wilhelm von, 226n8
scopophilia, 152
Screen, 6
secondary process, 12, 118, 120–121, 176–178, 181, 186
secondary revision, 152, 174, 196
seduction, 102, 110, 114
Seely, Sybil, 50
segmentation, 37
Seidman, Steve, 4–5, 79, 89, 91, 96–98, 100–101, 132, 134, 238n41
self-consciousness, 8, 21–24, 26, 28
Selig, Michael, 5
semiotics, 6, 123, 166, 171, 203, 230n8
Sennett, Mack, 1, 4–5, 11, 35, 42, 46, 48, 64, 125, 129–140 passim, 155–156, 178

sense and nonsense, 7–8, 10–12, 33, 44, 86, 88, 105–107, 114–117, 119, 121–122, 154, 158, 171–172, 175, 191, 195–196, 200, 211
Seven Chances, 64
Sherlock Jr., 10, 12, 44, 64, 66, 84, 87, 92, 94, 96, 97 fig. 11, 99–101, 102 fig. 12, 132, 141, 162–164, 166 fig. 17, 208 fig. 19, 224–225n9
Shklovsky, Victor, 38
short films, 46, 49, 57, 61, 63–66, 70
signifiance, 38–39
signification, 38, 113, 161–162, 164, 195, 203, 207
Silent Clowns, The, 129
simulacrum, 27, 30, 97, 106, 113, 207
simultaneity, 76, 154, 158–159, 173
singularity, 38, 96
slapstick
  1910s, 11, 125, 129–130, 132
  1920s, 1, 4, 11, 46, 125–126, 130, 132–133, 136
  and gags, 44–45, 54
  and narrative in cinematic comedy, 38–40, 45, 47, 50–51, 72
  and other comic and non-comic modes, forms and techniques, 7
  and physical comedy, 47
  and stylization, 48–49, 54, 56–57
  as an operation of the comic, 15, 106
  as cinematic attraction, 9, 72
  as the perfect contingency of time and space, 100–102
  Chaplin's, 95–96, 181–186
  choreography and editing, 140–144
  definition, 46–48, 139
  hiding thought, 192, 207, 210–211
  Keaton's, 35–36, 50, 64–65, 71, 83, 100, 139–144
  Lloyd's, 135–136, 232n46
  opposition to, 35–36
  Sennett/Keystone style, 12, 35, 48, 132, 137–140, 144, 155–156
  versus the sight gag, 155–156, 170
sophistry, 74

sovereignty, 2, 8, 10, 16, 18, 22, 25–33, 36, 40, 87–88, 92, 96–100, 102–103, 105–106, 132, 191, 196, 206, 239n1
spectators, 149, 152, 170
spirit, 19, 31
spoonerisms, 116
Staiger, Janet, 219n14
Stam, Robert, 218n3
star system, 132
Steamboat Bill, Jr., 64, 77, 78 fig. 8, 81, 82 fig. 9, 84, 144
Stettenheim, Julius, 115
Stewart, Garrett, 164
Strachey, James, 114–115
Strike, 192
structuralism, 12, 37, 171, 203, 206
style and stylization, 38–39, 48–50, 54, 56, 139
subjectivity, 6, 19, 21, 87, 91–92, 165, 171
subject-object relations, 10, 88, 91
superego, 10
superiority theory of the comic, 128
surprise, 9, 43, 53, 155, 211
surrealism, 17, 43, 51, 71, 101, 163, 189
Sweeney, Kevin W., 224n9
syllogisms, 121
synsign, 76–79, 81
Sypher, Wylie, 227n10
syuzhet, 38–39, 41–43, 50–51, 53

Tashlin, Frank, 214n18
taste, 15, 16, 129
Taylorism, 143
technology, 140, 144
teleology, 61, 66, 74–75, 85, 89, 183
television, 2, 6, 63, 149
temporality, 26, 38, 41, 69, 76, 101, 152, 158–159, 225n27, 236n33
tendentious jokes, 115–117, 122, 138, 151, 185–186, 188, 196
textual analysis, 171
"the is" and "the ought," 2, 11, 123, 141, 143, 156, 161, 180
themes, 15, 28, 87, 89, 91, 106, 210

thing presentations and word presentations, 161
Thompson, Kristin, 39
Three Ages, The, 66
Torrence, Ernest, 77
tragedy, 13, 15, 22, 26, 43, 125
transformation, 2–3, 11, 16, 21, 66, 70, 80, 92, 105, 109, 116, 118, 121, 123, 138, 155–159, 165, 170, 173, 177, 187, 193, 196
transgression, 12, 25, 27–30, 33, 43, 45, 95, 101, 123, 144, 148–149, 154, 156, 167, 171, 175, 234–235n18
travesty, 11, 113–114, 127, 183, 229–230n6
trope, 126, 182, 207
tropic vision, 182–183, 187–188
two-reelers, 36, 59, 61, 70–71, 133, 220n8
Tynianov, Juri, 38

ugly, 108, 126, 130, 137–138
Un chien andalou, 192
unconscious, the, 10–12, 105, 107, 109, 111, 114–123, 149–153, 157, 159, 161–162, 165, 167, 169–173, 175–178, 180, 188, 195–196, 228n34, 237n17, 239n11
universality, 36, 38, 48, 96, 101
unknowing and unknowledge, 16–21, 23, 25, 111, 119, 216n20
unmasking, 113, 127, 229–230n6

vaudeville, 5, 35, 78, 129, 133, 147, 201, 226n31
verbal communication, 153
Vischer, Theodor, 107
vision and visuality, 11–12, 31, 44, 47, 49, 68, 84, 126, 132, 134, 143–144, 148, 151–194 passim, 207–208, 210, 212, 231n32, 238nn37, 238nn42, *see also* pictoriality
vision and truth, 12, 156
visual abstraction, 11
visual communication, 153
visual intelligibility, 126, 144, 188

waste, 9, 24, 103, 172
Wead, George, 224
Weber, Samuel, 6, 106, 110, 114–115, 121, 149, 150, 228n31, 234n10
West, Mae, 5
White, Hayden, 9, 36, 53
Willemen, Paul, 6
Wilmeth, Don B., 47
wish fulfilment, 99, 170

wit, 3, 109, 138, 160, 227n13, 229n1, 230n8
Wittgenstein, Ludwig, 179
witz, 106, 148
Woolf, Virginia, 170, 188
words and images, relation between, 152, 167, 207

Žižek, Slavoj, 179–180
Zourabichvili, François, 206

www.ingramcontent.com/pod-product-compliance
Lightning Source LLC
Chambersburg PA
CBHW030532230426
43665CB00010B/854